Flying Colours

FLYING
COLOURS
The Epic Story of Douglas Bader

Laddie Lucas

Hutchinson

London Melbourne Sydney Auckland Johannesburg

Hutchinson & Co. (Publishers) Ltd

An imprint of the Hutchinson Publishing Group

17–21 Conway Street, London W1P 5HL

Hutchinson Group (Australia) Pty Ltd
30–32 Cremorne Street, Richmond South, Victoria 3121
PO Box 151, Broadway, New South Wales 2007

Hutchinson Group (NZ) Ltd
32–34 View Road, PO Box 40–086, Glenfield, Auckland 10

Hutchinson Group (SA) Pty Ltd
PO Box 337, Bergvlei 2012, South Africa

First published 1981
Reprinted November 1981

© P. B. (Laddie) Lucas 1981

Set in Linotron Baskerville by Input Typesetting Ltd, London SW19 8DR

Printed in Great Britain by The Anchor Press Ltd
and bound by Wm Brendon & Son Ltd
both of Tiptree, Essex

British Library Cataloguing in Publication Data

Lucas, Laddie
  Flying colours.
  1. Great Britain.   *Royal Air Force* –
  Biography
  2. Bader, Douglas
  I. Title
  358.4′13′320924   UG626.2.B/

ISBN 0 09 146470 6

Contents

Illustrations

Acknowledgements

I must record my thanks to those upon whom I have leant most heavily in establishing the detail of the Bader story.

I am greatly indebted to Air Commodore Henry Probert and his staff at the Royal Air Force's Air Historical Branch not only for their extensive help but also for the spirit in which it has invariably been offered.

I remember, too, the support of three senior and much respected Service friends – Marshal of the Royal Air Force Sir Dermot Boyle and the two Air Chief Marshals, Sir Harry Broadhurst and Sir Theodore McEvoy. Each touched Sir Douglas's life at moments of signal importance and each has thereby added strength to the story.

I am also obligated to three of Bader's former comrades-in-arms who flew alongside him in the great air battles of 1940 or 1941. To Air Marshal Sir Denis Crowley-Milling, Air Vice-Marshal 'Johnnie' Johnson and Group Captain Hugh Dundas my thanks are due for contributing the authority of their experience and knowledge.

Likewise I acknowledge gratefully the part which the late Group Captain Arthur Donaldson, Thelma Bader's first cousin and another fine wartime leader, played before his death last year in confirming certain tactical aspects of Sir Douglas's Battle of Britain concept. Nor can I overlook the assistance which Wing Commander W. J. Hendley has provided in aiding the early Cranwell narrative. One of the Royal Air Force College's first technical apprentices, 'Spanner' Hendley rose to become an outstanding engineer officer in Fighter Command.

I cannot complete the Service references without disclosing my debt to Lord Balfour of Inchrye who, as Captain Harold Balfour, for six cataclysmic years from 1938, served the Royal Air Force selflessly and with enduring effect as Parliamentary Under-Secretary of State. His political judgement and first-hand knowledge of events have been invaluable in assessing some of the more controversial features of the Battle of Britain theme. I thank him also for his permission to publish his verse, 'Biggin Hill, July 1947'.

In writing of Sir Douglas Bader's thirty-six years with the Shell Company I have drawn particularly upon the help of four people – Sir David Barran, a former chairman of the corporation, Jonkheer John Loudon, a senior and widely experienced managing director in Bader's time, Roy Snodgrass, Douglas' lifelong colleague and friend, and Maurice Guinness, whose long contact with the humanity of Shell's industrial and personnel relations enabled him to weigh the impact of Sir Douglas's personality and spirit on overseas staff especially those far away from home at the points of oil exploration and production.

I have trespassed upon their time and patience and I am grateful to them.

There are four further acknowledgements to make. To the Scot, Arthur Smith, for letting me reproduce his 'Address Tae An Auld Spitfire', to Kenneth More for talking feelingly about the problems of portraying Bader on the movie screen as, perhaps, no other world actor could quite have done; to my wife, Jill, Thelma Bader's sister, whose perceptive understanding of her brother-in-law's character and career has immeasurably aided the author's task; and, lastly, to the subject himself for allowing me the use of his private papers, documents and photographs – and for giving me the special privilege of his cooperation and confidence.

Laddie Lucas
London, July 1981

PHOTOGRAPH ACKNOWLEDGEMENTS
The author and publisher wish to thank the Imperial War Museum for their help in researching the majority of the photographs from their archives; other copyright photographs are acknowledged as follows: Ian Joy; Van Hallan; Middlesex County Press; Shell Oil Photo, Calgary Area; Keystone Press Agency Ltd; Canadian Forces.

Biggin Hill, July 1947

On Weald of Kent I watched once more
   Again I heard that grumbling roar
Of fighter planes; yet none were near
   And all around the sky was clear
Borne on the wind a whisper came
   'Though men grow old, they stay the same'
And then I knew, unseen to eye
   The ageless Few were sweeping by

                      LORD BALFOUR OF INCHRYE

'Douglas Bader's my name'

It was 0640 hours on the morning of Wednesday, 12 September 1945, when the telephone beside my bed murdered sleep. Summoned from oblivion, I was not at first sure whether the ringing I had heard was imaginary or real.

My doubt was readily explained. For the last three years a telephone erupting at this hour – or, more likely, a couple of hours earlier – had heralded some new and imminent operation against the enemy. To the receptive, but exhausted, mind of squadron or wing leader, the familiar voice of the Operations controller had brought reality to another day. It was the customary routine of a fighter pilot's life.

Now all that was changed. More than four months had passed since the surrender of the German armies on Lüneburg Heath. At home, a general election had intervened and Churchill, in the afterglow of victory, had been summarily dismissed from office by the British people. Those of us who had stood as parliamentary candidates in his support, and had been sent packing by the electors, were now obliged to return to the Service to play out time before being demobilized. Like cricketing 'night watchmen', put in to bat in the last minutes of the day, we were intent on keeping our end up until the close.

By a welcome and privileged piece of family patronage, my final innings for the Royal Air Force was being played out in the agreeable East Anglian countryside close to where, for centuries, my forebears had made their homes. The fighter station at Bentwaters, near Woodbridge, in Suffolk, to which I had been sent to command, was in the North Weald sector of No. 11 Group, made famous by the Battle of Britain. The sector commander was Group Captain Douglas Bader, recently returned from Colditz after nearly four years as a prisoner in Germany.

13

A few weeks before, I had become engaged to Jill Addison, the sister of Douglas's wife, Thelma. I had never met Bader until that first summer of peace when family ties had brought us together. Then, like some human nuclear device, he had exploded over the quiet of the Addisons' family home at Ascot. The resultant fallout had touched substantial areas of the surrounding country.

The air officer commanding 11 Group at the time was the perceptive and engaging Air Vice-Marshal Dermot Boyle, a talented officer of Irish stock, who was later to become the professional head of the Service, a knight and a Marshal of the Royal Air Force. Boyle had been an instructor at the RAF College at Cranwell in 1929 and 1930 when Bader was a boisterous and high-spirited cadet. The respect which each held for the other was mutual and enduring. At Bader's prompting, the two had, between them, contrived to deliver me from a dreaded posting to the Far East where the Japanese war was then still raging. Suffolk, in a traditional English autumn, had much more appeal for a defeated – and deflated – political candidate. Besides, the pheasants promised rather well that year.

A second and more persistent ringing of the telephone dispelled my doubt. 'It's the controller here, wing commander. There's a message for you from sector. Group Captain Bader is airborne from North Weald and will be landing in twenty minutes. He wants to be met and taken to the mess for breakfast.' There was just time to shave, dress and get over to the airfield before a speck in the western sky confirmed the approach of the sector commander's aircraft.

To the east, the sun, inflamed and bold, was breasting the horizon. Pockets of thin mist were forming over the fields as the moisture rose from the ground. The grass around the control tower, where I had parked my car, was heavy with morning dew. Out on the runways, hundreds upon hundreds of plover, heavily outnumbering the seagulls, were already alerted to the advancing throb of the Rolls-Royce Merlin engine. Above, a sky of thinly powdered blue was clearing to expose another day of Indian summer. It was a compelling morning for flying.

The Spitfire IX was flying at around 3000 feet when it passed overhead, going fast and looking rock-solid and steady in the fresh, stable air. There then followed a classical demonstration of the advanced art of flying. Three or four minutes of fluent, controlled aerobatics, performed noticeably above the regulation height, and the Spitfire, with speed now cut right back, was slipping easily into the circuit for a landing.

A final, tight, curving approach on to the runway was shaped within the perimeter of the airfield. With throttle closed, exhaust popping and speed falling to the point of stall, the aircraft settled on the ground as lightly as a butterfly. There was little run. A couple of touches on the throttle and the pilot was removing the Spitfire quickly from the runway and heading for the control tower.

I had seen similar sequences performed countless times in the last four years. Occasionally the pilot had been one of the Service's recognized exponents. Yet for blend, tidiness and comprehensive professional skill, nothing, to my discerning eye, had quite matched this. It was the first time I had seen Bader fly an aeroplane. The two seemed to be built as one. I never gave it a thought that the pilot had no legs.

I could not put this early morning incident out of my mind, nor could I analyse why these few minutes of superlative, scholarship flying should have made such an impact. I wasn't, after all, new to the business. On the contrary, by wartime standards I was widely experienced, with three tours of operational flying duty behind me. As an amateur airman (in at the beginning and out at the end), I never felt I flew an aircraft better than passably well. But I could recognize skill instantly I saw it in others. Perfection and profession-alism, no matter what the field, have always fascinated me. So why, I wondered, should this Cranwell-trained officer, who fourteen years before, at the age of twenty-one, had lost both legs in an appalling flying accident, be able to manoeuvre an aeroplane like this?

Thirty-five years on, the desire to answer the question remains. But now the urge extends much wider. Bader's accomplishments in the intervening decades, which have added new dimensions to his life, go far beyond his extraordinary flying ability. From being a wartime fighter hero he has developed into a world figure, a force in his own right, a champion of the disabled and the handicapped, known and recognized wherever he goes and sought after as keenly overseas as he is here in Britain.

New stories are there to be told, fresh questions to be answered, different assessments to be made. With them goes the belief that they *ought* now to be made as we approach the fiftieth anniversary of the crash which, by a hard paradox, set him on his way to creating one of the most astonishing human sagas of our time.

In 1946, a few months after the Bentwaters episode, Bader took the crunch decision to leave the Royal Air Force for good. He went back to the Shell Company which, thirteen years before, after the accident, had offered him an office job at £200 a year. A salary of £1250 was now far short of what others had said they would pay him.

There were doubters who said that his days of greatness were over. The human frame, devoid of two of its principal members, which had conquered marvellously in the great air battles over England and France, was not designed to reach the summit a second time. In one person's life, the highest peaks are seldom scaled twice.

In any case, they argued, war was one thing, peace was another. Bader's penchant for saying in short, simple words exactly what he thought instead of what others hoped they might hear – or even what they thought they were entitled to hear – would land him in deep trouble and bar the forward path. He might not himself have any toes to feel with, but others had, and an artificial foot stepping insensitively upon them could be exceedingly painful.

At the end of the day, these forecasts, as we shall see, were to be remarkably disproved; in some ways, unexpectedly disproved. It has taken guts, persistence and an innate resolve never, never, never to give in to have done it – just the qualities which are so often mistaken for overconfidence, arrogance, dogmatism and a disregard for the convenience of others.

Bader's life has been inseparable from difficulty and reverse. The legend is strengthened, not impaired, by exposing it.

There were the 1930s, the first years after the accident. As an 'exceptional' pilot (the rating appears in his log-book) and an outstanding young games-playing athlete, his legs had been cut off and the coveted chance to play Rugby football for England – which seemed to be there, literally, for the accepting – had been extinguished for ever. He had been obliged to leave the Service which he loved. His civilian job was humdrum. Each day, bringing its own hideous reality, was a struggle. It is at least arguable whether he would have got through those times without three attributes to sustain him – the judgement and wisdom of his wife, Thelma; his courageous and spirited humour; and, amazingly, his golf.

The troughs between the high waves, in those first, Shell years after leaving the Royal Air Force, were very deep. There were days when the tops on either side seemed as if they must curl and swamp him. And, all the time, the years were ticking away. Few remember now that Bader was thirty when he led 242 Squadron in the Battle of Britain. He was thirty-one when he collided with a German Messerschmitt over enemy-held France, wrenching off his right tin leg completely as he deserted his Spitfire for his parachute.

The cruelly testing years as a legless prisoner of war – years to which his restless, unyielding temperament never became attuned – came after no more than twenty months of glorious life. The crowded hour of 1940 and 1941 had passed in minutes. The glory was over, irrevocably. The letters he wrote home to Thelma from captivity were a manifestation, sometimes a poignant manifestation, of his unease and torment.

No sooner had he been released from prison and a brief interlude of bursting national publicity had followed than another irksome, challenging climb had begun. Bader was thirty-six when he returned to Shell, the age at which a successful man may feel he is on the threshold of top management, and he was having to contend with the incompatible process of adjusting his demanding mind to the flatness of civilian life.

True, the next eight or ten years to his middle forties were times of kaleidoscopic change, variety and travel. The flights for Shell to the Far East and Africa in a tiny, single-engined aeroplane with few aids, primitive radio, no navigator, no flight engineer – and often with Thelma sitting beside him, blithely and endearingly impervious to the hazards which lay about – were reminiscent in their way of the deeds of the pioneers of the 1920s and 1930s, of Alan Cobham, of Kingsford-Smith, of Jean Batten, of Amy Johnson and Jim Mollison, and the rest.

And then there was golf, which continued to be his ally in the bright days and the overcast. It supplied a great need and kept him in touch with his friends. Bader must have his friends about him. He relies heavily upon their company and the laughter and the fun it brings. 'A man', said Dr Johnson, 'should keep his friendships in constant repair.' No one ever followed the doctor's dictum with greater constancy. For Douglas, loneliness is the Black Death.

For the reader, these may well seem to have been days of varying pattern, excitement and colour. For Bader, they lacked fulfilment, the means of expressing his talents. What was missing amid all the activity was the opportunity to lead again, to accept authority and responsibility and discharge them. For all the glamour, these were not satisfying times.

There was, however, a mitigating factor. His work for the disabled, the extensive help he was bringing to them and the results he was achieving were becoming a feature of his life. He felt there was purpose in it. It transcended the other charitable work he was doing, worthy though it undoubtedly was.

Two constituents of mine in Chiswick, knowing my relationship with Bader, once wrote to me, as their member of parliament, asking if I could arrange for him to see their fourteen-year-old son who had had a leg amputated after a road accident; the other had also been severely damaged. The boy was in low spirits. A visit from a hero would, they felt, cheer him up.

Douglas and I called to see Derek Dimmer at 1 Mills Row, Chiswick, one evening on our way back to London from the country. His mother took us to the back room of the house. There he was, sitting very upright on the edge of the sofa, shy and wondering. Douglas walked across to him, hand outstretched. 'Hello, Derek, old lad. Douglas Bader's my name. How are you getting on?'

A few, halting words in reply were followed by the knockout question: 'Where's your football?'

Disbelief was written across the young face. 'Haven't got one, guv'nor.'

'Well, one of the boys next door must have one.' He wasn't getting away with that.

Within a minute or two a football had been found, other kids were out in the street and an uninhibited kick-about had been joined, tin pins, falls and all.

That was in November 1954. The *Brentford and Chiswick Times* reported Bader's parting words to the boy:

Good luck, old lad. Don't listen to anyone who tells you that you can't do this or that. That's nonsense. Make up your mind, you'll never use crutches or a stick, then have a go at everything. Go to school, join in all the games you can. Go anywhere you want to. But never, never let them persuade you that things are too difficult or impossible.

Within a week of the story's appearance in the paper, an anonymous approach had been made through a third party, offering the boy help with his training and resettlement to get him started on life's way.

With the middle 1950s, two things happened which re-established the buoyancy and impulse of Bader's career.

18

Danny Angel made the film of Paul Brickhill's book *Reach for the Sky*, the stirring and dramatically told story of Douglas's early contests with adversity, his exploits in the Battle of Britain, his days as a prisoner and the aftermath. Kenneth More, in a brilliantly conceived piece of character acting, played Bader in the film. The screening of the story, following quickly upon the publication of the book, brought him international renown. He was idolized, fêted and given VIP treatment everywhere. People who knew Douglas Bader only as a name soon recognized that he represented, as More put it to me, 'everything that an Englishman wants to be – courageous, honest, determined – but knows he hasn't either the nerve or the capacity to be'.

The fresh surge of publicity, which the book and then the film brought in their train, made not the slightest difference to the principal character's outward bearing and behaviour. He handled fame rather as a man deals with an uninteresting mail in the morning – perfunctorily. He was able to be offhand about it for no better reason than that that was how he felt. Bader behaves exactly as he feels; that's what some complain about.

Now and then he would tell some interloper, prying upon his privacy, or persisting with stupid questions, not to be such a bloody nuisance. He has been doing it for years. It is one of the more compelling traits of his character that, without implying any lack of respect, he is unconsciously able to talk in much the same way to a prime minister whom he happens to know as he will to the mechanic who looks after his motor car. He doesn't change his stance to suit status or personality. He just says what is in his mind and is openly natural about it.

What the gathering international attention did do was to confirm in him the recognition that by his example and endeavour his power of influence was now very great. His training at school and in the Service had taught him how to manage responsibility and how it must instantly be accepted.

Good breaks, like accidents, usually go in pairs. A second event of considerable personal importance now occurred. Quite soon after the film's release, with Bader still well short of his fiftieth birthday, the Shell Company responded to his repeated, restless urgings that it would be an advantage for the group to establish a vehicle of its own to deal with its worldwide fleet of aeroplanes. The new company was to be called Shell Aircraft Limited, and Douglas was appointed its first managing director.

Numerically, the fleet, with a strength of some seventy light and medium-sized aircraft – owned, rented or chartered – was not far short of the total which, in those days, the British Overseas Airways Corporation held on its books. It included helicopters and was engaged primarily in supporting the group's exploration and production work. All aircraft operations came under the managing director's broad purview.

Shell Aircraft, in terms of capital, was a small entity in a massive international organization; but this was not the point. What mattered was that Bader, once more, had his own responsibility, his own show. He was left largely alone, with his colleagues, to run it, since Shell practised to the full the principle of delegated authority. It suited his temperament and his training. There was an unmistakable affinity between the feel of the managing director's chair and command of a fighter squadron in the Royal Air Force. Mentally, it was satisfying. Things were looking up.

From this base, Douglas could pursue his lifestyle. Never one for getting bogged down with the paperwork, he found others (he had been doing it since his early days with Shell) to take care of that. Full in-trays, lying demandingly on the desk, were unwelcome. He painted on a broad canvas and accorded only limited weight to the administrative chores. He trusted his staff and they trusted him – to pass on the papers.

For the next twenty years or so, up to and beyond his retirement in 1969, indeed right through the 1970s into the 1980s, all his activities went on apace. His work for Shell, the flying all over the world, wherever oil was being drilled for or produced, and air transport of some kind was needed; his public speaking; his articles for the press and his authorship; his abiding interest in the physically handicapped both in Britain and across the globe; his talks with the world's leaders, to whom he was never averse from expressing his pungent and intensely patriotic views. When his time to retire from Shell arrived, the company let him keep his aeroplane so that his mobility might be maintained. It was an understanding gesture. It meant that the new commitments he had taken on for other companies, his work for the Civil Aviation Authority and all the travelling could go on much as it had done in the past.

No one was particularly surprised when, in 1976, his name appeared among the new knights in the Prime Minister's list, twenty years after it had last been there when he was made a Commander of the Order of the British Empire. Those of us who knew at first hand the extent of his voluntary work, most of which was never known outside a small circle, thought the honour was long overdue.

The knighthood had no effect on his demeanour. People may, from time to time, criticize his ways – justifiably. But none, so far as I know, has ever accused him of being pompous. The grounds do not exist. Pomposity and Bader are two most incompatible bedfellows.

It is easy to see now, in retrospect, that the parts Sir Douglas Bader has played on the world stage in the last quarter of a century make up a catalogue of endeavour scarcely less remarkable than the exploits which seized the imagination of his fellow countrymen in the fierce glare of war.

What has never been recognized in all this time is the contribution which the Shell Company, unheralded and unsung, has, by design, chance or the simple changes in corporate life, made to their fulfilment. It is not an asset which will be found in a balance sheet. It could not be claimed to be, in the accountants' well-known jargon, 'a material factor in the company's business'. What is quite undeniable, however, is that, without Shell's preparedness to invest for thirty-six years in its distinguished employee, the Bader Mission would never have got off the ground. Go back to the year 1933, the nadir of Bader's fortunes, and one is entitled to ask whether any other world company would have acted in the same way. The answer, I judge, must almost certainly be 'no'.

A lifetime, it seems, has been lived since that lovely September morning at Bentwaters thirty-six years ago when I saw, in a few treasured minutes, an aeroplane flown with such manifest flair and grace that its vision will remain for ever. In several ways, the Suffolk adventure was the precursor of this story, the juncture at which the journalist in me sensed that somewhere, somehow, sometime, the opportunity would come to contribute at first hand to the Bader legend. But, even in my moments of fantasy, I never thought then that things would quite turn out this way.

1

The impact of Cranwell

THE SEEDS OF SEPARATION

Douglas Robert Steuart Bader joined the Royal Air Force, not because he wanted to fly aeroplanes, but because he wanted to go to Cranwell. From the age of eleven, his mind was settled. Cranwell was the place for him.

The circumstances of this precocious decision were significant, its results far-reaching. The outcome was to influence his attitude to life, his personal standards and discipline, and the belief that, of all the human virtues, loyalty must come close to the top. A man may be forgiven many transgressions provided he is loyal – loyal to his country, his friends, his Service, his company, his staff, his servants, his family. Disloyalty, on the other hand, is a failing never to be countenanced. If a man gains the whole world and is disloyal, his achievements profit him nothing.

In the spring of 1921, soon after his eleventh birthday, Bader was invited by his aunt and uncle, Hazel and Cyril Burge, to spend part of the Easter holidays with them and their two very small children, Hugh and Suzanne, at Cranwell. He was then a highly promising pupil at Temple Grove, a well-known and conventional preparatory school at Eastbourne.

Cyril Burge, a flight lieutenant, was a regular officer in the Royal Air Force. He was an exciting and friendly uncle. As a First World War pilot, he had seen much of the fighting with the Royal Flying Corps over France and Flanders. Now he was adjutant to the Royal Air Force College which, with its airfield, lay just to the west of Sleaford in the flat Lincolnshire fenlands, 30 miles or so from the exposed North Sea coast.

It had been established only two years before to train the cadets who were to form the chosen cadre, the élite, of the Service. Winston Churchill, then Secretary of State both for War and Air, and the great Air Chief Marshal Sir Hugh Trenchard (later Marshal of the Royal Air Force Lord Trenchard), the Chief of the Air Staff, had been two of its most vigorous proponents.

For Douglas, who was the younger of two sons (there were no daughters) of Frederick Bader, a successful civil engineer working in India, and Jessie, whose father was also an engineer by profession, the environment of the college was immediately appealing. He was drawn to the place from the start. Its atmosphere and spirit, its pace and gaiety, its games and athletics, thrilled him. There was a welcoming friendliness about it and the Burge household which was somehow different from what he had known at home.

His upbringing had been anything but cosseted. He did not enjoy in his childhood the advantage of being one of a close-knit and constant family circle with all the affection and dependence that provides. His parents had come back temporarily from India with their first child, Frederick, or Derick, as he was called in the family, to await the birth of their second. Within weeks of Douglas's arrival, the Baders had returned again to India – without him. He was left behind with relatives until it was thought he was ready to face the summer heat of the Indian climate.

In the event, it was some two years before he rejoined them. By then the seeds of separation had begun to germinate. The reunion did little to stem their growth; rather the reverse. His parents' attention remained centred upon their first-born; the new arrival was regarded as something of a stranger. The reactions were to rumble on and on.

A year later, when the family left India for good to return to England and make their home beside the Thames at Kew, Europe was moving towards war. Within months of its outbreak, Frederick Bader was in France, serving with the Royal Engineers. As a sapper, he was soon in the front line and, in 1917, he received the head wounds from which, four years later, he was prematurely to die in hospital at Saint-Omer. Thus, at a stroke, Douglas was made fatherless at eleven and Saint-Omer became a place name which, prophetically, was to have a meaning in his life.

Major Bader had stayed on in France after the armistice in 1918 and was a member of the War Graves Commission when he died. His visits to the family in England during his last years had been few and spasmodic. Upon Jessie Bader, a woman of great attraction and determined mind, had fallen the burden of bringing up her two rumbustious sons. It was a task which was barely eased when, at the age of thirty-two, she married again.

Her second husband, the Reverend E. W. Hobbs – Bill Hobbs – was the rector of Sprotborough, a small Yorkshire village two or three miles from Doncaster. The reverend gentleman was no hand at curbing his stepsons, particularly the younger, who found little in vicarage life that appealed – and much in it that didn't. Douglas was clearly not his mother's favourite son and, being a bright and alert boy, he very soon began to sense that he wasn't wanted as much as his brother. By contrast, the warmth and closeness he found in his aunt and uncle's home, and the whole ethos of the college, were to leave their mark for ever.

Douglas passed well into Cranwell and was awarded one of the six prize cadetships which were then on offer. It wasn't surprising. He had earlier won an open scholarship from Temple Grove to St Edward's, the public school near Oxford, which became a cherished haven in his adolescent years. He had, moreover, been offered a place at Oxford and was considered to be a near-certainty for an award. But, had he gone to either university, Cambridge would have been his choice. The fact was he never had much difficulty with his work – so long as he could bring himself to concentrate, which wasn't too often.

His difficulty was the perennial problem of the outstanding school-boy games player for whom good performances for the 1st XI or 1st XV meant everything. He was noticeably more interested in whom he might be marking in the school match on Saturday than he was in sorting out the mathematical complications of calculus or unravelling the complex translations of Virgil's *Aeneid*, Book III.

There was a legacy that St Edward's bequeathed which could not be valued. Like others, he drew freely upon it. In the Reverend H. E. Kendall, the headmaster, or warden, as they called him at 'Teddy's', Douglas found a guardian spirit whose influence and example supplied an important need. The loss of a father in boyhood, no matter how thin-spun the relationship, creates a void which only those who have known it can truly comprehend. Occasionally it is filled by the substitution of a third party, an old family friend, a teacher, or even a step-parent. In Douglas's case, Henry Kendall probably came closer to standing in for a father than anyone else.

In the inter-war years, Kendall performed a service for St Edward's which was analogous to the job that the immortal Roxburgh was concurrently doing, by a coincidence of juxtaposition and timing, 40 miles away at Stowe. He understood a boy's mind and, like Roxburgh, he appreciated better than most that to show latitude and tolerance in treating the lesser, and inevitable, misdemeanours of youth was to improve immeasurably the chances of gaining acceptance of the larger principles of life. Let a boy have his head, leave him to use his common sense about the small things, without recourse to myriad rules, and the bigger issues have a curious way of taking care of themselves.

While others might tend to dwell upon the not infrequent indiscretions of the exuberant young Bader, Kendall preferred to look beyond to the qualities, attributes and potential which he believed were there. He did not allow the pinpricks, of which there were many, to prejudice the balance of the account. In return, he obtained co-operation, whereas, handled in a narrower, stricter way, the reaction could easily have been different. And probably a good deal less helpful.

In his formative and impressionable years, and, indeed, for much longer, Douglas was unusually susceptible to example – good and bad. He looked for a lead and expected to get it. In Henry Kendall of St Edward's he found a man who provided the first of the five major influences in his early life. Under him, his schooldays were successful and happy, a time of steady and uninterrupted advance. From such a base, the leap across the intervening abyss to Cranwell was accomplished confidently and without fear.

SUCCESS – AND ADMONITION

Bader was just the type of cadet the Royal Air Force was looking for: forceful, opinionated, dead honest, proud of his school, exceptional at games, undeniably and puckishly naughty at times and prepared to take unwarranted risks in the interests of a challenge. Here was a leader in embryo, someone whom other teenagers tended to admire and follow.

If he was cocky, which he was (success in youth can be a heady thing), the Service would very soon take care of that. There was nothing there which, in a couple of cadet terms, a hand-picked, senior NCO couldn't trim off and mould. What's more, there was already present a stomach for the fight, a touch of belligerence which was always ready to find its expression in a few evenly matched rounds of give-and-take in a boxing ring. Only there tended to be rather more give than take.

Equally important, perhaps, was the transparent and admitted desire to make Cranwell and the Royal Air Force the chosen career.

Few experiences in life fulfil our highest hopes. Too often is there a shortfall in the outturn of extravagant expectation. The old adage about travelling hopefully being better than to arrive has a tendency of repeating its truth. For Douglas Bader, Cranwell blew these concepts sky high. The two years he spent there from 1928 to 1930 – the notoriously difficult years when the teens are left behind and manhood waits hesitantly in the wings – were as agreeable as any he could remember. The college lived up to all his aspirations, and more. He loved his time at Cranwell, and, in return, Cranwell bestowed its favours upon him. His indoctrination was complete, blind and lasting. He wouldn't hear a word against the place. In the stories, experiences and impressions he retains to this day can be found some of the reasons for that establishment's extraordinary rise.

The two commandants of the college in Bader's time were both products of the Royal Navy and the Royal Naval Air Service, the forerunner to the modern Fleet Air Arm. In, first, Frederick Halahan (Air Vice-Marshal F. C. Halahan) and, then, Arthur Longmore (Air Chief Marshal Sir Arthur Longmore), Douglas found the leadership he hoped for and, at the time, certainly needed. Firm but reasonable, decisive but undramatic, disciplined but understanding, their authority was unchallenged. It never had to be worked for. They became, in Bader's eyes, models in their way.

There were, of course, the reverses. It was Halahan who struck first. His admonition is still sharp in the memory, the more so because it was at once accepted as being deserved. With Geoffrey Stephenson and a few others among his closer contemporaries, Douglas had been getting offside with the staff. The offences, individually, were minor; in sum they were causing gathering irritation. Coming early in the first term, they were by-products of the freedom from the regimen of school; like undergraduates in their first year at university, they felt a compulsion to exploit to the full their new-found liberation.

The summons to the commandant's office struck suddenly on a Monday morning without warning. There had been trouble about coming in late the previous weekend. Bader was regarded as the leader. Instinct told him he was for it.

It wasn't so much the words Halahan used as the way he delivered them which stunned. It was all quite quiet and unemotional; no threats, no warning. As he listened, motionless and in silence, to 'this lovely, square-faced man', Douglas was gripped by a sense of lowering humiliation. The simplicity of the message was devastating.

'Bader, I just want you to understand that we're getting a bit sick of you and your friends. This isn't a sort of school. What we want in the Royal Air Force are men, not boys.'

The pause seemed like an eternity.

'That's all.'

It was all over in less than a minute. As he withdrew, Douglas felt his small world closing about him.

If Bader had opted, originally, for Cranwell (instead of Cambridge) because he liked the place and longed to go there, rather than because he wanted to learn to fly, flying now took command of his feelings. 'How can they know that joy to be alive who have not flown?': the simple, sensitive words, written in an essay by a young cadet, typified his sentiments.

The sensation of flight drew him irresistibly to the air. He showed an aptitude for flying just as he had done for games as a small boy at Temple Grove. There is an affinity between the two. That he was able in his lifetime to exploit his instinctive gifts as a pilot and turn them exceptionally to his advantage, particularly after he lost his legs, was due in significant part to the doctrine of one man.

Flying Officer W. J. Pearson, his first flying instructor, was a precise, modest and pedantic man. The Service, by its well-tried habit of contradiction, called him 'Pissy' Pearson. The sobriquet was the antithesis of his personality, character and temperament. Indeed, with his reticent manner, his punctiliousness and his aversion to any form of histrionics, he made small impression upon his fellow men.

But he flew an aeroplane with the angels, and he had the blessed knack of being able to instil in the adaptable pupil the sense of coaxing, caressing and stroking an aircraft about the sky. His soft, persuasive hands turned flying into a continuous recital of fluid movements. And yet, for all his lightness and kindness of touch, he exercised absolute dominion over an aeroplane. He controlled it positively and possessively.

Bader's first flight with Wilfred Pearson in an Avro 504 took place on 13 September 1928. It lasted 20 minutes and merited only two words in his log-book: 'air experience'. He played no part at all in the practice. He was a silent and absorbed witness to man's mastery over flight and to the first-class pilot's enduring respect for its principles. The impression of sympathetic, urging hands was paramount.

The next twenty flights up to, but not including, his first solo covered a period of five months, from 14 September 1928 to 12 February 1929, including a short break for Christmas leave. His total flying time then was 11 hours and 15 minutes.

12 February, nine days short of his nineteenth birthday, was unforgettable. He had three flights that day in the Avro. Hitherto he had never flown more than once a day. Pearson took him up first for 25 minutes of circuits and landings. Then his flight commander, Flight Lieutenant Douglas MacFadyen (Air Chief Marshal Sir Douglas MacFadyen), gave him his final solo check. Like the dress rehearsal before the opening night, the solo check is always an edgy business. For Bader, the 10 minutes that he and MacFadyen were airborne together were a formality. No doubts, no criticisms; only a word or two of encouragement and advice.

Now he was taxiing out on his own, turning into wind, steadily pushing the throttle forward with his left hand while the right, with a light and gentle touch, kept a respectful forward pressure on the stick. His feet on the rudder pedals maintained the direction. Once off the ground, Douglas held the aircraft steadily down until the speed had built up. He felt swamped by an exhilaration of mind which knew no bounds. He was alone with an aeroplane. And utterly free.

There were no worries, no apprehensions about making it. For most of us, the first solo, like a maiden speech in the House of Commons, is prefaced by nightmares, anxieties and appalling visions of total collapse. Bader knew none of this. He much preferred knowing that the instructor wasn't there; otherwise it was all just like it had been when MacFadyen or Pearson was with him. But he was conscious of a feeling that, at last, he had come of age.

THE LEGACY PEARSON BEQUEATHED

Towards the end of his first cadet year, Bader flew with Pearson, a flight lieutenant now, for the last time. The entry in the log-book was quite factual: '8.7.29 F/Lt Pearson, 30 minutes, 2 loops, 3 forced landings, 1 landing into wind'. By now, his total flying time had

29

reached 47 hours and 45 minutes, of which 25 hours had been dual instruction, almost all of them with Pearson. The experience with him had been invaluable, the time priceless, for it is in the first fifty hours of a pilot's flying that the foundations and habits are irrevocably laid.

Dermot Boyle, who was a cadet wing officer at Cranwell in Bader's time and who, in his own right, became one of the Service's outstanding pilots, has lent his authority to that belief:

The fact that Douglas thought as much of Pearson bears out one of my best-established theories. A pupil will normally worship his first instructor, and this carries an enormous moral responsibility for the instructor because everything he does and says in the air and on the ground will automatically be what the pupil will afterwards emulate.

Pearson's influence was not restricted to flying. It extended to his pupil's vocabulary. He heard Douglas refer one day to a 'plane'. Straightaway he took him to an Avro, parked beside the hanger. Touching the lower wing of the biplane, he said in his precise and pedantic way: 'This – *this* – is a plane. That – *that*', pointing to the whole aircraft, 'is an aeroplane.' He would allow 'aeroplane' or 'aircraft' but nothing else. The other bastardized abbreviations – kite, plane and, no doubt, the Americanism, ship – were absolutely forbidden.

Equally forthright was his rejection of his pupil's somewhat irreverent reference one morning to 'that french letter over there', meaning the wind-sock, as it fluttered, condomlike, in the breeze from its mast at the end of the airfield. Pearson challenged the analogy immediately. 'That *isn't* a french letter,' he retorted dryly, without the trace of a smile, 'that is a *wind-sock*.'

Unlike a majority of the flying instructors, Pearson was not himself a Cranwell graduate; but his standards were similar. At the end of 1929, after four proficient but undramatic years, he left the college for No. 84 (Bomber) Squadron in Iraq. Ten years later, in August 1940, when his old pupil was rising to a crescendo of endeavour in the Battle of Britain, he was struck down by ill health and invalided out of the Service. He was still a flight lieutenant, having temporarily left the Royal Air Force in the interim when his engagement ran out.

He died on 22 January 1943, from tuberculosis. He was barely forty. Few were aware of his passing. Bader, a prisoner in Colditz by then, did not know what befell him. But he never forgot the start Wilfred Pearson had given him in their enlightened year together.

'It's a pity', he said, 'that a fellow like that couldn't know what I felt.'

It wasn't long before Douglas had placed MacFadyen, the officer commanding 'A' Flight in 'A' Squadron, alongside Kendall of St Edward's and Halahan as a model to emulate. Understandably, it was his manner and the easy authority with which he imposed his will that Bader noticed so particularly. The ability not only to make a pupil see the sense of his diktat, but to do so humanly and with reason in such a way that foolish behaviour was made to appear beneath the dignity of an adult man, contrasted with some of the more brash and exhibitionist methods (seldom seen at Cranwell) employed by lesser commanders. Respect, obtained by example, good manners and grace, and without apparent effort, carried so much more effect.

Bader saw MacFadyen display these characteristics in an unexpected context. An instructor in the flight had shown a pupil how to do an unusual manoeuvre which, in the flying trade, is known as a 'bunt'. It is not an aerobatic that is commonly performed because it tends to put unnatural stresses on an aircraft, not least a biplane like an Avro.

It consists of flying round the outside of a loop – a normal loop turned inside out. It's like following the outer surface of a globe right round until the bottom, or the underneath, has been passed with the aeroplane upside down; the pilot may then roll out. With the stick being shoved persistently forward, pushing the nose down, down, down and eventually underneath, it isn't one of the more agreeable flying sensations. Of course, if a bunch of new pilots, who have just gone solo, hear that someone has done a bunt, then all will want to try it. Thus it was in 'A' Flight. In the interest of reasonable safety, something had to be said.

MacFadyen called the cadets into his office and put his thoughts to them. 'When I was flying yesterday, I saw two or three of you doing bunts. I know it's good fun trying these things, but you haven't had much experience. I don't want you to start being careful or anything like that but this does put quite a big stress on an aircraft. So please – *please* – think about it before you start doing these things. We don't want to have to stop it all with a fatal accident.'

There was nothing more; no ticking off, no warnings. Just 'watch it', and then 'we don't want people getting killed, so keep it in mind'. MacFadyen made his appeal to common sense and reason. It was all done without effort and without striving for effect. Douglas found it impressive.

The fact was, of course, that the staff and the instructors at Cran-well were a hand-picked lot, well above the general run. The evidence is to be seen in the record and the names in his log-book: Flight Lieutenant Boyle, Flying Officer Constantine (Air Chief Marshal Sir Hugh Constantine), Squadron Leader Coningham (Air Marshal Sir Arthur Coningham), who had brought with him from the First World War the DSO, an MC and a DFC. It was an impressive stable.

Some pupils – relatively, only a very few – fell short of the mark. Those who achieved it were handed a visiting card for life; they found it opened most doors in the Service and set them climbing a stairway to the stars.

The competition among the cadets for the top spot – the Sword of Honour – at the end of the two-year course developed into a two-horse race. Bader was beaten into second place by a young officer cadet named Patric Coote. 'I didn't really mind,' he said. 'Paddy Coote was a splendid man; very good all round – at games, at work, at flying, at everything.' Commissioned on the same day, 26 July 1930, each went to a fighter squadron – Bader to No. 23, and his conqueror to No. 43. Coote, then a wing commander, was killed in 1941 leading a low-level attack against the enemy in Greece.

THE NAVAL AND MILITARY INFLUENCE

Cranwell's foundations were driven deep into the ground which the Royal Navy and the British Army had prepared. Naval and military tradition permeated the Royal Air Force in its early days.

In the First World War the college site had been used for a naval station formed to train pilots for the Royal Naval Air Service. Its nautical atmosphere had prevailed long after the sailors had gone. Those who served on the staff of Sholto Douglas (Marshal of the Royal Air Force Lord Douglas of Kirtleside) at Fighter Command in 1942, and remember the meetings he chaired with the Navy about ship and convoy protection, still recall the commander-in-chief's reflections about the mariners' influence at Cranwell.

Sholto Douglas had been sent there in 1918, fresh from his exploits as a fighter pilot in France, to look after the flying training. The college had not yet been born, and the senior officer was a colonel in the Royal Air Force who had earlier held the rank of captain in the

Royal Navy. He had not forgotten it. With a commendable prejudice and obstinacy, he had allowed the nautical terms to endure. Officers and other ranks still referred to him as 'the captain'. They did not go on leave, they 'went ashore'. The Air Force transport which took them to the railway station was known as 'the Liberty Boat'. Naval uniforms were still much in evidence.

When the college eventually came to be established, it relied significantly upon officers who had transferred from the Navy and, to a lesser extent, from the Army. Like the Service it was supplying, it absorbed the concepts and disciplines of the other two Forces. For the first ten or a dozen years, its character and personality owed much to this external influence. Bader regarded it as a factor of capital importance in the emergent period. It had a noticeable effect upon his own attitude and respect for his naval and military friends. He reserved a privileged place, in the battles which were to follow, for the Fleet Air Arm pilots who, to gain fighter experience, were seconded by the Royal Navy to his squadron and wing.

The special and quite unmistakable individuality with which the Royal Air Force – and Cranwell – subsequently became endowed (a character to which Bader himself, by example and performance, made his own contribution) was built on these beginnings. They brought strength and incalculable advantages to the youngest Service.

In Bader's mind, there was another mentor who has to be added to Halahan, Longmore and MacFadyen as a signal influence in his time at Cranwell and for years afterwards. When Arthur Longmore, a lifelong friend of Bader, succeeded Halahan as commandant at the beginning of his last year, Douglas Evill (Air Chief Marshal Sir Douglas Evill), a group captain then, remained for some months as the college's number 2. 'Strath' Evill, as the Service knew him, had been trained as a cadet at Dartmouth. There was a strong naval influence about him and, like Longmore and Halahan, he too could claim fighting experience with the Royal Naval Air Service in the First World War.

These four officers, with Kendall before them, became models in the impressionable years. When the tests came, their image, silent yet still dominant, was there in the background to counsel and to guide. Their collective and individual leadership, coming when he had a real need of it, affected Bader profoundly.

There is an important and illuminating comparison to be made between the flying instruction which Douglas received as a cadet and the training process which the Royal Air Force, by the impact of circumstance, introduced in wartime. It is the key, or, at least, one of the keys, to the superiority which the peacetime professionals normally enjoyed over their 'amateur' counterparts who came into the Service from civilian life in 1939 and left again, having played their part, after the war.

Douglas's first flying log-book, well thumbed and tattered now with the years, tells its own story. When Evill, as the assistant commandant, placed his neat and familiar signature to the record in July 1930, Bader had then flown a total of 104 hours and 45 minutes in his two years as a cadet. 104 hours flying between 13 September 1928 and 16 July 1930 – an average of no more than 52 hours a year, or not quite 5 a month and rather less than 2 a week – make, on the face of it, a remarkably small tally when set against the time and the totals achieved in the comparable training programmes of the Second World War. True, at Cranwell, the cadets were learning to do many things other than just fly aeroplanes. Certainly there were the longish periods of leave between the terms. Granted the flights in the old Avro 504 seldom averaged more than 30 minutes apiece and that the weather in Bader's first winter at the college was exceptionally unfavourable for flying. Make allowances for all these factors and still, in a strictly comparative sense, the total of hours flown in relation to the timetable appears, by latter-day standards, strikingly unhurried and leisurely.

To make a judgement, I set this picture against the comparable details in my own wartime log-book. In 1940, in the beautifully crisp, clear and sunny days of a Canadian fall, far removed from the firing line, the same (or much the same) initial stages to the first solo were completed not in five months but in ten days. In terms of training time, the first 100 hours embraced not two years but four months – and *that* with liberal weekend passes for pleasant skiing excursions into the Laurentian Mountains and an extended Christmas leave spent in the rugged loveliness of northern Quebec. Seven months after the first flight, the 'amateurs' among us were reporting for operational duty with our first squadrons; some did it in less. With Bader, *two years* elapsed between the initial gentle swing round the sky with Pearson and his posting, on 25 August 1930, to 23 Squadron at Kenley in Surrey.

But the bread cast on those slow-moving waters returned in due time. The opportunity to assimilate all the teaching – in the air as well as on the ground – to absorb it all without rush and bustle, conferred many benefits. In sum they amounted to professionalism – plain, undiluted, unadorned professional skill.

Other conventions contributed to the college's special ethos. It was essentially a bachelor establishment – a state which enhanced the spirit of 'dining-in' nights in the mess. As a general rule, no officer in the Royal Air Force took unto himself in those days a wife until he was thirty, or a squadron leader, whichever was the earlier. It followed that no cadet was married.

Douglas has no doubt about it.

Cranwell was half a university for us. It gave us time to read, to think, to listen, to talk and to make friends. We drank it all in – the flying, the intimacy of the place, the gaiety, the walks, the messing about with motor bikes, the games, the disciplines, the leadership. It was all there. And there seemed to be time for everything and this, undoubtedly, was reflected in our flying. We absorbed the instruction rather than learnt it.

In the hangar at Cranwell in Douglas's time there hung an old First World War picture which has always stuck in his mind. It was a drawing of a fighter, caught at the top of a 'victory' loop, as the pilot, flushed with a success over the enemy, gave vent to his joy. A wing had just broken away and was beginning to flutter earthwards. A three-word caption completed the story: 'The Last Loop'.

Years afterwards, Bader never allowed his squadron or wing pilots, in the first ecstasies of victory, to repeat the folly. The customary beat-up of the airfield, the steep climbing roll to the right and then one to the left – the classical (and normally imaginary) expression of victory – was not for him. How could a young pilot be sure that his own aircraft hadn't suffered weakening damage in combat?

He had absorbed Cranwell's lesson; no one had taught it.

THE GAIETY OF LIFE

If the sterner side of life at the Royal Air Force College cut the deepest marks, the lighter moments are secured for ever in Douglas's memory. 'The gaiety of life', as he has it; the simple, straightforward acts of fresh, playful minds; the events and outings which so often seemed to end in unlikely and even ridiculous complications: this was the stuff of which cadet humour and jollity was made. It was the spice of young men's lives as they served in comradeship together.

For Bader and his friends, it was the escapades on their motor cycles and the goodnatured banter of the senior NCOs which made for much of the fun and the laughter. They never stopped tinkering with their bikes – the Rudges and the Nortons, the AJSs and the BSAs, the Douglases and, here and there, the Brough Superiors. They stripped them down and reassembled them, changed the pistons, fitted new rings, bored them out, lifted the compression ratios, polished the surfaces – anything to coax another two or three miles an hour out of them in the split-arse dashes up and down the length of the neighbouring Ancaster straight.

One Sunday afternoon, Douglas, his friend Geoffrey Stephenson and another cadet named Fairtlough – Fairey Fairtlough – with throttles wide open, were passing and repassing one another on the road to Newark when the world very nearly stopped still. It was the time when long woollen scarves, in club, school or college colours, were the fashion. They were wound loosely round the neck, and the long, tassled ends dangled down to the knee. These were the days, also, when the primary chain system on a motor cycle, connecting rear wheel, gearbox and crankshaft, was left oily and exposed. They hadn't thought then to case it all in. Fairtlough, on his AJS, his Cranwell scarf, with its light blue stripe on a grey background, wrapped round his neck, was travelling fast alongside Bader on his prized, flat-twin Douglas. With the speed steadily being pushed up to near the maximum, Douglas was suddenly conscious of seeing his companion's head snap down on to the tank of his bike, as machine and rider left the road.

'That's bloody funny,' was the somewhat insensitive comment, as they bent quizzically over the luckless Fairtlough, his face now purple with near-strangulation. 'Whatever happened?' The question was hardly necessary.

With the ends of the scarf frantically disentangled from the offending chain, Fairtlough was able once again to fill his lungs. Not long afterwards he transferred to the Royal Navy.

Rather more bizarre, and certainly a great deal more complicated, was Douglas's strange adventure with Massey's 500cc BSA and torpedo sidecar on the same Newark road. Peter Massey, a contemporary, had had to go to Nottingham by train, so Bader was invited to ride the combination up later in the afternoon to foregather at some prearranged rendezvous with the inevitable 'girls'. ('There were the hell of a lot of damned good-looking girls up there in those days, old boy.')

Adept on a solo machine, Douglas had never before ridden a motor cycle and sidecar. As he was speeding up the shallow hill approaching Newark, two fellow cadets, bent on a similar mission, and giving appropriate gestures, passed him on their solo machines. A complimentary burst on the throttle took him too fast into the left-hand bend at the top of the hill. Up came the empty sidecar in protest. To correct, Douglas had no alternative but to straighten out and head for the wooden fence on the opposite side of the road. With the fence and hedge offering scant resistance, he crossed a broad and well-filled flower bed before coming to rest, still in the saddle, on the edge of a freshly cut lawn of a comfortable, middle-class Nottinghamshire home. A tea party, with an immaculate white tablecloth and best china tea service laid out on it, was in progress in the warm afternoon sunshine.

'Difficult to know, really, what to say, sitting there by oneself on a BSA and sidecar . . .'

With ready and instantly willing help from the somewhat surprised guests, Bader and mount were soon pushed back on to the road. In addition to the snout of the sidecar being well dented, the throttle cable had come adrift in the mêlée. The local garage agreed to have the repairs done so that the machine could be collected on the way home.

In the darkness, five or six hours later, with the rain now pouring down, Massey didn't notice that the mechanic had inadvertently reversed the throttle linkage. When he thought the lever was marginally open it was, in fact, set wide open. With no response from the kick starter, they elected to push the machine with Douglas behind the sidecar and Massey on the handlebars. As the speed built up, the engine caught. Away it went like a shot into the darkness and the rain. Not expecting the response, Massey let the handlebars go. As the sidecar mounted the pavement, the wheels of the motor cycle ran along the gutter, keeping it on course – straight for the plate-glass window of a motor car showroom at the far end of the road. A dimly lit street lamp was sufficient to expose the impending disaster.

Suddenly there was a shattering crash, followed by the sound of a revving engine. As they hurried down the road, they came first upon a man lying flat on his back on the pavement. 'I shall always remember it,' said Douglas. 'He was perfectly dressed, mackintosh smartly buttoned and belted up, gloves – fawn gloves – on his hands, cap pulled slightly down over his face. A cigarette was burning in his fingers.'

37

Flying Colours

As they shook him, the victim gave an unpromising grunt. Further on, the combination had overturned after hitting a pillar box. Close by, a policeman was hopping about on one leg and rubbing the other. His comment was not unreasonable: ' 'Ello, 'ello, I said to myself, 'ere's some bugger pissed.' It was a fair, if inaccurate, assumption.

Having established that Bader and Massey were Cranwell cadets, the constable, at once on their side, then turned his attention to the victim who was still lying stretched out on the pavement. 'You all right?' he asked, shaking the unfortunate individual, determined to get the answer 'Yes', no matter what condition he might be in. 'You're all right. . . . Come along now, up you get.'

With that, the motley crew repaired to the police station. Over cups of strong tea the Law put in a call to Cranwell. 'Got two of your cadets here,' he said. 'The usual. No transport.'

Within less than an hour, the customary Trojan van, which on Saturday nights was in the habit of collecting cadets scattered about at divers points in the surrounding countryside, was bowling along with Bader and Massey in the back, reflecting upon their strange adventure. Nothing more was ever heard of the incident, although rumour had it afterwards that the wretched victim, having been off work for weeks, had made a settlement with the insurance company under which he was to receive £3 a week for life.

Such was the understanding between college and constabulary in those days that seldom was anything ever heard of any incident involving a Cranwell cadet within the boundaries of the neighbouring shires.

If the outings on the road supplied their quota of fun, the rare days out with the Belvoir and the Blankney added to the variety. The two hunts normally used to meet at Cranwell once or twice a year.

Bader wasn't a horseman, but a few of the cadets like Geoffrey Stephenson and John Chance had, in the course of their upbringing, learnt to ride well. Stephenson, knowing it would take little to spur Douglas into having a go, made light of it. 'There's nothing to it, old boy. Just remember to go up when the horse's front leg goes forward.'

After a ride or two on horses hired from the local stables, Bader had mastered a few rudimentary principles. The Blankney were due to meet at the college the next day. 'Come on,' said Stephenson, 'we're going to hunt tomorrow.'

The day was noteworthy for the tolerance, forbearance and steady-

38

ing qualities of the Master, 'a really splendid man'. 'Just imagine it,' recalled Douglas, 'seven or eight cadets, aged eighteen or nineteen, most of us out for the first time, going at it just like we used to ride our motor bikes.' He remembers vividly four of them, pounding along, almost abreast, taking a grey stone wall at full tilt. 'Just like Balaclava, old boy.' As they went over, he recalls catching a glimpse of the cadet on his left, Doran, parting company with his horse. As he came off a plaintive cry rang out. 'Catch my horse, somebody, catch my horse will you?'

Doran seems to have been accident-prone. He was later to meet his end in curious circumstances. Someone slow-rolled an aeroplane in which he was a passenger. He had omitted to strap himself in.

'THEY WERE LOVELY, LOVELY MEN'

Flight Sergeant Curtis was cast in the traditional mould of the outstanding senior non-commissioned officers who gave the Service its peacetime core and enabled it to contain the great expansion when war came. In Bader, Curtis soon found his man; just the sort of foil the experienced disciplinarian was always on the lookout for. A tendency to get into scrapes and to be a bit admired by the others for doing so. The spirit to take in good part anything that was coming. A touch of cockiness which left scope for pricking. A temperament which would bounce back from any well-aimed barb. A disposition, unless otherwise ordered, to take up station in the middle of the middle rank with two very similar characters on either side.

'That gentleman there in the middle of the second rank': he became an essential butt of the resourceful flight sergeant's repertoire. 'The bugger kicked me round from pillar to post. He never let up. And he became a great chum in my Service career.'

Seventeen years later, in 1945, Douglas, then a group captain and the sector commander at North Weald, went to a dance at the headquarters of what, for most of the war, was called Fighter Command. He met Curtis again. He was now a wing commander with a son in the Royal Air Force – a flight lieutenant with the Distinguished Flying Cross. His pride was manifest.

Much later still, when Bader was nearing the end of his time with the Shell Company, he took a call in his office from the King Edward VII Hospital for Officers in London – 'Sister Agnes'. 'We've got a friend of yours here,' they said. 'Wing Commander Curtis has just

39

had a leg amputated. We thought you might, perhaps, like to come and see him.'

Douglas called round that afternoon at teatime. Curtis was sitting propped up in bed. The banter was on the other side now.

'It's all those years at Cranwell, flight, drilling the life out of us, that's what's done it. Too much of all that "HALT ... ONE TWO ...", bang, bang. That's what's messed your leg up.'

Other senior NCOs were to figure notably in his life. Bernard West of 242 Squadron, J. W. ('Tubby') Mayes of Coltishall, and then another who, with Curtis, was to scale the heights and see his family's connection with the Royal Air Force continue. W. J. Hendley, one of the first of the young engineering apprentices at Cranwell in the early 1920s, became a wing commander and kept the aircraft flying at Coltishall where 'Knocker' West and 'Tubby' Mayes first made their names. Like others of his generation in the Service, 'Spanner' Hendley is a believer in maintaining contact with old comrades. A message reaches Douglas each Christmas.

In 1979, by way of providing a caption for two faded yellow photographs of the old hutted buildings of the original college, a personal memoir captured, as well as any words could do, the mood of those times:

I shared a royal suite in this five-star Hilton with twenty other lifers. The padre told us to wait until we were married; the discip. corporal said we were 'orrible little boys who had never seen our fathers. He taught us only four-letter words.

The CO was a splendid fellow.... I saw him personally twice. The interviews were short. 'Seven days on fatigues and I do not wish to see you again ...'

Our schoolmasters were dedicated men. I still write to one, Captain Fanstone, AFC. He must be in his nineties now.

We ate a lot of hard biscuits for tea – twice weekly. They were surplus to World War I requirements.

I got my wing colours for shooting and football and an average passing-out mark.

Most of us were very happy and proud to have been associated with Cranwell.

Bader embellishes the legend of the Curtises, the Wests, the Mayeses and the Hendleys. For Cranwell's senior NCOs he offers the ultimate accolade: 'They were lovely, lovely men. I learnt more about being an officer from them than from anyone else.'

*

The impact of Cranwell

On 25 July 1930 Douglas reported to the commandant's office for the last time. Nearly two years had passed since that fateful Monday morning when, in less than a minute and with a few simple, quiet sentences, Halahan had turned him from boy into man. What he had learnt from that humbling experience and in the months that followed became the platform upon which he was to build his astonishing life.

Arthur Longmore passed his confidential report across the desk. 'You may as well read this,' he said.

Three words caught Bader's eye: 'plucky, capable, headstrong'. Half a century on, they still fit pretty well today.

2

Fighter squadron

A pilot's log-book, like a company's balance sheet, tells its own story. One feature is common to both. The good things are put in the window; the nasties get tucked away.

Not even a nitpicking auditor, examining Bader's books of account, could deny that they represented a 'true and fair view' of the state of the pilot's affairs. Everything was revealed. Nothing was hidden. Terse explanatory notes abounded.

After the last Cranwell balance had been struck and Evill had countersigned the account, Douglas appended a rider. Set out boldly in double spacing and underlined twice for special effect, it was written in a swift, well-slanted, flowing hand. The Greek 'e's, paying deference to the classics, were a feature of the manuscript. 'Posted to No. 23, Fighter Squadron, RAF, Kenley, from Cadet College, Cranwell. Reported for duty: 25.8.30'. It was the second milestone along the Service highway.

Bader was six months short of his twenty-first birthday when he joined 23 Squadron. He played his arrival quietly. Cranwell and St Edward's had taught him that. But inside there was a pent-up, surging enthusiasm which could not long be disguised. Had he been given the chance to make his own choice, he would not have picked differently. The moment he set foot in Kenley, sited pleasantly between Croydon and Caterham in the Surrey hills, he knew there wasn't another squadron like it. In his eyes it was the best, the nonpareil in a distinguished few.

There were captivating aircraft to fly. The Gloster Gamecock – in his words, 'a beautiful, unstable biplane, just right for aerobatics and lovely to handle' – still had a year to run before the squadron was re-equipped with Bristol Bulldogs. It was one in a line of classical fighter aircraft, chubby, compact and squat. In the late 1920s and 1930s, these manoeuvrable aeroplanes caught the eye of every air-minded youth in the land. For a generation of young Britons growing up, the Gamecock, the Bulldog and, then, the Gladiator, the last of the biplanes, offered irresistible appeal.

Like the Bentleys of Birkin, Benjafield and Barnato at Le Mans and the overhead-valve Nortons of Woods and Guthrie, tearing down the Mountain in the TT races in the Isle of Man, these aircraft confirmed the consummation of the marriage between Britain's inter-war design genius and her workmanship. No thoroughbred ever came from sounder stock. The flying was expected to match the progeny.

Life in a peacetime fighter squadron in the Royal Air Force was delicious. It suited Douglas Bader from air to ground. He couldn't think there was another job like it. Everything, or almost everything, was right. The daily routine unfolded in a measured, well-ordered, unhurried way. Service standards and discipline were certainly there, but the demands of the early 1930s were hardly a pointer to what war was soon to bring. There was time to do the things that young men want to do, 'to smell the flowers along the way'. And Kenley was a base of many attractions.

The established stations of the peacetime Air Force, with their solid, angular buildings, were planned on a comfortable and functional pattern. They seemed to have been pressed out by die-stamp and then run off the conveyor belt. They were secure and tidy places which looked as if they were permanently awaiting the commanding officer's inspection.

Closely tended lawns were offset in summer by flower beds of blazing colour. Red geraniums, bright as Dayglo, were the preferred plant; the roses ran them a close second. Edges and grass verges were kept cleanly trimmed, and formidable, whitewashed corner-stones were set to protect them from the ravages of the squadron pilots and their curiously assorted means of transport.

Entrance gates, guardroom and flagstaff, railings, posts and chains wore fresh traces of the painter's brush. Like the Forth Bridge, the painting was never done. Whiteness was brightness; yet, paradoxically, what could not reasonably be deemed to be white seemed destined to be black – glossy and decisive black. There was no compromise, not as the Royal Navy had found with its characteristic grey.

Days began civilly around 7 a.m. with a cup of tea brought to the bedside. Uniforms, buttons and shoes were placed in the attentive care of a batman. For a young officer, commissioned in the 1930s, domestic chores were happily assigned to other, and trusted, hands. The relationship between officer and servant was very close, and built on mutual respect.

The mornings when the weather was kind were normally given up to flying. Reporting to their flights after breakfast, at an hour when other men would be reaching their offices, the pilots received their orders for the day. The flight commanders who issued them were men of authority and decision. The ground crews who made the aircraft ready – the fitters who tended the engines and the riggers who looked after the airframes – were part of the team. The proficiency and example of the senior NCOs, whose word was God, permeated the flight.

Aerobatics, formation flying, simulated fighter attacks, forced landings and the occasional flights at night when conditions and the moon were right: the pilots spent their days going through the gamut. The sequences were as predictable as the visits which were paid to friends at other airfields. A social interlude and lunch at midday made a congenial digression in a carefully planned cross-country flight.

The steady pace of life was such that there was time to assimilate the precision and advice of the senior squadron pilots. The opportunities to practise, practise and practise again the exercises to be found in the flying manuals, and to emulate the mighty, were numerous. It was an invigorating atmosphere in which to lift personal performance and flying skills.

For its younger members, the mess was a focal point of squadron and station life. Great store was laid by it. The regular dining-in nights, when all officers wore mess kit and protocol was strictly observed, were invested with proper decorum – and fun. The food was good, well cooked and inexpensive. The fresh vegetables and fruit, picked that day, came from the station's extensive kitchen garden. The fare was enhanced by the way it was served by the mess staff, by the immaculately polished silver and glass, by the softened lighting and by the squadron's trophies and spoils, proudly displayed on the long tables. Watching in judgement over it all, like examination invigilators, were the great fighter heroes of the First World War – Mannock, Ball, McCudden and others – whose portraits gazed out from the walls.

Douglas always considered himself a teetotaller, although now and then he would allow himself a special glass of champagne. But he needed no stimulant for he entered *fully* into the spirit of the evenings. He loved them for their happiness, gaiety and friendship. He had taken to them from the very start at Cranwell. Dermot Boyle, the first Cranwell cadet to become Chief of the Air Staff, recalls the occasions. 'I remember how I used to enjoy his company and spirit during dining-in nights. He had the remarkable gift of being able to be naughty and still be absolutely loyal to authority.'

Games, like dining-in nights, were important in the Service, and to the squadron, and Wednesday afternoons were reserved for them. An outstanding games player like Bader quickly caught the selectors' eye. Rugby football was his game and, playing outside the scrum either at stand-off half or centre three-quarter, he made an instant mark. The matches that he played for the Royal Air Force, the Combined Services and the Harlequins at Twickenham were the high spots; an England cap was now within his grasp.

There was cricket, too, for the Service, but, adept though he was at the willow game (he was a strong, combative all-rounder), it was rugger that he preferred. Cricket – two-day matches at the Oval and elsewhere, against the other two Services, the universities, the MCC, the Foresters, and the rest – took too long. It kept him away from flying and flying now came first.

The affinity between games and flying, like a flair for riding a motor cycle and flying well, is surprisingly close. The gifted games players always seemed to make good pilots and able and resourceful fighter leaders. They had a facility for flying aeroplanes and a natural feel for leading squadrons and wings. Certain denominators are common to both pursuits.

The accomplished player of games, by eye, anticipation, footwork and an innate sense of position, places himself ready to strike. He is seldom off balance or hurried. He gives himself more time than the others to fashion his fluent strokes. This is what sets him apart. Tilden, Perry, Laver and Borg in lawn tennis; Bradman, Hammond, Sobers and Vivian Richards in cricket: in their respective times, they have seemed to have had an age in which to make their sallies. Time and position – and, of course, boldness – have been their friends.

In the make-up of a great fighter pilot, the lethal thrust, the fast overtaking speed, the short penetrating burst at close range – all this flows from good initial positioning. And adroit positioning, for its success, demands that allegiance be paid to height and to having time to deal in the currency of surprise. Bader, Malan, Tuck, Johnson, Caldwell and Beurling for Britain and the Commonwealth; Blakeslee, Gabreski, Zemke, Gentile and Godfrey for the United States; Galland, Moelders, Steinhoff and Marseille for Germany: their sense of position in the air, of being in the right place, and ready, was to give them their chances and the time in which to take them. It had been the same story with their forerunners in the earlier war, with Mannock, Ball, McCudden, Bishop, Richthofen and Boelke. The principles of air fighting, and games, do not change.

By the time Douglas had spent a year with 23 Squadron, he had digested the writings and the sayings of the First World War heroes. There wasn't an autobiography or a biographical sketch of any of them that he hadn't devoured. Their strategy and tactics became the gospel in which he placed his trust. Its theme was position. It suited the playing field as appositely as it did the daylight air.

Bader was lucky with his flying in 23 Squadron in two other significant respects. Harry Day, or 'Pricky' Day as the squadron called him, was a successful First World War pilot, operationally mature and older than most of the others. As a flight commander of stature and experience he was a good foil for an enthusiastic and forceful young pilot officer.

When he had to tell Bader off for doing unwise things with an aeroplane, his background and status gave the message an added impact. Moreover, Day, like Boyle, Pearson and the other exponents of the flying art, who had riveted their expertise upon Douglas's mind, was another master of an aircraft. He was an accomplished aerobatic pilot, and aerobatics were 23 Squadron's speciality. Four of its pilots, Jones, Purvis, MacDougall and McKenna, flying the pair in the Hendon Air Display in each of the two years (1929 and 1930) before Douglas's arrival, had defeated all comers. Within a year of his joining the squadron, Bader had been picked by the commanding officer, Squadron Leader H. W. Woollett, to partner Day in 23's defence of its Hendon title. Geoffrey Stephenson, his Cranwell contemporary and, now, almost his equal in the air, was first reserve.

Having prevailed again, to make it three in a line, Day and Bader treated the crowd of 170,000, packed round the airfield, to two 15-

minute demonstrations of the advanced and imaginative art of aerobatic flying. It was a spell-binding display.

Douglas remembers that the same afternoon 43 Squadron, with its aircraft tied together, flew a sequence of tight formation aerobatics with an ease that hid the remarkably small margin for error that such a synchronized exercise offered. Since their aircraft lacked the power thrust and impetus of the later low-wing monoplanes like the Spitfire and the Hurricane, the danger of a subordinate pilot falling out of a manoeuvre for lack of speed was always in the mind of the proven leader. It was a feature which was lost on the massive audience, but it restricted severely the extent of 43's repertoire.

If the truth be told, 23 gained its third successive Hendon victory with something to spare, for Stephenson, by any test now an exceptional aerobatic pilot, had already got the edge on Pricky Day, undeniably expert though the flight commander was still recognized to be. Two months later, on 22 August, in a second display, this time at Cramlington in Northumberland, Bader and Stephenson, flying the pair together for the first time in public, fashioned a sequence over the top of the airfield which set the great northern crowd alight. With speeds barely touching 150 m.p.h., even at the bottom of a dive, the demonstration could all be completed well within the perimeter of the airfield. In the case of Hendon, most of it was performed right in front of the royal box and no distance at all from the vast concourse of spectators gathered for the display. It was the intimacy of it all which raised the temperature and stimulated the thrills.

Bader and Stephenson, now flying frequently together, had lifted their dual and individual skills to a level which was out of reach of all save a small handful of Service pilots. Squadron pride and the quest for perfection – to be, in a word, the best – was their spur.

Some of the flying with 23 was, of course, primitive and in keeping with the stage aviation had reached in those times. There were no navigational aids, the barest minimum of instruments in the open cockpits, no comforting controller to talk to by radio, no electronic means of fixing position over the ground, no one to help a lost pilot with a face-saving vector to fly for base. The gyro compass, which was to transform the process of turning an aircraft on to the right heading and keeping it there, was yet to come.

What assistance there was, was, to say the least, rudimentary. There was an indicator to tell the aircraft's speed; something which looked uncommonly like a carpenter's spirit level to give an impression of the attitude of the aeroplane in the air; and then there was a compass, a sensitive instrument whose needle floated all over the place as the aircraft turned and banked. There was little else. It was a hard way to learn to fly.

A pilot did not willingly fly into cloud, get his head down inside the cockpit and instrument-read his way out of it. The means to do it weren't there. If there were no gaps in the overcast to go up through (and come down through), the place to stay was underneath. This was what Bader, always 'a light aeroplane man', called 'real flying'. Flying by feel and sense and intuition lay at the base of it all.

Pearson had taught him some good dodges. If he felt the wind in the open cockpit blowing on his right cheek, the aircraft was skidding to the right. If he sensed it on his left cheek, the skid was to the left. The corrections could then readily be made. It was a different world from even the elementary admonition we used to hear from our instructors in the early days of Hitler's war: 'Now come along, I've told you this before. Needle, ball, airspeed. Do you hear me? Needle, ball, airspeed.' Their strictures could have been put on tape. Needle, to show whether the nose of the aircraft was turning left or right. Ball, to tell us whether we were banking, skidding or slipping. Airspeed, to warn us about getting too fast or too slow. Like a juggler keeping all the balls in the air together, the trick was to keep the ball in the middle and the airspeed on the ordered mark. It was made quite simple; Douglas and his contemporaries did not enjoy the same advantage.

The comparatively low airspeeds and, particularly, the low stalling speeds of the fighter biplanes greatly strengthened a pilot's chances of making a successful emergency landing if the necessity arose.

One day, in the late autumn of 1931, Bader was doing some local routine flying practice. Haze and smoke quickly turned into pockets of fog as the smog from London drifted south and east over the ground. Unable, now, to pick out the familiar landmarks, it wasn't long before he was lost. He decided to put the Bulldog fighter down in what appeared to be a promising field. A tight, low circuit, with the speed reduced to the safe minimum, and the aircraft was settling, feather-light, on to three points.

A man was walking alone along the adjoining road. He met Bader's inquiry in the customary manner. 'As a matter of fact,' he retorted, 'I'm a stranger here myself. But, if it's of any help, I know that the Crystal Palace is somewhere over there,' pointing to the north-west.

It was quite enough for Douglas. 'I knew', he recalls, 'that if I could find and line up the two tall masts on the high ground at the Crystal Palace and then fly due south for a few minutes, it would take me over the top of Kenley.' Ten minutes later, in the murky gloom, he was landing without trouble on the friendly grass airfield, with no one the wiser about his enforced stop.

All round, life in a peacetime fighter squadron in the Royal Air Force was made for him. 'It was enormous fun. . . . The most enormous fun.'

It is a sombre reflection that, in the few years before Day and Bader gained their Hendon success for 23, the fatality rate among the members of former winning pairs had reached a disturbingly high level. It might well be thought that such an unusually comprehensive flying ability would have the opposite effect and that the skills of outstanding pilots would have tended to insulate them against disaster. Yet this was not so. The reason lies in the human mind.

There arrives a time in a pilot's career – and this was certainly true of Douglas – when the exhilaration of flying begins to lose its strength. It is not that the allure of flying is lessened, for to be alone in a man-made machine in God's sky will ever retain its sensation. Intercourse with the air will always remain one of man's indulgent pleasures. It is when the natural orgasm of flight ceases to be regularly achieved that troubles begin and satisfaction is sought in what the sexologists rather picturesquely call 'deviations of aim'.

When once the authorized aerobatic manoeuvres are mastered and become a commonplace, when the charade of low flying on the tops of cloud – chasing round the corners of great dollops of billowing cumulus to see what's on the other side, going over the peaks and nipping down through the imaginary valleys – when this has been exposed for what it is, a mildly titillating exercise in the Sky of Make-Believe, it is then that a pilot, in search of kicks, will start turning to the hard stuff.

In the final analysis, euphoria will only be found close to the ground. That's the devil of it. Low flying, real low flying, right down on the deck; beat-ups of the girlfriend's house; making the picnic party in the country field run for cover, just for the hell of it; flying upside down, in Johnnie Johnson's splendid epithet of Bader at

Hendon,[1] 'with his head almost brushing the grass' – this is the heroin of flying.

Somewhere between 400 and 600 hours is usually the danger span. Addiction, however, tends to be short-lived. Like the young with drugs, experiments are tried, results are felt, hallucinations are falsified, the phase passes, normality and common sense return. For most, a wiser, happier life then ensues and the past takes an understandable place in personal history.

There was, however, another and more insidious problem to face. In some ways it was much harder to combat. It only affected, persistently, those of Bader's and Stephenson's calibre who, *by achievement and performance, had earned* reputations as outstanding aerobatic pilots. Victory at Hendon in the 1920s and 1930s carried the ultimate cachet. The demands for repeat performances tended to follow the victors wherever they went. They became the rule rather than the exception. It was very difficult to refuse.

The analogies are numerous: the pianist is asked to please the other guests after dinner, the composer to play a few of his favourite works; the professional comedian, enjoying his first evening off for weeks, is pressed to 'give them a few of your jokes'; the soloist is invited to oblige, the politician to say a few words off the record to the gathering (to be leaked the next day). If the request is declined, varying reasons will be attributed to such refusal, mostly uncharitable. People, seeking a privilege, do not like to be denied it, however courteous the refusal.

This was the familiar lot the Hendon winners knew as they flew over to visit their friends at other airfields. If they relented, it wasn't because they wanted to show off their wares; it wasn't because they were provoked into it in the teeth of a challenge ('I bet you can't do a bunt followed by two upward rolls, a roll off the top and . . .'). It wasn't usually that at all. More often it was that refusal would be construed in quite the wrong way. 'He's stuck up now that he has got so good. Nose in the air. They're all the same. Gone to his head.'

So, brimful of confidence – overconfidence maybe – the relentless repertoire had to be pursued again to the limit. It had to be, otherwise they would start saying he'd lost his nerve or wasn't as good as the last time he was here. The trouble was that the best of them made

---

[1]. Air Vice-Marshal J. E. Johnson, *Full Circle: The Story of Air Fighting* (Chatto & Windus, 1964).

mistakes; and errors doing that sort of thing could be very costly indeed.

It was drilled into every pilot, right from the start, that unauthorized low flying and low aerobatics carried unreasonable risks. Harry Day, wiser, more understanding and experienced in this field than most, had spoken to Douglas about it; once very sharply. But at that age and stage, and with that kind of confident ability and temperament, the chances of the words being heeded for long were worse than poor. Ladbroke's wouldn't have quoted a price.

Monday, 14 December 1931 started like any other Monday morning for 23 Squadron at Kenley. After breakfast in the mess, the pilots in Douglas's flight – 'C' Flight – had reported as usual for their orders. 'Pricky' Day had authorized Bader to go up for a spell of aerobatics. It was now midwinter, the days were short, the glory of Hendon was more than five months behind, and no other displays loomed ahead. Christmas leave would soon be coming up. All the same, just as a Guards regiment keeps itself in trim for short-notice calls for ceremonial duty, so 23 Squadron maintained an advanced state of aerobatic readiness. Reputation demanded it, and Douglas was now its principal contributor.

The squadron had had its Bristol Bulldogs for some two or three months. They were fine fighter aircraft, not, perhaps, quite as receptive as the Gamecocks to the more extreme aerobatic manoeuvres, but none the less beautiful handling aeroplanes; right out of the top drawer. Douglas had completed 32 hours and 20 minutes on the new type and was thoroughly confident with it. Another 1 hour 30 minutes that morning brought his total flying time up to 492 hours and 20 minutes, within gunshot of the magical 500 but only a nibble at the 7000 hours or so he was later to amass.

As he walked back from his aircraft to the flight hut, one of the other pilots, G. W. Phillips, a flying officer, said he was about to fly over to Woodley, near Reading, for lunch. His brother was involved with the flying club there. It might be an idea if Douglas and Geoffrey Stephenson made up a threesome. The two responded at once.

What followed, as a result of that fateful invitation, is written indelibly in the annals of the Royal Air Force. Yet the detail of the appalling accident may not be precisely known.

After lunch, there was the usual request for the repeat performance. Would Douglas oblige? One or two had seen him at Hendon. Others would be thrilled just to have the chance. It would be marvellous if he would. The familiar urgings were there. How the hell could he say no? After all, it was Phillips's brother who had given them lunch. How could he deny them the chance?

Douglas took the Bulldog off with Phillips and Stephenson flying to his right. Holding the aircraft down to let the speed build up, he then pulled it up into a steep climbing turn to the left through 180 degrees. He was now heading back at the airfield, gathering additional speed as he approached the bottom of the dive. All eyes were on him.

He had about 125 m.p.h. on the clock – no more – as he went into a slow and very deliberate, straight and level, roll to the right. He was at little less than the normal height of a room. Call it 10 feet, no more.

At this point two vital factors have to be noted. Whereas, with the later high-powered, low-wing monoplanes, there was ample speed to allow the nose of the aircraft to be shoved well up as it rotated on to its back and round, with a biplane the same manoeuvre would be accompanied by a noticeable drop in flying speed. The penetrating forward thrust of a Spitfire or a Hurricane wasn't there.

This hazard – and a very real one it was low down – was compounded by another. A Bulldog was normally never rolled above 120 m.p.h. – 125 top weight. So Bader was keeping the aircraft to this limit. At that speed the margin for error was very small. Not enough top rudder (to hold the nose up) going in; or not enough stick forward (again, to keep the nose up) going underneath; or not enough top rudder as the aeroplane rolled out – a minor handling blemish at any one of these points – and precious feet would instantly be lost. Given that the rest of the act was spot on, speed was the critical factor.

It was a knife-edge exercise. But Bader had done it many times before. And no one, neither Day nor Stephenson, nor any of the other first-rate aerobatic pilots in the Service, had it better buttoned up. It is possible that at that moment he was the best aerobatic pilot in the Royal Air Force.

Going slowly and smoothly into the right-handed roll, the starboard (right) wingtip passed comfortably above the ground. Underneath, with half the roll completed and the aircraft now on its back, the stick was pushed well forward to hold the nose up and maintain height. There was a marginal fall in flying speed. Even so, there was still something in hand.

Coming off the second half of the roll, with the speed now falling perceptibly, positive use of the top rudder to hold the height was not quite enough. A slide had begun. It was irretrievable. The speed wasn't there to allow corrective action to take effect. The left wingtip brushed the ground, braking the forward speed, and the aircraft slid catastrophically into the ground. For a moment, the dust obscured the extent of the dreadful wreckage.

'I just made a balls of it, old boy. That's all there was to it.'

3

Triumph out of tragedy

A devastating, overwhelming experience – mental or physical or both – can irrevocably change a person's character and attitude to life. It is nature's way of accommodating the holocaust. The earlier it comes in years, the deeper and more extensive will be the repercussions.

The 2- or 3-foot error over Woodley airfield, and the shattering weeks in hospital which followed, were to mark Douglas Bader far beyond the immediate and appalling physical consequences of the crash.

But survival was the first concern. The thoughts of those who received the torn body from the ambulance were riveted on the present. They were dealing in minutes, not hours. To the surgeon, Leonard Joyce, one of the best in the orthopaedic business, there was no option. Without amputation there could be no life.

He took the right leg off at once above the knee; he allowed a couple of days to pass before he severed the left below it. The flex he preserved with the knee and the little extension he left below it (the spread of a hand would cover it) were to prove invaluable assets in the later struggles for mobility.

What Douglas suffered in the aftermath of disaster took him to the precipice of human endurance. There were times when his mother prayed that the Almighty, in His infinite kindness, might spare her younger son his torment and agony and bear his soul quietly away. Only his exceptional fitness and superhuman courage gave him the strength and the will to resist the last fatal step into oblivion. His accumulated reserves of buoyancy and spirit were the last savings he possessed to fund recovery.

But other forces were now being marshalled behind him. A gathering and lasting resolve never to succumb to negative noises began to rouse and fortify his mind. The more he heard it suggested that something could not be done, the more resolute he became for its achievement. Out of the traumas was born a ruthlessness of purpose which decreed that nothing and no one should stand between him and his chosen goals. The impulses that were being loosed, however, could never be the ingredients of an 'easy' man.

In his wilderness, three challenges were to mock his purpose. They served only to brace his defiant spirit. The first came within days of the accident as he lay in bed drifting from waking into unconsciousness. 'There's a boy dying in there.' It was the plaintive voice of a nurse appealing for quiet outside his room. Through a blurred haze of understanding, Douglas picked up the significance of the message. Although he was barely holding his own, his mental response was emphatic. Symptoms of death might well be there, but they were reckoning without the antidote. The will to hang on and live, dormant since the port wing of the Bulldog had grazed the ground at Woodley, began to stir again. Militant now, it moved into the attack. Once he had heard the aside, there was no way, he thought, that he was going to die. He was in business to trade life, not death.

He was sustained in his determination by a nurse of limitless spirit. His battle was her battle. She fought it for twenty-two hours, give or take an hour, of every tenuous day, seven days a week. The longer he kept his rally going, the greater was the inspiration she drew from his example. Her dedication to him was total. Dorothy Brace was the first person Bader had inspired to the full extent of personal endeavour. There would be others; but Brace, as he called her, was the pioneer. Her place in the legend is secure.

The mental shock of the surgery, heaped on top of the reaction after the accident, would have killed most mortals. As the weeks passed, for a young man of Bader's physique, temperament and athletic flair, the cold realization of what had been done to his limbs compounded the crisis. It could not be reconciled with the past. There was no purpose in contemplating the future.

But, slowly, a mumbling, grumbling, growing steadfastness was being assembled to start him rolling forward towards new aims. At last, the civilian hospital at Reading, where he had passed the previous four, searing months, was exchanged for its Service counterpart at Uxbridge. It hastened the day when he would be able to travel over to the hospital at Roehampton to be fitted with his first pair of artificial limbs.

Robert Desoutter masterminded the job. None was more knowledgeable or experienced in this work. Even so, the next critical stages, when Bader was learning to walk afresh, were agonizing and protracted.

> For while the tired waves, vainly breaking,
> Seem here no painful inch to gain

the moment eventually came when Desoutter, pressed persistently by his patient, agreed reluctantly that he could stump away on his two tin pins. The staff at Roehampton could scarcely credit what they saw. No more than six months had passed since Joyce had operated on Douglas in the theatre of the Royal Berkshire Hospital, yet here he was, moving about erratically – but unaided – on artificial legs, doing what no one had ever done before him. Several characteristics had brought him to this pass.

His determination to get there was, of course, top. Running it a close second were other features. The games player's balance and an inherent instinct for quick recovery. A total absence of fear about falling. (His early gymnastic training as a small boy at Temple Grove, on the parallel bars, the horse and the rest, had taught him to fall and think nothing of it. In any case, he tended now to fall forward and break the impact with his powerful hands, forearms and shoulders. That could never be so deranging as overbalancing sidewards or, worse, backwards.) The ability to brush difficulties aside as being expected and, therefore, of small import and to meet them with penetrating chortles and guffaws. An outward disposition to turn pathos into laughter and even hilarity and to use them to play off embarrassment. A nicely developing knack of being bloody obstinate when it suited him and telling anyone who was being the faintest bit defeatist that he didn't know what the hell he was talking about. (Later, it was this spontaneous and enduring habit of saying exactly what was in his mind, irrespective of the consequences for himself or the feelings of others, which set his detractors by the ears and sent them away muttering darkly about his being damned rude and inconsiderate.) A refusal to allow the tiniest trace of self-pity to intrude and to treat his lot as being commonplace and much the same as the next man's. Finally, a preparedness to accept that once he was set up with his new equipment it was then up to him – and no one else – to get on with it. He was on his own, and it was for him to learn to live with his problems and make his way.

It was this acceptance of the essential quality of self-help which subsequently developed in him an intolerance of the moaners and the whimperers, those who sought sympathy or who were reluctant to act for themselves. Difficulty and hardship swelled an already generous heart; but his open generosity was not extended to embrace the groaners.

Most of the traits which were to be identified with him in later life, to be both admired and criticized according to the whims of choice, found their derivation in these first tortuous months and years of struggle. They were the impedimenta of battle. Without them tragedy could never have given way to triumph.

Desoutter had a talk with him as he was preparing to leave Roehampton complete with new legs. 'You may as well face it now,' he said. 'You'll never walk without a stick.'

From that instant forward, Bader was utterly resolved. He would never, never use crutches or a stick. Never.

For half a century, the resolution has remained inviolate.

The third challenge to the integrity of Douglas's purpose would have split a heart of stone, coming, as it did, after all that had been endured – and conquered. Yet it was this, the unkindest cut of all, which triggered the dramas which were to follow.

Towards the end of the summer of 1932, Sir Philip Sassoon, for twenty-seven years the member of parliament for Hythe and for eleven of them, in two spells, the Under-Secretary of State for Air, asked Douglas to spend the weekend with him at his home near Lympne, hard by the south-east coast of Kent.

Sassoon was a man of wealth and remarkable kindness. His concern for the Royal Air Force far exceeded the normal call of parliamentary and ministerial duty. The Service found in him a benevolent friend, and the junior officers a genuine custodian of their interests.

Port Lympne was the third of Sassoon's three homes in England. In all of them he enjoyed a lifestyle which fitted his fortune. His exquisite taste was everywhere apparent. Everything was of the best, and comfort was paramount. The impression gained was of resplendent luxury and *haute cuisine* of a standard rarely found outside the great homes of Europe.

At 45 Park Lane in London, now the somewhat incongruous abode of the Playboy Club; at Trent Park, to the north of the capital; and at Port Lympne, with its commanding prospect across the historic marshes, to New Romney and Littlestone, Lydd and Dungeness: it was in these houses that Philip Sassoon entertained his friends. Cabinet ministers and politicians, writers, actors (Noel Coward was a close friend and neighbour) and actresses, national figures in business and the professions, the arts and sport, serving officers, the young and the old whose names would never make the headlines – all at one time or another enjoyed his hospitality; and all were thrown together in a splendidly indiscriminate galaxy of haphazard choice and left to do, during their stay, exactly as their curiously assorted spirits moved them. Sassoon gave happiness to many.

For Douglas, the weekend was important. His gaze was now fastened on his return to active Service life; he wondered where this would lead him. In his extraordinary recovery, he had quickly mastered the technique of driving a motor car – quite a task for one with a 100 per cent disability. The boon of the automatic gearbox was yet to come.

His longer left leg was made the workhorse; the right was the backer-up. He solved the footwork problem by transposing the pedals. The clutch was switched to the right, the brake to the left; the accelerator was placed in the middle. The left leg, with its flexing knee, nimbly managed the 'life and death' pair of accelerator and brake; the right could pump up and down on the clutch.

All was well until some overconfident and unwitting idiot got into the car to whisk it swiftly away. Minor incidents seemed to be strewn in its path. The safest answer for others was to sit at the wheel with the legs crossed and work the pedals that way.

Having secured the driving (accidents occurred because he usually drove 10 m.p.h. too fast), flying, thought Bader, would be a piece of cake. The question was how would the Service react? No one had ever flown an aircraft solo without any legs.

Sassoon was his ally. He had asked, typically, to be kept informed of Douglas's progress. After all, this was no ordinary pilot officer, and 23 was a rather special squadron. The Under-Secretary of State had been in the royal box at Hendon a year before when 'Pricky' Day and Bader, flying the aerobatic pair, had set the display humming.

Those who came to know Philip Sassoon in pre-war days for what he was – a generous, feeling man – would discern a motive when he asked his young guest to bring his friend, Peter Ross, from the squadron with him. 601, the colourful and talented County of

London, Auxiliary Air Force Squadron, of which the Under-Secretary was the Honorary Air Commodore and Nigel Norman was the commanding officer, was doing its summer flying at Lympne at the time. Among its Demons, the squadron had an Avro 504. Sassoon fixed it with Norman that Ross and Bader could take it up for a good swing round on Sunday morning.

It's a fair bet that, at that moment, with Douglas only just over his convalescence and with his legs still untried, no one else in the Air Force would have accepted responsibility for trusting him in an aeroplane. It was a sure-fire certainty that he, and not Ross, would be doing the flying. If anything went wrong . . .

Sitting in the rear cockpit, Bader had control from the start. Taxiing out to the downwind boundary of the grass airfield, perched on the high ground with Dover and Folkestone to the east, taking off, climbing and then landing over at Kenley where they called in for lunch – it was all as smooth as stroking a mink coat. Coming back, it was the same story. No trouble at all. Ross hadn't touched the controls once. Legs didn't matter. Hands were the thing. And Douglas's hands on the control column were special. No girl, in the flowering of her first affair, could ever have felt such irresistibly gentle and compelling hands searching the extremities of her virgin body.

One fact had been established beyond all reasonable doubt. Bader could fly. Of all the things he wanted to do, flying an aeroplane was the activity which came easiest to him. Flying, for him, was like eating sponge cake.

While the two of them had been away, John Parkes, one of the flight commanders of 601, who was later to become head of the Alvis Motor Company and one of Bader's lifelong friends, asked an airman where the squadron's Avro had gone.

'Dunno,' he said, 'Some officer with no legs took it away.'

Bader now directed his restless mind to convincing the Service that he could fly aeroplanes as well without legs as with them. Sassoon helped things along. After the medical board at the Air Ministry had given him a restricted (dual flying only) category, he was posted to the Central Flying School, then at Wittering in the east midlands. Here he was among friends, some of them from his Cranwell days. Constantine, Selway, Leach, Carey – no doubt about whose side the instructors would be on if he could prove himself.

The last, ghostlike entry had, by now, been entered in the

log-book. Terse and blatant, the facts were made to speak for themselves. '14/12/31. Bulldog K.1676. Pilot: Self. 1 hour 5 minutes. Cross-country, Reading. Crashed slow-rolling near ground. Bad show.' The 'Bad show' was underlined three times.

The four weeks spent at Wittering between the end of September and the end of October 1932 served only one purpose. Formal proof was given to the Air Council that, in the view of the Central Flying School, Pilot Officer Bader could still fly aeroplanes to the necessary standards. After 14 hours and 25 minutes flying in Avros, Siskins and Harts, going through all the practices, the chief flying instructor delivered his verdict. It was sharp and brief. 'You're wasting your time here only doing dual. You can fly perfectly well. We intend to say so.'

It made no difference to the medical board's decision. An officer without legs could not fly solo. The rules, in effect, said that; there was no way round them. Then what on earth, fumed Bader, was the point in sending him to Wittering if they knew that all along? Maybe they thought (and hoped) he would fail and that would let them off the hook. Indignant, and rocked by the conclusion, it was days before even his resilient mind could absorb the reality. His short life was at its nadir.

1932 was in its closing weeks when, prophetically, they posted Douglas to Duxford. He was put in charge of station transport. For all his outward bravado, the let-down was complete. These were sombre days.

With time on his hands, he could hardly be expected to shut out the 'might have beens'. He might, so well, by now be approaching his second season for England, playing at fly-half outside 'Tinny' Dean of the Army. Twenty-three years old, he knew that he would still have had another couple of years or so before he reached his peak.

His greatest hurt was being deprived of his beloved games. Nothing yet had been found, physically, to take their place. Young, fit and aggressive as ever, he found the mental torment akin to torture. All that was bad enough, but, now, after months of uphill struggle, the medical board had snatched away, at a stroke, the one thing he longed to do. By its decision, he had found his Calvary.

This third counter-thrust was the worst because he had so little control over it. Even his positiveness could not show him how to meet it. And yet, amid his despair, something told him that somehow, somewhere, he would fly again. He forced himself to believe it. Unlikely though it all might seem, he was determined not to buckle under the challenge.

His friend Joe Cox, a contemporary in the Service, was at Duxford at the time teaching the undergraduate members of the Cambridge University Air Squadron to fly. When nothing much was going on, he would take Douglas up for an hour or so in an old Atlas. As with Peter Ross and the Avro at Lympne, it was the 'passenger' who took the controls.

One day, with Cox in the front cockpit and his arms upstretched as if in mute surrender, the officer in charge of station transport put the aircraft down on the apron in an immaculate spot landing right in front of the main buildings. It was a beautifully slow manoeuvre with the aeroplane stalling, light as a fairy, on to all three points. Other pilots, who had been tipped off beforehand of the intention, applauded in jeering admiration. It was in keeping with Bader's current luck that the station commander, a man of no special humour or humanity, should be rounding the corner of the hangar just as the Atlas, with Cox's hands still held high in the air, was about to touch down.

However, as with other brushes with authority, all was soon forgiven.

Cambridge, the Backs and the Cambridgeshire countryside came into their own as the spring of 1933 gave way to summer and Douglas took his leave of Duxford and the Royal Air Force. The grounds given for his retirement were officially described by the Air Ministry in their correspondence as 'ill health'. It is questionable whether there was a fitter officer in the Service.

His disability pension and retired pay came to, roundly, £200 all in. This was all the income he had. With no legs and trained only to be a good officer and fly aeroplanes well (which he wasn't allowed now to do), his prospects could hardly be said to be bright. That a chapter was closed was irrefutable. No good, now, dwelling upon that. There would be others, he felt, to follow.

Within seven years, he would be back again at Duxford, answering the third challenge. By then, he was Page One news.

4
Shell

Only a mile or so separated Unilever's London offices at Blackfriars from the Asiatic Petroleum Company's premises at Great St Helen's, off Bishopsgate, in the City. In Bader's mind in midsummer 1933, there was probably little to choose between the two companies. As a prospective employer, each controlled a large international organization, and a desk job would most likely be as tedious with one as with the other. He was therefore surprised by what he found at St Helen's. He called there second after getting a most civil reception at Unilever.

A. P. Grey was Asiatic's overseas staff manager, a man of feeling and experience of the world. A former – and successful – general manager of Burma-Shell in India, he could have been cast in the part of a benign and respected headmaster or principal of a university college. He radiated humanity which encouraged the young and dispensed confidence. Always susceptible to first impressions, Douglas felt drawn to him immediately.

With the pleasantries over, Grey came to the point. 'With those legs of yours,' he said, 'we obviously can't send you to the hot countries. That wouldn't do. But there *is* an aviation department which we are now expanding here in London. Would that be of any interest?'

Having received a quick and positive answer, Grey took Douglas along to see Walter Hill, the head of the department. Though not an easy or engaging man, Hill was efficient and lived for his work. He was recognized to be a good picker. 'Yes,' he said, after a talk, 'I would like you to come and join us. I'll recommend that you be taken on.'

It was left to George Engle, the exceptionally able head of the group's financial operations, 'a great leonine-headed, white-haired

Jew, a marvellous character', to put a formal stamp on the appointment.

'Do you think you can do the job?' he asked, eyeing the candidate for his reaction.

'I don't know yet, sir,' retorted Douglas, showing a touch of realism, 'but I'll try.'

'All right, then,' said Engle. '£200 a year. Start on Monday.' That was all.

And so there began a relationship, at once bizarre and unique, which was to last, with only the interruption of war, for the next thirty-six cataclysmic years of the twentieth century.

One thing can be said for sure. The company, soon to be absorbed into the great Shell Transport and Trading enterprise, was never to encounter another recruit like Douglas Bader.

5

The climb back begins

Does the road wind uphill all the way?
Yes, to the very end.
Will the day's journey take the whole long day?
From morn to night, my friend.
(CHRISTINA GEORGINA ROSSETTI, 1830–94)

The six years to the outbreak of war in 1939 were, for Bader, hum-drum, testing and immensely frustrating. Driving into the City each morning from his lodgings in St John's Wood, close by Lord's Cricket Ground, and then back again in the evening, with the 9–5.30 stint sandwiched in between, wasn't stimulating. Life in an office, after the games, fresh air and excitement of 23 Squadron and Kenley, was flat and incompatible. Colleagues remember him in those days as a very square peg in a well-rounded hole. There were times when it took all the personal disciplines which Cranwell and the Service had instilled – and more – to make him stay the course.

For one thing, he disliked paperwork. Administrative detail, and the usual chores which a dogsbody in the office is expected readily to handle, were never his meat. Within a year of his starting, other newcomers had been appointed to the company. In no time at all he had used his winning ways to press one or two of them quietly into his service. He quickly became adept at off-loading the bumph. It was a procedure he followed with unvarying success during the next thirty Shell years. But, for the moment, he was well ahead of the game. The marvel was that he was able to get away with it. Those on the receiving end rather envied him the knack.

However, a new shaft of strong light was now cutting through the pall which hung heavily over the routine and tedium of Bader's daily life. Without it, it is doubtful whether even his own resilient mind would have stomached the rest.

Douglas had met Thelma Edwards quite by chance a year earlier when he and a couple of his friends from the hospital at Uxbridge, Victor Streatfield and John Peel, had driven over to the Ascot–Bagshot–Sunningdale district for an afternoon out. This motley crew of flying officers, one with a broken arm, another with a broken leg and the third without any legs at all, had called at a pleasant little eating and refreshment establishment on the left-hand side of the road from London, a couple of miles out of Sunningdale, past the golf club.

The girl who had served them had caught Douglas's eye as soon as he saw her. She was rare in several ways, not least because, as things turned out, she was to become for the next four decades the strongest single influence in his life.

Thelma, whose mother was a Donaldson, had a stunningly lovely face, rounded, well proportioned, with classically high cheekbones and deep-set and appealingly large blue-grey eyes. Her skin and complexion, touched with the faintest splash of colour, blended easily into a head of fair and very fine hair, so fine and soft in fact that it seemed as if a comb must break the strands.

She was small but she looked taller than she was because her back was straight and her carriage regally erect. She smoked cigarettes through an elegant holder to an extent which was eventually to prove lethal. Her voice was unusually deep, and now and then she contrived a low and surreptitious little chuckle, notably when she saw the funny side of something which plainly wasn't intended to be. She had an artful habit, too, of passing it off with a roguish sideways turn of the head and a noncommittal shrug. A twinkle was never very far away, particularly when things were serious. Thelma Edwards liked fun and laughter and gaiety.

But within this captivating person was a mind of purpose. Like Douglas, she was greatly determined. If she wanted something, she tended to get her way mainly because she could turn on at will a look of such melting wistfulness that it was virtually impossible to deny it.

She was working part-time at the Pantiles (that was the name of the roadside restaurant) partly to satisfy her independence and partly for something to do. It was an incongruous occupation because she was living happily at the time at Hatton Hall, her maternal grandmother's fine home at Windlesham, a village only a stone's throw away.

Thelma always enjoyed staying at Hatton with its spaciousness, its well-tended lawns and gardens and commanding trees. There, with 'Little Granny', as the family called Gertrude Donaldson, she found all the comforts of the times, good and easy living with servants, gardeners and chauffeur. There, too, she found horses to ride and dogs to care about. She doted on dogs and loved them as a child does.

Hatton was a symbol of two generations of the Donaldsons' commercial and professional success in the Far East in the early years of the century. With its forebears' adventurous spirit and their connection with the East India Company and the law, the family was well established in the Orient. Between them, Thelma and her mother displayed an amalgam of arresting Donaldson attributes. They were to be supplemented in the Second World War by the legendary ways of the exceptional brothers (first cousins of Thelma), Jack, Teddy and Arthur Donaldson, whose names became synonymous with some of the Royal Air Force's epic deeds. The three were to add lustre and uniqueness to the family when each in turn won the Distinguished Service Order and other coveted awards besides.

Students of genealogy, heredity and character will find much to ponder in the Donaldsons' recorded history – and rather more, perhaps, in what may possibly have been left out.

This, then, was the picture and background of the girl with whom Douglas was to set out on the long climb back from his Slough of Despond.

It was an impressive feature of Thelma's nature that no trace of jealousy ever entered her soul. Her philosophy was impervious to it. She enjoyed success for herself, and was grateful when it came, but she wanted her friends to be successful and happy and was genuinely pleased when they were. She liked nice things and hoped one day she might have them, but, if others possessed them and she didn't, she accepted that life will always be unequal.

When her mother's first marriage ended in divorce and, by her second, she had a son and another daughter, Thelma bestowed an affection upon her young brother and sister seldom seen in a much older child. She was twelve when her mother remarried, and the object of all the spontaneous attentions lavished on an only child.

When these were transferred to her brother Jock and her sister Jill (my wife-to-be), she bore no grudge, but rather compounded them in full measure by willingly adding her own.

When Douglas was about to make his first appearance at the family's London home, Thelma, somewhat anxious that all should go well, told Jock and Jill about his legs and made them promise on their honour that they would make no remarks about them. He was a very important friend. The instructions were followed – as children will – to the last comma and full stop. All through tea they sat, side by side on the settee, prim and silent, staring at the man's legs. Out came the dumpy pipe from his jacket pocket. A couple of sharp metallic raps on the right trouser leg, accompanied by great haw-haws and chortles of uninhibited laughter, and all was at once easy and natural. Here, they thought, was something really extra special.

There was a human rock now on which Bader knew he could lean. At the inevitable moments of remorse and doubt, Thelma was there to add her courage to his in a merger of indomitable wills. When the office and the job seemed overwhelming in their irksomeness, she was ready with patient encouragement and advice. For a girl in her mid-twenties (she was two years older than Douglas), her judgement and perception were surprisingly mature. With them she could deter headstrong action. These were days when people changed their jobs rarely and only then for some exceptional reason; yet without this supporting – and restraining – hand on his shoulder it is at least arguable whether he would have packed the City in and gone off to some other occupation.

The question may well be posed: why should a girl like Thelma Edwards, with so much going for her, and who had always enjoyed her full share of suitors, some of them among the wealthy (she had once been engaged to an upstanding and well-placed Australian), succumb to the persuasions of a young, retired flying officer whose liabilities, in a material and physical sense, seemed likely to exceed his assets? There is no doubt about the answer. Bader was a strikingly handsome young man and unfairly attractive to women. A pair of penetratingly blue eyes looked out of a square, slightly freckled, compact face which essentially gave the impression of being solid. Here and there there were traces of the pugilist that was in him. It is often said that in a long and devoted relationship master and favourite dog each take on something of the likeness of the other.

Bader's head and face, connected to the body by a short, strong neck, seemed to owe something to the squat and dumpy design of the finely proportioned biplanes, the Gloster Gamecock and the Bristol Bulldog, which he had now left nostalgically behind. Even those stubby pipes, with their abbreviated stems, which he has always smoked, might have been tailored to suit his image. Above a deep and broad forehead there was a thatch of shortly cut, curly black hair. Tidy and clean-shaven would have been the epithet to fit a police description.

Here was the healthy and robust, heterosexual character whose appeal for the girls went beyond a man's reasonable deserts. When he set his mind to it, he could be very fetching indeed. Legs or no legs, his success in this field was, as the bankers say, undoubted. There was ample proof.

Thelma played her feelings, as was her custom, deliberately close to her chest; yet the brute fact remained: this unconventional man was a bit of a knockout. And, what is more, she believed utterly in him; she felt somehow that he would succeed.

Young people in love don't worry much about life's difficulties. Douglas certainly didn't. His temperament, anyway, wouldn't countenance it. Close the deal, he thought, and sign the contract. Circumspect and decisive, Thelma did not demur.

They were married secretly at Hampstead Register Office, the nearest one to Douglas's lodgings, on 5 October 1933. Two days later they announced their engagement in the London *Times*. It was fairly typical Bader behaviour. Four years – to the very day – were to elapse before they went through the motions of a church wedding, at St Mary Abbott's in West Kensington. The interim was a period of rather more shade than light.

6

'How will you pay it back?'

The decade of the 1930s – in retrospect, perhaps the most tormenting in world history – was a golden period for flying. It was a time when aviation became the Art of the Possible. Flights in light aircraft around much of the globe, which none would have credited in the years immediately following the First World War, were now being splashed across the front pages of the international press under banner headlines a couple of inches deep.

Alan Cobham and Charles Lindbergh had touched the fuse in the mid- and late 1920s. Indeed, Lindbergh, by his solo flight across the north Atlantic in 1927, had probably done more than any other to set a new dimension in individual aerial endeavour. Alone with his tiny high-wing monoplane, the Spirit of St Louis, and God, he had covered the journey from Long Island to Paris in 33 hours and 39 minutes to make an impact upon peacetime aviation which was not to be equalled until, some forty years later, his compatriots Neil Armstrong and Buzz Aldrin stepped out of their spacecraft and, before millions of television viewers, took a walk on the surface of the moon.

In the wake of such achievement, a young Yorkshire girl named Amy Johnson made it on her own to Australia and South Africa. Jean Batten, the New Zealander, compounding her sex's challenge in the skies, reduced the south Atlantic to a single flight. Francis Chichester, one of mankind's adventurers, defying the Tasman Sea and its sharks, crossed from New Zealand to Australia in his diminutive De Havilland Moth – the first time it had been done solo from east to west.

To these examples of human and mechanical endurance were added the exploits of Jim Mollison (Amy Johnson, his wife, was often with him), Kingsford Smith, Campbell Black, Charles Scott and

69

others who were ready to pit their courage and their aircraft against the elements and set fresh horizons for others to master.

At the same time, a trinity of manufacturers – Hawker, Supermarine and Rolls Royce – sustained by their dedicated designers, were, between them, preparing the marvellous flying machines in which a handful of our young, fighting élite would, quite soon, bloody Hitler's nose and give notice to the world that Britain was in the business of war to win.

Imperial Airways, with their C-class flying boats, were opening new services to the Far East and Africa, while, nearer home, small and enterprising firms like Hillman Airways and Instone, usually with a single, dynamic character at their head, were throwing aerial bridges across the Channel and telescoping the journey to Paris, Brussels, Amsterdam and other continental towns and cities into the space of a single morning or afternoon.

One Suffolk dawn, just as the first horse-drawn farm carts were setting off down country lanes, the villagers of Mildenhall, joined by a cluster of Cambridge undergraduates, became incredulous, silent witnesses to the start of possibly the most imaginative long-distance air test ever flown – the Mildenhall–Melbourne air race. At the end of it, the colourful but vanquished American, Roscoe Turner, held out the hand of capitulation to Scott and Black, the winners. 'Congratulations,' he said, 'I was glad to smell your exhaust smoke.'

Those were the days when the spirit of interdependence and chivalry was abroad in the air; when one helped another and all pooled hard-won knowledge – and mistakes – as the frontiers of experience were forced back; when personal ideas and theories were exchanged and meteorological data were amassed; when the hazards of the air drew a new fraternity together into a band of generous, selfless, resolute pioneers. Few experiences in life are better calculated to foster the brotherhood of man than the facing together of common risks and dangers. As Shell steadily increased its share of market sales, so the company began to build its dossiers of information to help this new breed of adventurers along the freshly charted ways.

In the aviation department, they now started to compile, as part of their service to the air, air route schedules to the continent, to the Near and Far East, to Australasia and to southern Africa. These represented, in a sense, the pilots' flying primers which told them, in potted form, what landing strips to look for and what facilities (if any) were available, what areas to avoid and which seasons to miss, what weather to expect and dangerous line squalls to skirt, what heights to fly and where the company's agents would be found *en route*. The information, gathered at first hand, was widely culled. Such was the spirit of the times that pilots, operators, agents and interested parties of all kinds *wanted* to add to the library of knowledge. This way lay survival and advance. Maps were updated, experience was revised; all details were recorded, checked and separated into individual guides for specific routes. The schedules became a bible for those flying in the northern and southern hemispheres.

Bader played his limited part in their build-up. Unconsciously, and certainly undramatically, the work added significantly to the sum of his knowledge. It was to be years before he would draw on the resources which were now being tucked away in his mind. But, for the moment, it was the ethos which counted. Things were stirring. Even for a comparatively new dogsbody, sitting behind an office desk, these were historic times in which to be living with aviation.

Visits overseas, infrequent though they were, relieved the tedium of the City. Their purpose was to make contact with customers, actual and potential, with operators and with representatives of such national airlines as there were. The flight to Sweden with Jerry Shaw, following one to Denmark, stuck particularly in his mind. Shaw had joined the aviation department from Shell-Mex after a spell of flying with the Dutch airline, KLM. He was an experienced First World War pilot and a character with whom Bader established an easy rapport. His handling of the Vega Gull, in which they travelled, disclosed the competence of his airmanship and the extent of his knowledge. He was impressively sound and his regard for detail and flight planning was to find an echo in Douglas's invariable habits in later years.

The visit to Poland in 1939, as Europe was slipping hopelessly into war, was weird in its novelty. The last stage of the journey from Berlin to Warsaw, where the headquarters of Lot, the Polish airline, were located, was covered in a German Junkers 52 which was already the Luftwaffe's standard troop- and supply-carrying transport. Little did Bader think that this aircraft would become the fighter pilot's target to end all targets as it lumbered its steady way across eastern, western and Mediterranean skies.

More than half a dozen, momentous years were to pass before the bread cast on those pre-war, Shell waters began to return. Then, with the war over, Douglas was to remember vividly an incident, small in itself, which had occurred in 1934, soon after he had joined the company. Its effect upon his mind was ingrained for ever.

Hard pressed at the time on his salary of £200 a year and his small pension and retired pay from the Service, he asked the manager of the department one day whether the company would be prepared to lend him £50. Walter Hill passed him on to Hunt, Engle's number 2, on the finance side.

'Ah, Bader,' he said, as Douglas entered his office, 'I gather you want to see me. What can I do?'

Bader came straight to the point. 'I wanted to ask, sir, whether the company would lend me fifty pounds?'

Hunt's face was expressionless. 'How will you pay it back?' he asked.

'Well, sir, my salary is two hundred pounds a year. I wondered whether it could be deducted from that?'

'Ten shillings a week all right?'

A clerk answered Hunt's bell. 'Will you please make out a cheque for fifty pounds for Mr Bader and bring it to me now?' He signed the cheque and handed it to Douglas without comment.

'Thank you very much, sir,' said Bader. Hunt gave an understanding nod and the matter was closed.

Douglas never forgot the episode. He was asked only one question. 'How will you pay it back?' '*How*', not 'when' or 'why' or any of the other probing questions that seven accountants out of ten would have asked in the circumstances. Half a century on, recalling the incident he said, 'You don't forget those things.'

Whatever might be the outside diversions, it was now apparent to his colleagues (and the truth enhances rather than diminishes the legend) that Douglas, in the second half of his restless twenties, and the job he was doing for Shell were incompatible bedfellows. If they admired him for his resilient courage and unflagging spirit, they saw him in those days as a misfit, cast in an unsuitable role.

At heart, he was still a serving officer in the Royal Air Force. It flavoured his thinking, his attitudes and his judgements. Nothing could match the Service where he had been so happy; its methods and simple efficiency were the yardstick by which he measured company procedures and routine. For all his breezy bravado, he seemed to be without a defined purpose – and, indeed, without a discernible future. His light-hearted jesting, which was sometimes introduced at

moments of pressure when others might be at full stretch and engaged
with some departmental crisis, was symbolic of an unsatisfied and
unfulfilled mind.

There was always, however, his manifest capacity for friendship to
draw on. He collected friends easily. Two that he found during those
first, trying Shell years were to become numbered among the closest
and most enduring of his life's companions. They probably had a
more acute appreciation of the whims of his insatiable temperament
than any of his other colleagues. They understood his ways better
than most.

Roy Snodgrass had been with the aviation department for three
years before Bader arrived. He had joined Asiatic in 1928 straight
from Sedbergh where he had been at school. His first two years, spent
in the accounts department, were to stand him in solid stead in the
days ahead.

But then, in 1931, at the height of the depression which had caught
the country by the throat, the axe had fallen. In company with 140
of the group's eastern staff, he had been sacked with six months' pay.
Sometimes, however, courtesy finds its reward. As a lowly member
of the house committee of the company's sports and social club at
Teddington, by the Thames, he went along to say his farewell to the
chairman and thank him for past interest and help – not, perhaps,
the customary action of a young man who had just been dismissed.

The embarrassment of his superior was matched only by his genuine sadness. Within an hour, Snodgrass received a call to report to
Greenslade, number 3 to Engle in the finance department, whose
responsibilities also included staff. 'The aviation department want
you back,' he began. 'Don't tell me what to do with my job, but I
strongly advise you to accept the offer.'

Within three years he was editing Shell's journal, *Aviation News*,
and only wartime service with the Royal Fusiliers interrupted an
otherwise unbroken span of four decades of employment with the
company.

Snodgrass's association with Douglas, which was to survive the
vicissitudes of war and peace, proved to be of capital importance to
Bader's career with Shell. In a personal sense, it revealed characteristics of a rare and unusually perceptive nature. For much of their
time together, and particularly in later years, they worked harmoni-
ously as a pair. The one owed much to the other. And when Bader
retired from the aircraft company, it was to Snodgrass that he handed

over his managing director's job. Such a relationship is the exception rather than the rule in a corporate context.

They had the advantage of being opposites. Snodgrass, or 'Snoddy', as Douglas habitually called him, was precise yet patient. He had a clear and uncomplicated mind which could be very firm when necessary. He was an able administrator who was prepared to accept and absorb detail. Where Bader was boisterously extrovert and opinionated, he was reserved, circumspect and undramatic. He deliberated before reaching a conclusion, giving himself full opportunity to balance the arguments. It would have been difficult – in fact, probably impossible – to find a man better suited to act as a foil and counterweight to his colleague's more demonstrative and intuitive ways.

He had, moreover, two special attributes which were to contribute conspicuously to the success of their work together. A selfless man, he did not covet, nor, I suspect, did he particularly want the limelight. While he would be ready, in their later years, when Douglas was abroad, to accept responsibility and discharge it with all the force of fully delegated authority, he did not seek the mantle for himself. Whatever his inner feelings may have been, his outward disposition allowed him to play the back-up role without giving any impression that he wanted things to be otherwise. It was a stance which was based upon mutual loyalty and personal regard.

Equally important to the relationship was Snodgrass's humour, an essential quality in a Bader intimate. It enabled him to see amusement in much of Douglas's style; although there were plainly times when the vagaries of his colleague's customs stretched even his patience, it wasn't long before the funny side of the eccentricity had taken possession, and other sentiments had been banished from the mind.

The fact was that by the end of their extraordinary working association Snodgrass was ready for anything; nothing that Bader did or said surprised him. Humour and respect have a special part to play in human understandings.

Geoffrey Darlington, another close friend in Shell, though not in the aviation department, brought mirth and laughter to those prewar City days. Whereas Roy Snodgrass was cast in a very different mould from Bader, Darlington's temperament and individuality bore, in several ways, a striking resemblance to his friend's. There was an affinity between them which was reflected in the way they blended their interests together.

Darlington was a games player and an athlete, fit, spare and agile.

He was also a golfer. A winsome sense of fun and an outgoing, infectious humour enabled him, like Douglas, to make friends easily. He enjoyed his life and his eyes were usually smiling. He took nothing very seriously, and his stories, customarily about the oldest topic known to man, rivalled Douglas's in variety, detail and colour.

Their approach to office life was not dissimilar, and when Geoffrey indicated a preference for Walter Hill's department, with its publicity, public relations and advertising functions, Bader co-operated to the full in trying to engineer a move. The machinations failed but the lack of success may well have been a blessing, effectively disguised, for these activities, which were Darlington's *métier*, were soon to be separated from aviation and placed in a compartment of their own.

The first head of the publicity department, to which Darlington was quickly transferred, was Alexander Wolkoff, a White Russian, whose sister was to stand trial for alleged spying. Wolkoff later changed the spelling of his name to the rather more manageable English version of Wolcough. Under him, Geoffrey was able to deploy his talents which, in due time, were to find their expression in one of Shell Oil's most brilliant advertising ventures in the United States.

It was no surprise that Douglas should invite Darlington to be his best man when, four years after the first rituals had been completed in secrecy in the register office, he and Thelma went through the marriage ceremony in church in the autumn of 1937. The Shell pair made a rather engaging duo as they waited at the chancel steps for play to commence. None could say that either looked particularly nervous or serious.

It stands to the credit of Geoffrey Darlington and three others that Bader should have been encouraged to take up golf in the mid-1930s and persevere with it in the face of daunting physical odds. Darlington and Tinny Dean, the England scrum half, with whom in the halcyon days Douglas had played for the Combined Services, were the earliest influences. Very shortly they were joined in their purpose by another persuasive pair who were ready to add the weight of their formidable support.

Horton Martin Row and Henry Longhurst had partnered one another a few years before in the university match at Sandwich, an event which was to achieve immortality by Longhurst's description of his partner's nerves and his vain attempts at eating an ice-cold grapefruit on a frigid March morning, an hour or so before walking on to the first tee for their foursome against Oxford.

Horton Martin Row, who at breakfast, what with the cold and the natural feelings of one about to play in his first University match, had ordered grapefruit and, though securing a number of segments in the spoon, had failed to get any as far as their objective, some merely dropping off, others going over the shoulder, as with a man dropping a provisional ball . . .[1]

Through their golfing background and the unforgettable friendship which each was to provide, the two of them contributed notably to the cause of setting Bader going down the fairway. Once he had made this start, golf was to become, for the next half-century, a light to lighten his life and an example by which others would be inspired.

For the record, the Royal and Ancient game took Bader into custody in 1934, two years after Desoutter had fixed him up with his new legs. He can identify the moment and place of his arrest. Every golfer, from the first, tentative motions, will know the experience.

Douglas had been trying to get the hang of hitting a golf ball one weekend when he and Thelma were staying with Audrey and Adrian Stoop at their home in Hampshire. Adrian Stoop was one of the great figures in Rugby football, an outstanding player and administrator. He and his wife were to bestow many kindnesses upon the Baders in the hard years following the accident.

The first attempts at making contact with club and ball were not promising. Even for an able-bodied beginner, the golf swing and the related contortions of the body present problems of balance. For one relying on two artificial supports, the process at once falls into the unplayable category. Such connections as were achieved – hard, unpleasing and metallic – left no compelling sensation.

Then it happened. Douglas caught a single, isolated ball on the sweet spot of the 7 iron. The speed which he had generated in the down-swing, with his immensely strong forearms, wrists and hands, sent the ball flying off the clubface like a rocket-propelled missile. Exquisite feel and elation sang out in unison.

As a natural games player, he had known the sensation of hitting a half-volley plum on the driving spot of a cricket bat; of striking a tennis or squash ball with the sympathetic square inch of the racquet; of screw-kicking a Rugby football with the hard outer part of the foot, sending the ball rifling away on its fore-and-aft axis, with just the

1. *My Life and Soft Times* (Cassell, 1971).

faintest touch of draw at the end. The games player in him had so often 'tasted' these moments.

But this stroke with a golf club was, somehow, different. No contact had ever felt quite so tantalizingly enthralling as this impact with a small, white, rubber-core ball which had soared away into the air, clearing the extensive lawns, shrubs and bushes and the boundary fence beyond. The feel was squeezy and delicious. That it could not be repeated at will (or even at all, so it seemed) didn't matter. What he had felt just once was enough. Like a puppy introduced to chocolate for the first time, one taste was sufficient. The craving for more would be there for ever.

Bader was now hooked on golf. Weekends in Hampshire – at the North Hants club at Fleet and at nearby Liphook – took on an altogether new meaning as he moved from individual shots and practice to the real thing, playing actual holes on the course. First it was three or four holes; then nine; then eighteen. Later, and almost incredibly, it was thirty-six – two rounds of eighteen – in a single day. It meant that on the artificial masterpieces[1] which Desoutter had given him only three years or so ago he was now covering six or seven miles on a Sunday with all the additional exertion of hitting the ball on the way. It was an astonishing physical achievement – even if Thelma *was* always ready and willing to carry his clubs.

Douglas wasn't taught to play golf in the sense that beginners usually are. True, Horton Row and Longhurst offered advice – jocular, ribald, but none the less wise advice – but mostly he picked things up for himself. His natural ball sense, his innate instinct for balance, the flair for co-ordinating mind, eye and hands and, above all, the ruthless, unyielding determination to improve and never to give in or be dismayed by the bad days of which there were plenty – these were the characteristic qualities which drove him on.

The facts are indisputable. They can be coldly stated. Within four years of having hit that magical 7 iron shot on the Stoops' lawn, Bader had been allotted a genuine club handicap of 10. By that time (the summer of 1938) he had reached a standard which thousands of golfers, in full possession of all the physical faculties, will never know.

With Thelma at his side and this new stimulus of golf to absorb his mind in the leisure hours, his life was gradually being transformed. The initial frustrations of learning to play golf which, to begin with,

1. The right leg was made $^1/_4$ inch shorter than the left to prevent the toe of the shoe catching the ground on the forward stride. Indirectly, it helped Bader's golf by shifting his weight more on to the back foot.

made a comforting antidote to the frustrations of the office and the job, were now in retreat. As his game developed, so its fascination held him in a tighter and tighter grip. The weekends had now become green and lush watering places in an otherwise parched land.

To satisfy his desire for normality and his inflexible resolve never to concede a millimetre to his physical disability, he contrived to move his body about a tennis or squash court with spectacular dexterity. But the results for a games player of his distinction could be no more than a travesty of what he had achieved before. His efforts represented a commendable, even admirable, demonstration of will, but the outcome, in terms of enjoyment, was no substitute for the real thing. It was a palliative, no more.

With golf, however, things were totally different. For one thing, he had never played the game before he lost his legs, so there was no pristine yardstick, no nostalgic thoughts, no longing to recapture what he had known in the past, no troublesome antecedents to torment the mind. This was new. A green fairway, virgin, untrodden and entrancing, was stretched out ahead, winding its way through inland woods and then into open country, among lovely dunes and sandhills. A beckoning finger was calling him forward, coaxing him on. He had not been this way before. He was immensely taken with what he found. What's more, there was a host of new chums about, dozens of them, with the hand of friendship outstretched, wanting to draw him along with them. The welcome was important.

One round of golf is marked for ever in his memory. It was the day his patron saint turned up to watch him play and tell him to put all his other leisure pursuits aside and stick to golf; this was now the game for him. He said the Good Lord had told him to say so.

It was the summer of 1939. War was only a matter of weeks away. Douglas went to stay with Geoffrey Darlington and his parents near Hoylake, in Cheshire, close to the links of the famous old Royal Liverpool Golf Club where so much championship history had been made. Cecil Darlington, Geoffrey's father, was an old member of the club and a keen golfer. He and his family had moved there from Hale when he retired from his business in Manchester. A mining engineer, he was determined now to get as much golf as he could at Hoylake. He had worked hard all his life and he felt he was owed it. But now he was intrigued to see how Bader would make out.

Douglas had never seen Hoylake before, so this three-ball game with the two Darlingtons was to be quite a personal examination. He still remembers everything about the day. The sun beat down from a cloudless sky; the flags hung limp on the greens; heat waves quivered across the links; out beyond the eleventh hole and the big sandhills they call the Alps, the waters of the Dee estuary, as far as Hilbre Island, sparkled and danced to the glory of the day. Hoylake seemed intent on doing Douglas proud. It wasn't usually like this.

He completed the round in 77 strokes. For the likes of Cotton, Sarazen, Padgham, Snead, Nelson and the rest, par for the 6700-yard course that day was probably 70 or 71. It was the first time he had ever broken 80, and to do it at Hoylake, of all places, was almost beyond his comprehension.

It was the opening hole which set him clicking. This is a testing, 420-yarder with a disturbing out-of-bounds boundary running along the length of the right-hand dog-leg. It was an old-time Scottish professional, Jamie Anderson, who paid a lasting tribute to the difficulties of the hole. 'Ma God,' he cried to the spectators as he hit his fifth consecutive ball out of bounds into the field, 'it's like playing up a spout!'

A drive straight down the centre of the fairway, a second hit daringly across the corner of the field and Douglas was left with an 8 iron to the green. His approach, to the left of the flag and away from the boundary, finished 12 yards from the hole. Out came his old hickory-shafted, rusty-headed putter and down went the putt for his par 4. The ball is still in his eye now, running on and on over the beautifully true surface, until at last it pauses agonizingly on the lip before toppling in.

On he went in much the same manner all the way round. His memory is of putts going in from everywhere on those perfect Hoylake greens. Darlington's recollection, however, is of his father's mounting excitement as the holes began to run out and it looked, for all the world, that, barring some terrible catastrophe, Douglas must break 80 – the magical barrier.

As the final putt went in on the eighteenth, cheers and relief turned into silent incredulity. It was as if the ghosts of Hoylake's past, of John Ball, Harold Hilton, Jack Graham, Horace Hutchinson and others, in their narrow caps, tight-fitting Norfolk jackets and knee breeches, were gathered by the last green, wanting to make their mute acknowledgements to one of the most astonishing private rounds of golf ever played.

For Douglas, there were to be other extraordinary rounds to come in the years ahead, some in company with the game's mightiest figures. But none – none – was to give him such a fillip. Coming when it did, rather less than eight years after Leonard Joyce had severed first his right leg and then the left in the hospital at Reading, it represented a milestone of incalculable consequence in the forward march. He had proved to himself beyond all doubt that he could make himself into a good enough golfer to be able to play anywhere and with anyone. His legs would never stop him from doing that so long as he remained fit and there was strength in his body to do it. That was the measure of the Hoylake achievement.

He knew now that he had succeeded against all the odds. It was a suitable prelude to other battles which were soon to come.

7
Breakthrough

Europe, like a car in neutral coasting downhill, was now running on unchecked into war. In Britain, the advocates of peace-at-a-price vied for the headlines with the hawks who saw no merit at all in appeasement. Beaverbrook's *Daily Express*, with the brilliant Arthur Christiansen in the chair, led the optimists with the daily chant: 'No war this year, or next year either.' Churchill and Eden, without the constraints of office to inhibit them, took a harder, unequivocal line. Stand up to Hitler and make Britain strong. Aggression cannot be allowed to pay.

Whatever the counter-arguments, the fact was, of course, that one of the by-products of Munich and the quest for a 'lasting peace' was to buy time in which to set the production (such as it was) of Hurricanes and Spitfires rolling. These were the aircraft on which Bader's gaze was now fastened.

The work in the office at St Helen's Court went on for the rest of the summer in much the same humdrum way as before. There was one difference. Instead of driving in each morning from St John's Wood, the journey now started from West Kensington. Douglas and Thelma had taken a flat in West Kensington Court in the North End Road on the way out to what is now Heathrow. It was on the right side of London for weekends with Little Granny at Hatton and for golf at Fleet and Liphook. The drive eastwards each morning into the City didn't bother Bader. An early riser, he always left for the office well ahead of the rush-hour traffic. The habit was to stick for a lifetime.

The government's decision to expand the Services had stimulated his resolve to get back to flying. Like a telephone call from an old flame, it had rekindled thoughts of the past. The urge to return to the Royal Air Force was now beginning to dominate his mind. He was utterly confident he could fly and, if necessary, fight.

Ever since that weekend at Port Lympne seven summers ago, when Philip Sassoon had arranged for him and Peter Ross to have 601 Squadron's Avro, he knew he could do it. And, what's more, do it just as well, if not better, than most. The time at the Central Flying School at Wittering had confirmed it. Flying was made for his disability. 'Flying an aeroplane', he was once to say, 'is the easiest thing I can do.' Like his new love, golf, he wanted to be with it and, actively, a part of it.

The impulse was strengthened by the knowledge that other young men in the office were preparing for the inevitable. John Longley, who had learnt to fly with the Air Squadron at Cambridge, was getting ready to be 'refreshed'. Darlington had made his move to join the Royal Air Force's Volunteer Reserve. Snodgrass was already in the Territorial Army. Like thousands of others, they were already giving up spare time at weekends or in the evenings for training with one of the Services. Young Britain was on the move. It was wholly uncharacteristic for him to be out of it.

Bader badgered his friends at the Air Ministry to be given the chance to prove himself. That's all he asked – the opportunity to show that he would be capable of flying operationally. He had made up his mind that he would go on until he got his way. There was to be no question of taking no for an answer, no matter who might say it. He didn't care how much trouble he caused ringing up and writing. He was resolved to get there somehow.

Thelma was dead against his going back to flying. They had been together now for six happy, but testing, years. Mostly it had been an unrelenting struggle. To think of him in combat, perhaps being shot down, and then, because of his legs, being unable to get out of the aircraft, was more than even her brave heart could stand.

She was backed up by her mother. Olive Addison so much resembled Thelma that, at one time, they had often been taken to be sisters. As a girl, she had been arrestingly beautiful and much sought after. The features of her oval face, with its pale skin, large blue eyes and straight nose, were finely drawn. The faintly golden hair bore traces of the Donaldsons' Scottish ancestry. 'Missus' (it was Douglas's name for her) was a mother who fussed and worried over her brood. To have an artistic and highly talented son just of military age was anguish enough; but then to find this dogmatic and aggressive son-in-law doing what she thought was not only unnecessary but unreasonable, thereby causing Thelma endless turmoil, was the last straw. She was distraught at the awful prospect.

Mervyn Addison, Thelma's stepfather, was, on the other hand, more understanding about it. His philosophy was that of a professional soldier with a long family association with the British Army. A colonel in the Gunners, he had an impeccable Service background. From Wellington and the Shop (as they called the cadet college at Woolwich in his time), he had gone straight off to fight the Boers. He was still only nineteen when his troopship left England for South Africa.

The carnage of the First World War had followed. Gallipoli, and years in the mud and trenches of France and Flanders, had brought hard experience of war and fighting men. Three times he had been wounded and each time, after a spell in hospital, he had gone back into the line. He spent over a year in hospital and he reckoned this probably stopped him from being killed.

Subsequent service in India in the 1920s under the Raj, with the polo, riding, shooting, the grandeur of the ceremonials, the servants and good living, and the clear beauty of Kashmir, had been a halcyon period. For this tall, pencil-thin, humane man, who had given so much for so little reward, the respite was heaven sent.

It was not surprising that, with such a background, and with a first-class brain to supplement it, Mervyn Addison should understand Bader as well as, and probably rather better than, anyone save Thelma. Before all the argument started, he knew that nothing, absolutely nothing, anyone said would have the least effect if he wanted to fly again and was passed fit to do so. It was a waste of time worrying about it. Better to accept it for what it was, his own decision. The reading was exactly right; but it brought no comfort to Thelma and her mother.

Bader's association with Cranwell helped him now in pursuing his single aim. Just as the Eton Society seems, to an outsider, to be a bond of unusual strength which draws past Etonians together, so the graduates of the Royal Air Force College stand rock-solid for one another. It is a manifestation of their pride in the heritage.

Several of the instructors in Douglas's time were in posts of influence. Men of the calibre of Boyle, Constantine, MacFadyen and Coningham had obviously been marked out and were on the way up. Additionally, there were several among his own contemporaries, close friends like Geoffrey Stephenson and Rupert Leigh, who were in a position to be useful and certainly to try to help. Stephenson, a staff officer at the Air Ministry, beavered away for him behind the scenes.

Best of all, his first commandant at Cranwell, Frederick Halahan ('Bader, what we want in the Royal Air Force are men, not boys'), was also at the Air Ministry. An air vice-marshal, he carried some responsibility for personnel – not aircrew, but that didn't matter. The important thing was that he was there, in Kingsway, at the centre of things.

From the early days, it has always been Bader's practice, if he wanted something badly, to go to the top. He has never been hesitant about taking the shortest route along the corridors of power. The habit has caused some raised eyebrows, and even some sore toes, but results are what count; and results are what he frequently seems to get. Where he does not succeed, and request is met by refusal, the reaction is usually forthright and spontaneous. And, normally, not particularly complimentary. He tends to see decisions in terms of coal black and Persil white. If they go against him and they're black, on the whole they are most probably wrong. If they're favourable and white, the likelihood is that they are wisely conceived. Grey areas and compromises are not a currency he cares to deal in.

But now, with August hurrying on, and peace dangling over the precipice, he tried again for a hearing at the summit. His allies had prepared a way. For once, he was to see some worth in a temporized response.

The Air Member for Personnel, the man who held responsibility on the Air Council for principal selections and postings, was Charles Portal (Marshal of the Royal Air Force Viscount Portal). Known as 'Peter' Portal to the Service, then an air marshal. In little more than a year, with the Battle of Britain won, he was to succeed Cyril Newall as Chief of the Air Staff, a post he was to hold with well-modulated and impressive distinction until the end of the war. As the professional head of the Service, it would fall to him, on the instructions of the Secretary of State, to address a most surprising and unusual letter about Bader to the outgoing Commander-in-Chief of Fighter Command, Hugh Dowding.

Meanwhile, on 31 August, three days before the British government declared war on Nazi Germany, Portal wrote a straight, personal note to Douglas in terms which were at once disappointing and yet promising. He told him (a) that he was too busy to see him; (b) that the Royal Air Force couldn't employ his services now; but (c) that, if war should come, a new situation would arise and he would then almost certainly be used in a flying capacity, if the doctors agreed.

It was characteristic of Portal's intellectual resilience to stick his neck out so far.

Nothing but immediate acceptance would have satisfied Bader. But this was something. The great thing was that he felt he had been to the top, he had made his mark and staked his claim. He could do no more for the time being. The umpire had pronounced. But he got the feeling that one more heave would do it.

Halahan was the next to catch the draught of Douglas's persistence; it was he who paved the way for his former cadet to return to active service with the Royal Air Force. In a succinct and authoritative note to the head of the medical board at the Air Ministry, the Air Vice-Marshal made his opinion quite plain. He remembered Bader at Cranwell. He was the type of officer the Service needed. If found fit, apart from his legs, he should be sent forthwith to the Central Flying School and given the chance to prove himself.

The doctors had no difficulty in accepting the brief. Within days he was reporting to CFS, now at Upavon in Wiltshire, to where it had moved from Wittering while Douglas had been with the Shell Company. There, on Salisbury Plain, were assembled some of the leading exponents of the technical art of flying, professional pilots who were among the Royal Air Force's élite. You had to be a real pro to be an instructor at CFS.

If luck had been on Bader's side in finding Halahan ready to unlock doors at the Air Ministry, fortune smiled again when he arrived at Upavon. Rupert Leigh, a squadron leader now, was in charge of 'A' Flight of the Refresher Squadron over which Wing Commander George Stainforth, the Schneider Trophy pilot, presided. Douglas had come to know Leigh at Cranwell as well as he knew Geoffrey Stephenson. He was numbered among his Service intimates. Amusing, good company, inclined, when in the mood, to take the mickey (without being disloyal) out of senior officers, Rupert Leigh was a gentle, feeling man, who cared about his fellow men. He had always been devoted to Bader. He knew his temperament and was not at all surprised when he became fractious and cantankerous if he didn't get his way. He was also well aware at first hand that he could fly aeroplanes with the angels.

Off they went together on the first morning, in a North American Harvard trainer, a low-wing monoplane, with all mod. cons – retractable undercarriage, variable-pitch airscrew, flaps, heater and a cockpit full of instruments and gauges, many of which didn't have to be bothered with, anyway. The Pratt and Whitney engine hummed on take-off like a speedboat going at full bore. It was a smooth, stable aircraft to fly and it embraced many of the aerodynamic advances which had been made since the days of the Avro 504, the Gamecock and the Bulldog, with their simple, functional designs and economy of gadgets.

It had been nearly eight years since Douglas had had what might be described as formal, or official, control over an aircraft. But the gap seemed to melt away in minutes. Half an hour and the feel and sensitivity were back. Flying, for a pilot of his instinct and flair, is like driving a motor car or riding a motor cycle; once learnt, and while fitness endures, the facility is there for ever, waiting to be picked up and dusted off, almost at will.

One unexpected problem, however, had to be met. With artificial legs, neither foot has any flexibility from the ankle; there's no up and down or sideways movement. Nor is there any contrivance which can compensate for the absence of toes. While this caused him no trouble at all when operating the pedals on the rudder bar (a straightforward pushing action with either leg was quite sufficient), working the brakes on the Harvard was another matter. The trainer, unlike the fighter aircraft in service with the Royal Air Force, had its brakes on the rudder pedals. They were operated by the pressure of toes and feet, flexing from the ankles – just the sort of movement that Douglas can't manage. In the Hurricane and the Spitfire and, indeed, in British training aircraft like the Miles Master, the brakes were operated by squeezing a hand lever on the control column. The difficulty hadn't occurred to Bader – or Leigh – until they went through the cockpit drill together. There was no blinking the difficulty. It was a teaser.

It needs little imagination to visualize what some instructors would have made of it – caveats introduced into assessments of pilot ability, and so on. It wasn't Leigh's way. 'No difficulty,' he said, brushing the problem lightly aside. 'You won't have foot brakes on any of the operational aircraft you'll be flying, so I'll work them. Leave them to me.' It's easy, now, to dismiss the point as being of no consequence. But how many others would have played it that way? It's a good question.

Rupert Leigh did the first circuit and landing, talking Douglas through the various procedures. Then he sat back and told him to get on with it. The first circuit and bump was adequate; the rest began to get closer to the required standard. It all went off uneventfully. It was rather like a first-class games player working himself in again – in a net, on a court, on a practice ground or kicking about on a field. In a few moments the old feeling began to return. The first hurdle had been cleared.

Like Douglas, Leigh never had any doubt that he would make it. Others, however, were less sanguine. Arthur Donaldson, who was an instructor at Upavon at the time teaching others how to instruct, recalled quite clearly what the feeling was like among the staff who didn't know Douglas's flying. No matter how able a pilot he might have been before his accident, they couldn't see how, with his 100 per cent disability, he could measure up to the standards CFS would demand. In the event, the verdict was just the same as it had been at Wittering after the accident and before he had retired from the Service. CFS was satisfied that Bader could fly aeroplanes rather better than the next man.

For the Air Ministry, however, there was a small difference. There was now a war on. Little things like the lack of a suitable instrument in King's Regulations to cover his case, the inability to accept postings to hot countries, the doubtful expectation of length of service, pension considerations and the rest, these were small beer now. Moreover, there was Portal's written statement of 31 August to fall back on: 'if war came we would almost certainly be only too glad of your services in a flying capacity . . . if the doctors agree'. Both provisos had been met – and more.

Thelma was becoming resigned to the course of events. Nothing was going to deflect Douglas from his purpose now that things had reached this pass. But it didn't stop her from worrying terribly about him.

At Shell there was concern, bordering on dismay, at his decision to pursue a return to the Royal Air Force. Walter Hill did his best to dissuade him from taking this decisive step, arguing from all the obvious points of view and adding a further consideration of genuine substance. The supply of aviation fuel for the Royal Air Force would be a wartime necessity of first priority. The company and the department would have a role of capital importance in the prosecution of the national effort. Without a continuous and effective supply of petrol, Britain's air capability would be as nought. Shell, and the other petroleum companies, would be making a maximum contribution to the country's needs. There would therefore be vital work to do. Such well-meant persuasion had not the slightest effect on Bader. It was exactly as his father-in-law had forecast. He was resolved in his purpose. His place, provided he could justify it, was in a Hurricane or Spitfire squadron. That was to be *his* war work.

After getting the report from Upavon, the Air Ministry wasted no time in restoring him to the active list and sending him back to CFS for a full refresher course, including some experience on operational fighter aircraft. His stay was to last two months. Between the end of November 1939 and the end of January 1940, he did 54 hours and 15 minutes' flying, going through the gamut of the various practices. 6 hours and 20 minutes of it was dual, mainly with one or other of his two 'instructors' in the Refresher Squadron, Squadron Leaders Leigh and Constantine, after Flight Lieutenant Clarkson had checked him out.

The seven flights he squeezed in by himself between 27 and 30 November, which totalled 3 hours and 50 minutes, were as exhilarating in their way as his very first solo flights had been at Cranwell in February and March 1929, after Douglas MacFadyen had given him his final 10-minute solo test and spoken the unforgettable words: 'All right, that'll do. It's all yours.'

George Stainforth, as the commanding officer of the Refresher Squadron, signed Douglas's Form 414 (A), 'Summary of Flying and Assessment for Year commencing 1st June, 1939' on 2 February 1940. Under 'Assessment of ability as a fighter pilot', he wrote one discerning word which is used sparingly in the Royal Air Force: 'Exceptional'.

Five days later, on 7 February – eight years, one month and twenty-seven days after the ambulance crew had lifted his critically injured body from the wreckage of the Bulldog on Woodley airfield and eased it gently on to the stretcher – he was posted back again to a fighter squadron: No. 19 at Duxford in 12 Group of Fighter Command. It was equipped with Spitfire Is.

It looked to be rather more than a coincidence that Flying Officer Bader's commanding officer should now be his old aerobatic partner from 23, and Cranwell contemporary, Squadron Leader Geoffrey Stephenson. Less than five months later, Douglas had caught him up.

8
'We were learning, old boy'

War, it used to be said, is made up of long periods of unremitting boredom interspersed with brief moments of intense excitement and fear. It didn't seem much like that to Bader at Duxford in February 1940. Life in a fighter squadron, like a stew on the hob, simmered away. Certainly things were quiet. The attacks which Fighter Command had been expecting since the declaration of war hadn't materialized. Another two months were to pass before the German armour crashed through the Low Countries. Douglas didn't mind. Just to be with aeroplanes and pilots again, talking shop, flying whenever the weather allowed it and absorbing the atmosphere, was exhilarating.

He felt a bit strange at first, like starting a new job; and he knew very well that, without legs, he would have to prove himself before he could win the confidence of the pilots who hadn't know his flying before. It didn't trouble him because he was certain he could do it. The important thing was to be with a squadron again in the Royal Air Force with its effervescent spirit and morale. He had broken loose from his City bonds.

A close-knit family has a character of its own. The special jokes and secrets; the childhood nicknames; the funny words and expressions; the spoiling of the last-born; the simple, choice dishes (especially the sweet things) which mum makes better than anyone else; the favourite stories that dad goes on telling at bedtime; the regular programme which keeps time like the best-made Swiss clock . . . happy is the clan which is cocooned within its own personality. It was like that in a fighter squadron in the early days of the war. Its soul was common only to itself. Its members did things together and, like a family, relied on each other for company, succour and support. It was much the same on duty as off it.

With a well-trained, competent professional like Stephenson to lead it, 19 could hardly help being contented. A fighter squadron tended to be as good – or as indifferent – as its commanding officer. A first-class leader, provided he was given a free hand to make changes, could pull a ragged or demoralized squadron together in a fortnight; a poor commander could let a successful unit slide downhill in a month. The premium on personal leadership was very high, but then a fighter squadron was a personal, possessive thing.

The relationships between commanding officer, flight commanders, pilots, senior NCOs, ground crews and administrative personnel were close. They had to be if there was to be a well-mixed amalgam of discipline, humanity, morale and respect. Misfits got in the way like a bandaged finger.

The adjutant of a good squadron counted for much. He shouldered the burden of staff work and took care of myriad details. In the war years (it was different in peace) an experienced, worldly, understanding figure was only a little less important than the CO to a young, high-spirited and aggressive unit. He had to be a lot of things all rolled into one – Father Confessor, Dutch uncle, strict and firm tutor, approachable guardian, psychiatrist, organizer, reliable friend. He mattered greatly when a squadron was up against it. Pilots would remember a good adjutant for the rest of their lives.

To sense the ethos again, and, in his own rather special circumstances, to be serving under an old and trusted friend like Geoffrey Stephenson, was a wonderfully invigorating experience after all that had gone before. There was, of course, the other side of the coin.

Bader, like Stephenson, had first been commissioned in July 1930, nearly ten years before. Even allowing for the interim away from the Service, in terms of age, personality, flying ability and status he was a senior member of the squadron. He may have been only a flying officer, but judged by personal qualities, experience, undiluted professional competence and skill he was more like a supernumerary squadron leader. It was the last impression he wanted to give.

It took him no time at all to master the Spitfire, to fly, aerobat and handle it as if Supermarine had run him one up specially, made to measure. It seemed to fit him like a well-cut Savile Row suit. One of the things he noticed particularly about the aircraft was its speed and the confidence which speed brought. It was a big change from the biplanes he had flown in 23 Squadron. Speeds in excess of 300 m.p.h. – twice that, and more, of the Bulldog – ensured a comfortable margin to work with. There was always plenty in hand for slow rolls low down, upward Charlies (upward rolls) off the deck, nice, wide loops and rolls off the top. There were no disturbing worries about the speed falling away halfway through a roll like there had been with a Gamecock or a Bulldog. The forward thrust was such that, provided things were managed right, when the aircraft was on its back and the stick was shoved well forward, there was an immediate and positive response as the nose held up nicely above the horizon. It induced confidence and made it all the more tempting to transgress the law about low flying and low-level aerobatics. It felt so safe at those speeds.

One March afternoon, just before dusk, Douglas slipped off to do a night flying test on his aircraft. No one was about. The pilots of 19 Squadron had gone to the mess. Duxford was deserted. As he brought the Spitfire back to the airfield after a 20-minute stint, he felt just in the mood to give it the treatment with two carefully fashioned, very deliberate, straight and level slow rolls – one to the right followed by another to the left – right down on the deck. (It was Woodley all over again.)

He did it immaculately, just below hangar-height level. A steep and tight climbing turn to the left brought him neatly into the last, crosswind leg of the circuit, just right for a final curving turn in for landing. It was a typically smooth blend of rhythmical movement.

Rather pleased, Douglas walked off across the tarmac to the flight hut, parachute slung across his shoulder, flying helmet in his hand. A dark and momentarily indistinguishable figure came towards him in the gathering dusk. It was 'Pingo' Lester, the station commander, an agreeable and stylish officer with an affected, and rather engaging, manner of speech. 'Oh, Douglas,' he pleaded, and the emphasis was on just the right words, 'I *do* wish you wouldn't do that. You had *such* a nasty accident last time.'

Bader's broadly based flying experience showed up, as it was bound to do, when it came to leading aircraft in the air. He found that some of the section and flight leading in 19 fell well short of what he had been accustomed to expect in the peacetime Service. He had been through it all in 23 as a pilot officer. Under Woollett and Day, there had been chances to lead other aircraft. It was part of the thorough training routine. It's easier to make mistakes when you're young and junior. And, anyway, having made them once, you tend not to repeat them when it really matters.

Few things are better calculated to unsettle an experienced hand

91

than to be led by a 'green' and unpractised leader, particularly if he fancies himself at the art. It's an unnerving business, like being a passenger with a driver who hasn't got competent control over his vehicle.

Bader had a taste of it one morning when he was coming in for a formation landing beside his flight commander at the end of a session of aerobatics. He had his wing tucked in tight beside the leader's and was concentrating hard on keeping close station. Instinct suddenly told him they were too low coming over the perimeter of the airfield with wheels and flaps down. Looking up, he saw a building right ahead of him. Pushing the throttle through the 'gate' and whipping up the undercarriage, the engine surged into a great roar. It was in time to avoid the worst, but the experience left him protesting vehemently and permanently uneasy about flying behind untried leaders. He didn't have to do it for long.

The fact was, of course, that within a month the pilots of 19 Squadron had forgotten about his disability. It clearly made no difference in the air; he had proved that by performance. He was a square peg in a square hole, all right. The trouble was the hole wasn't really big enough to take the peg. He did his best to conceal it. He was at pains not to give a contrary impression. But there are some things which cannot be hidden and no one saw it more quickly than Stephenson. He expected it, anyway. He knew Douglas and his flying from A to Z.

Even so, like every other pilot, Bader made his mistakes, elementary and bad ones at that. For a perfectionist of his calibre they were the ultimate humiliation; and yet, after a lay-off of eight years, and coming back on to new and advanced types of Service aircraft, it wasn't easy to remember everything and get the drill right each time. There was a lot more to think about than there had been with the stubby biplanes in the early thirties, with their simple designs and their lack of complications. There was little to do except fly them.

The unkindest cut came on the last day of March 1940. He took a Spitfire off from Horsham St Faith, another 12 Group airfield close to Norwich, on a routine mission. Without thinking, he left the airscrew (propeller) control lever in coarse pitch instead of fine, the necessary setting for take-off. Instead of the airscrew biting into the air as the speed built up and helping the aircraft to lift off, there was no grip. Clinging obstinately and clumsily to the ground, the Spitfire hadn't enough forward speed to get it airborne. It hit the boundary fence at the far end of the field, still at a formidable rate of knots, with most unfortunate results to the aircraft.

It was a relatively commonplace error; but, having done it once and having been mercilessly bawled out both by flight and squadron commander, a raw pilot seldom did it again. Once made, the mistake could usually be spotted and corrected before the aeroplane was halfway down its take-off run. Later on, when an airfield was under attack, and bombs were descending, pilots developed a second sense for this sort of thing. Few essentials were forgotten in the heat of battle.

The experience made Douglas wish that the ground would open up and swallow him and his Spitfire. The ignominy was horrible.

There was only one other gaffe which he would have preferred to forget. It occurred a few weeks after he had taken over a flight in 'Tubby' Mermagen's 222 Squadron. Treble-Two was also stationed at Duxford at the time. In bad weather at night, with the visibility lowering all the time, he messed up a landing, overshot the flarepath and finished up, out of bounds, in an uncharacteristically inelegant attitude. The conditions would have excused the average pilot; but Bader wasn't average. In his precise eyes, the performance fell well below standard. Mermagen took the same view.

Neither of these two incidents had anything to do with his disability. But the fact that he *had* no legs, and was managing so demonstrably well without them, only made the lapses more irksome. They pricked at Douglas's pride. Like the prang at Woodley, both crashes, such as they were, were given full prominence in the log-book: '31 March 1940. Spitfire K 9858. Self. Crashed at Horsham.' The 'Crashed at Horsham' was underlined twice. '13 June 1940. Spitfire D. Self. Night flying patrol, crashed landing.' 'Crashed landing' wasn't underscored. This time, he may well have thought that the conditions had mitigated the error. It hadn't been a heinous crime like the coarse-pitch take-off at Horsham.

Within weeks of the German surrender in 1945, Britain was enveloped in a general election. In its strange circumstances, with the forces' votes spread across the world, the count was unusually delayed. When, eventually, the results began to flood in, it soon became clear that the Socialists would form the next administration. The British people had rejected their leader in his moment of supreme triumph.

Mrs Churchill tried to console her husband. 'It may well be', she said, 'a blessing in disguise.'

The Prime Minister was not to be comforted. 'If that is so, my dear,' he retorted, 'then all I can say is that at the moment it seems quite effectively disguised.'

It was the same with Bader in the first months of war. The unreal inactivity had brought some well-camouflaged blessings. While he and the other pilots were fretting to get to grips with the enemy, the period of uneasy quiet gave him full opportunity to hone and fine-tune his flying, to debate tactics and generally prepare himself for the holocaust which was about to flare. Routine shipping patrols and reconnaissances off the east coast; formation flying; interceptions (often abortive); mock attacks; co-operation with the Navy; exercises with the gunners and the searchlight batteries . . . the menu was unattractive. But Douglas used the time well. His eye was now well in, and any doubts about his ability to fly operationally had been dispelled.

Only towards the end of his command of 'A' Flight in Treble-Two did the battle really spring alive. The last week of May and the early days of June, when the British Expeditionary Force was fighting its way back to Dunkirk and the sea, and avoiding capture by the advancing German armies, saw intense activity in Fighter Command. It shot through the quiet like a muscular spasm.

Covering a British withdrawal, followed by miraculous evacuation, wasn't the kind of work Douglas or any other fighter pilot much relished. But it provided him with action – and his first taste of blood. As a young gun will always remember his first partridge, pheasant, grouse or mallard, so a pilot will ever retain the picture of his first aerial victory.

If Bader's first Messerschmitt 109 didn't actually fall into his lap, it was certainly popped into the bag with surprising ease. It was clearly no November partridge, more an undergrown September bird. His own modest description, deliberately played down, catches the mood. It was the first day of June. 'I was flying at about 3000 feet when an Me 109 appeared straight in front of me, [going] in the same direction and at about the same speed. . . . [The pilot] must have been as inexperienced as I was since he continued in that position while I shot him down . . .'

They weren't all going to be as accommodating as the first.

*

For all Fighter Command's lack of combat experience, the fighting in the daylight air over Dunkirk in those fine May and June days confirmed Bader in some of his long-cherished beliefs. He was satisfied to think the proof was now there. Beyond anything, he was convinced, from what he had seen with his own eyes, that the tactics which his great predecessors had employed in France in the First World War still stood.

He had never ceased to mistrust the stereotyped, textbook approach to combat to which, for years, the Royal Air Force had blindly adhered. He preferred to rely on history. The time he had spent as a cadet at Cranwell studying the writings, experiences and tactical doctrines of heroes like Ball, Mannock, McCudden, Bishop, Richthofen, Boelke and others had persuaded him that the principles upon which they had rested their combat faith must still apply.

The speeds of the aircraft they flew were very slow by comparison with those of the latter-day Spitfires and Hurricanes. But that, he felt, was irrelevant. Speed, after all, was only relative. Tightly circumscribed manoeuvres flown at 100 or 120 m.p.h. simply became wider patterns traced at indicated airspeeds of 225 to 250 m.p.h. The lessons and methods hadn't changed in twenty years; they had just been forgotten in the clamour for progress and a uniform system.

After Dunkirk, he was certain that the three basic articles of a First World War fighter pilot's faith had been reaffirmed. Forty years on, he can still recite them like a piece of catching doggerel:

> He who has the height controls the battle.
> He who has the sun achieves surprise.
> He who gets in close shoots them down.

If the fighting over the beaches had proved his point, the Battle of Britain was soon to provide the double check.

On the aircraft side, subject to height (which was critical), there was, at this stage, not a lot to choose between the Hurricane 1, the Spitfire I and the Messerschmitt 109E *in actual combat*. There were pluses and minuses in each case. Beyond that, pilot quality counted for much – much more than most would credit.

The German fighter, with its fuel-injection system, which allowed the control column to be pushed hard forward without the engine cutting, initially could outdive its British counterparts. This evasive tactic, which the German pilots exploited to the full, made an effective early getaway. By comparison, the carburetion process of the Rolls Royce Merlin jibbed at accepting a firm, forward shove of the stick.

The negative 'G' force halted the flow of fuel to the carburettor and the motor cut instantly. The severance was disturbing in combat.

Set against this, the British fighters, at their best respective heights, held the advantage in manoeuvrability. Each aircraft could outturn the Messerschmitt. Indeed, up to 18,000–20,000 feet, the Hurricane had the edge on the Spitfire in a drum-tight turning-circle; but above that height its performance fell quickly away. It was then that the superiority of the 109 and the Spitfire at once became apparent. At near-maximum altitudes, the speed advantage rested with the 109 which, with its faster rate of climb, was the better attacking aircraft of the two. But, at around 25,000 feet, the margin between these two fine aeroplanes was tissue-paper thin, although the Spitfire, like the Hurricane lower down, was a steadier, more stable gun platform. Both British fighters were made of stronger, sturdier stuff, and the robustness of the Hurricane allowed it to be used in a variety of roles, unmatched by the other two.

The pendulum of aircraft performance was to swing back and forth throughout the war just as it had done over the skies of France in the previous conflict.

The other feature of the first, intensive bout of air fighting which struck Bader, and which found its derivation in history, was the reliance which the Luftwaffe placed upon line-abreast formations. It was a tactic which he was himself later to refine and adapt for the Tangmere wing when he formed it in 11 Group in the early spring of 1941. He was the first wing leader in Fighter Command to use it. Others, including the United States Eighth Fighter Command, would later adopt it. But the British patent belonged to him.

Whereas the Royal Air Force clung for a while to the old air-display concept of a relatively tight vic of three aircraft – three aeroplanes flying together in an upturned V formation – the enemy was employing an altogether looser and more open pattern. It allowed the pilots more elbow room, offered more latitude for manoeuvre and, combined with the cross-overs on the turns, it provided a greater margin for security and safety. Based upon the principle of a pair of aircraft flying together in line abreast 100 to 150 yards apart (later in the war the spacing was widened appreciably), with each pilot looking inwards at his mate, it was the least vulnerable, and most opportunist, formation of them all.

The mechanics were remarkably uncomplicated. The pilot on the left, in addition to leading and navigating, kept his eyes traversing the sky to his right. His number 2, on the right, concentrated his attention exclusively on his leader to the left. This way, two pairs of eyes held the whole sky under scrutiny, up and down, in front and behind. The dependence of one pilot upon the other was complete. It promoted comradeship in the air.

Oswald Boelke, a thinking pilot and tactician, had originated the pair of aircraft flying in line abreast – the *Rotte*, as the Germans called it – in the First World War. With the slower aircraft, the spacing was closer and the turning-circles tighter. But the principle was the same. As the Royal Air Force had expunged from its manuals in the 1920s and 1930s the findings of the pioneers in favour of a theoretical glossary of fighter attacks, so the Luftwaffe had turned its back on the heritage which Boelke had bequeathed. It took the Spanish Civil War, which began in 1936, and the German Air Force's support of Franco against the Republicans, to revive his teachings.

It was the arrival of the Messerschmitt 109 in Spain, and the battle experience that was obtained with it, which changed things almost overnight. In 1938 Adolf Galland's old ground-attack squadron was re-equipped with the new fighter. Led by the talented Werner Molders, then the best tactical brain in Wolfram von Richthofen's Condor Legion, it set about applying the lessons to practice. Out went the tight and tidy vics of three aircraft and in came the less inhibited, and operationally more practical, *Rotte* – the pair in line abreast. It was a fundamental transformation.

Upon this the Luftwaffe built the four, the *Schwarm*: four aircraft (two pairs, flying in touch) spread out across a thousand yards of sky, like the fingers of an outstretched hand. The leader usually led from the centre – from the position of the long middle finger – while scope was given for other supporting fours to be stepped up and down to the side at varying altitudes, to suit tactical needs. This was the formation which, despite Goering's misguided attempts to interfere in the Battle of Britain, was to sustain the Luftwaffe's fighter arm for the next four, throbbing years of war. With it, its two outstanding protagonists, Adolf Galland and Werner Molders, were to make their indelible mark.

Bader was now applying his questing, practical mind to the tactics of air fighting, searching for anything which might be new. Theory was all very well; what mattered was what was actually happening in the air – what worked and what didn't. Fighter Command, without the proving ground of the Spanish Civil War behind it, was feeling its way.

97

Every patrol over the beaches which made contact with the enemy brought something fresh. Between 28 May and 4 June inclusive – eight days' fighting – Douglas completed 26 hours and 10 minutes' flying at the head of his flight and often under Tubby Mermagen's overall command. His total flying time was now 767 hours and 25 minutes; it made him an experienced pilot at this stage in the war.

Some of the patrols which the squadron flew were surprisingly protracted. They bore testimony to the Spitfire's flight duration – another signal advantage over the much shorter ranged 109: 2 hours 10 minutes; 2 hours 15; 1 hour 50; 2 hours 20; 2 hours; 1 hour 55; 2 hours 15; 2 hours 10; 2 hours 10; 2 hours 20. When account is taken of the short outward and return legs across the Straits of Dover, these sorties represented long and exacting spells over the battle-sensitive target area.

As Treble-Two earned its daily bread and moved about from Duxford to forward bases in 11 Group – Martlesham, Hornchurch, Gravesend, Manston and Tangmere – there were notes to compare and experiences to trade with other squadrons as they returned from their own engagements to refuel. There was usually something unexpected to pick up, some new development to ponder. It was a hard 'blooding' period.

'We were learning, old boy. . . . That was the point. . . . We were learning.' Dogmatic, opinionated, unyielding though he might be in deploying his views on sundry affairs of state, amid all the outward aggressiveness and confidence there was an almost incongruous humility about his approach to the mastery of the daylight air. He respected knowledge, and knowledge could come only from the hardest school of all, the school of experience. If a pilot thought he knew it all after half a dozen successful sorties, that was the time to watch it. The air was the eternal leveller.

'We were learning.' It makes rather a different picture from the dictatorial, assertive, adamant image in which the Bader of 1940 has so often been cast.

Treble-Two were whacked when Dunkirk was over. Days which started around 4 a.m. and went on, without respite, till maybe 9 or 10 o'clock in the evening seemed to be endless. It was difficult to unwind. Moreover, for Douglas at the beginning and the end of the day there was always the small matter of his artificial legs to attend to. It just added to the burden.

Since he had taken over 'A' Flight, at Mermagen's request, seven weeks before, he had struck up one of those specially close relationships which have been a feature of his life. T. A. Vigors – Tim Vigors – came from Eton and Tipperary, an interesting mix. He loved horses and dogs in the nature of his countrymen. He had a lurcher named Snipe, a companionable and engaging dog. In this, animal took after master.

Vigors and Bader found much in common, not least the ability to destroy enemy aircraft in the sky, a facility Vigors later applied to the Japanese with the same infectious spirit he had reserved for the Germans both now and in the Battle of Britain.

In the brief lull which followed the British Expeditionary Force's providential return from France, the two of them sought the sanctuary of a weekend's rest at the Pantiles, where Thelma and her family were staying, having decided to leave London ahead of the bombs. It was 9 and 10 June. Jill, Thelma's sister, remembers their arrival. It had been most eagerly awaited. No sooner had they sat down and had a cup of tea than they were both fast asleep in their armchairs.

'Well, look at *that*,' exclaimed Thelma, standing there, hands on hips, eyeing them indignantly. 'They haven't been in the house ten minutes and there they are – *asleep. That's* a nice thing, I *must* say.'

A fortnight later, Trafford Leigh-Mallory (Air Chief Marshal Sir Trafford Leigh-Mallory), the air officer commanding 12 Group, sent for Bader to tell him personally he was giving him a squadron of his own. It was to take immediate effect – on 24 June 1940. He didn't try to disguise the extent of the problem he would be tackling. 242 (Canadian) Squadron had had a rough ride in France; it had had losses; now it would have to be pulled together; this would require determined leadership, a quality he knew Bader possessed.

Leigh-Mallory was very good at that sort of talk. Here was a squadron commander's AOC. A solid, upstanding man of forty-eight, a product of Haileybury and Magdalene, Cambridge, he seemed to work at the business of conveying authority. Always trim and spruce, he guarded his dignity with care. It was important to him. At first he could give the impression of stiffness, even pomposity; but this was an outer crust. It could just have been a cover for some inner uncertainty or doubt.

L-M was a First World War aviator, but, unlike his opposite number in 11 Group, he hadn't been a fighter pilot; reconnaissance and Army co-operation was his business. Although, by 1940, he had already had some three years in command of 12 Group, this deficiency in fighter experience may well have weighed in his mind and caused him to adopt a somewhat elevated stance to disguise it. All the same, his pride would never blind him from seeking and, if convinced, adopting a squadron or wing leader's advice. Behind a determined and rather haughty exterior, there was warmth, kindness and loyalty. When L-M was satisfied and confident with a commander, he would stand at his shoulder and never leave him exposed. Difficult he might be, but for those who served him he possessed the virtue of dependability.

He could make a squadron commander feel that he was 'walking tall'. Bader was not, of course, in need of verbal encouragement. The offer of command was quite enough. At last he had a squadron of his own. The news was richer than the richest alchemy. It was pure elixir. The bigger the challenge, the more he wanted the chance to match it. It was made for him. Cranwell had taught him ten years ago how to do it and accept responsibility without demur. He had no doubt whatever – no doubt whatever – that he would be equal to the task. It was as if all the training and all the adversity of the last decade had been a preparation for this moment.

He made an effort to give the AOC an extra-specially smart salute and stumped out to his destiny.

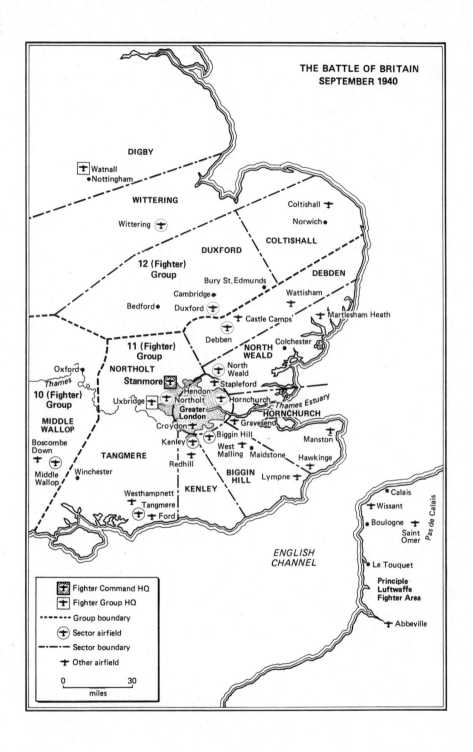

THE BATTLE OF BRITAIN
SEPTEMBER 1940

DIGBY

+ Watnall
● Nottingham

WITTERING

Coltishall +
Norwich ●

COLTISHALL

Wittering ⊕

DUXFORD

12 (Fighter)
Group

Bury St. Edmunds +

DEBDEN

Cambridge ●
Bedford ● Duxford ⊕

Wattisham +

Martlesham Heath +

+ Castle Camps

11 (Fighter)
Group

Debben +
Colchester ●

NORTH
WEALD

Oxford ●
Thames

NORTHOLT

Stanmore ⧆

+ North
Weald

⊕

Stapleford +

10 (Fighter)
Group

Hendon +
Uxbridge ⊕ Northolt +

Greater
London

Hornchurch +

Thames Estuary

HORNCHURCH

MIDDLE
WALLOP

Croydon +

Gravesend +

Boscombe
Down
+ ⊕

TANGMERE

Kenley ⊕

Biggin Hill ⊕

Manston +

West
Malling +

Middle
Wallop

Winchester ●

Redhill +

Maidstone ●

Hawkinge +

BIGGIN
HILL

Lympne +

KENLEY

Westhampnett +
Tangmere +

Calais ●

⊕ + Ford

Wissant +

Pas de Calais

ENGLISH
CHANNEL

Boulogne ●

Saint
Omer

Le Touquet ●

Principle
Luftwaffe
Fighter Area

⧆ Fighter Command HQ

+ Fighter Group HQ

- - - - - Group boundary

⊕ Sector airfield

-·-·- Sector boundary

+ Other airfield

+ Abbeville

0   30

miles

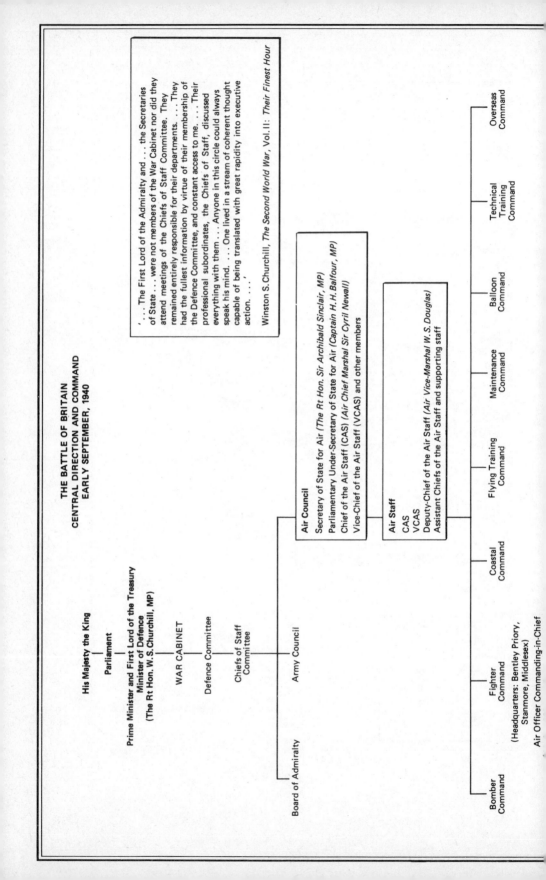

THE BATTLE OF BRITAIN
CENTRAL DIRECTION AND COMMAND
EARLY SEPTEMBER, 1940

His Majesty the King

Parliament

Prime Minister and First Lord of the Treasury
Minister of Defence
(The Rt Hon. W. S. Churchill, MP)

WAR CABINET

Defence Committee

Chiefs of Staff Committee

Board of Admiralty

Army Council

Air Council

Secretary of State for Air *(The Rt Hon. Sir Archibald Sinclair, MP)*
Parliamentary Under-Secretary of State for Air *(Captain H. H. Balfour, MP)*
Chief of the Air Staff (CAS) *(Air Chief Marshal Sir Cyril Newall)*
Vice-Chief of the Air Staff (VCAS) and other members

Air Staff

CAS
VCAS
Deputy-Chief of the Air Staff *(Air Vice-Marshal W. S. Douglas)*
Assistant Chiefs of the Air Staff and supporting staff

'... The First Lord of the Admiralty and ... the Secretaries of State ... were not members of the War Cabinet nor did they attend meetings of the Chiefs of Staff Committee. They remained entirely responsible for their departments. ... They had the fullest information by virtue of their membership of the Defence Committee, and constant access to me. ... Their professional subordinates, the Chiefs of Staff, discussed everything with them. ... Anyone in this circle could always speak his mind. ... One lived in a stream of coherent thought capable of being translated with great rapidity into executive action. ...'

Winston S. Churchill, *The Second World War*, Vol. II: *Their Finest Hour*

Bomber Command

Fighter Command
(Headquarters: Bentley Priory, Stanmore, Middlesex)
Air Officer Commanding-in-Chief

Coastal Command

Flying Training Command

Maintenance Command

Balloon Command

Technical Training Command

Overseas Command

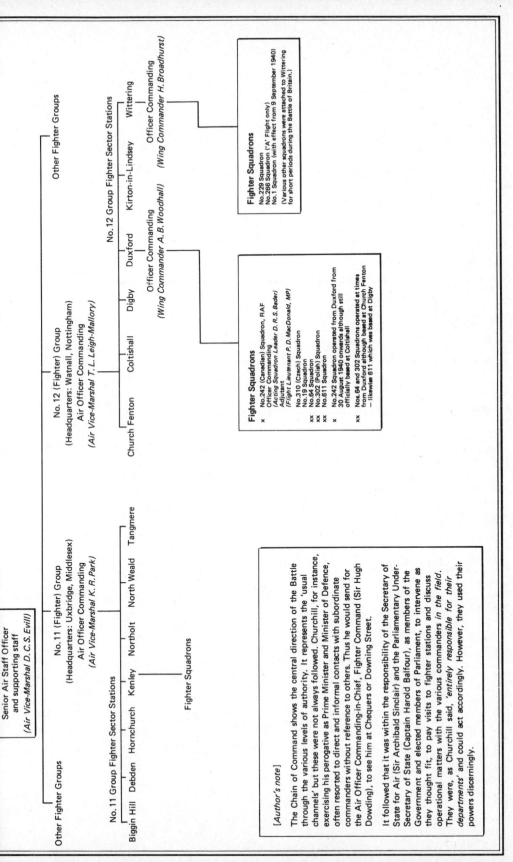

Senior Air Staff Officer
and supporting staff
(Air Vice-Marshal D. C. S. Evill)

Other Fighter Groups

No. 11 (Fighter) Group
(Headquarters: Uxbridge, Middlesex)
Air Officer Commanding
(Air Vice-Marshal K. R. Park)

No. 11 Group Fighter Sector Stations

Biggin Hill   Debden   Hornchurch   Kenley   Northolt   North Weald   Tangmere

Fighter Squadrons

No. 12 (Fighter) Group
(Headquarters: Watnall, Nottingham)
Air Officer Commanding
(Air Vice-Marshal T. L. Leigh-Mallory)

No. 12 Group Fighter Sector Stations

Church Fenton   Coltishall   Digby   Duxford   Kirton-in-Lindsey   Wittering

Officer Commanding
(Wing Commander A. B. Woodhall)

Officer Commanding
(Wing Commander H. Broadhurst)

Other Fighter Groups

Fighter Squadrons

x   No. 242 (Canadian) Squadron, RAF
     Officer Commanding
     (Acting Squadron Leader D. R. S. Bader)
     Adjutant
     (Flight Lieutenant P. D. MacDonald, MP)

     No. 310 (Czech) Squadron
xx   No. 19 Squadron
xx   No. 302 (Polish) Squadron
xx   No. 611 Squadron

x   No. 242 Squadron operated from Duxford from
     30 August 1940 onwards although still
     officially based at Coltishall

xx   Nos. 64 and 302 Squadrons operated at times
     from Duxford although based at Church Fenton
     — likewise 611 which was based at Digby

Fighter Squadrons

No. 229 Squadron
No. 266 Squadron ('A' Flight only)
No. 1 Squadron (with effect from 9 September 1940)
*(Various other squadrons were attached to Wittering
for short periods during the Battle of Britain.)*

[Author's note]

The Chain of Command shows the central direction of the Battle
through the various levels of authority. It represents the 'usual
channels' but these were not always followed. Churchill, for instance,
exercising his perogative as Prime Minister and Minister of Defence,
often resorted to direct and informal contacts with subordinate
commanders without reference to others. Thus he would send for
the Air Officer Commanding-in-Chief, Fighter Command (Sir Hugh
Dowding), to see him at Chequers or Downing Street.

It followed that it was within the responsibility of the Secretary of
State for Air (Sir Archibald Sinclair) and the Parliamentary Under-
Secretary of State (Captain Harold Balfour), as members of the
Government and elected members of Parliament, to intervene as
they thought fit, to pay visits to fighter stations and discuss
operational matters with the various commanders *in the field.*
They were, as Churchill said, *'entirely responsible for their
departments'* and could act accordingly. However, they used their
powers discerningly.

9

Squadron commander

The circumstances of Bader's appointment to command 242 are of capital importance to the events which followed. When the squadron put down at Coltishall in mid-June 1940, it was demoralized, shot through with reverses and utterly deranged. The fighting in France, which had been a near-catastrophe, had left it in tatters. As the French armies had fallen back, impotent against the floodtide of the German advance, the unit had been forced to withdraw, first from Châteaudun, where it had been operating with 1 Squadron, then from Le Mans and, finally, from Nantes, hard by Saint-Nazaire, on the Atlantic coast. When it reached this westernmost point, it was without effective direction, without cohesion and without its ground crews.

The leadership was deficient. The pilots were servicing their own aircraft. The adjutant had become separated from the aircrew. Peter Macdonald – 'Boozy Mac' to the pilots – who represented the Isle of Wight in parliament in the Conservative cause, was busy rounding up the ground personnel somewhere between Le Mans and the coast, hotly pursued by the advancing German forces.

In such a situation, there were bound to be tales of individual courage and resource; but, if the rough truth be told, little worse could have befallen the squadron at that juncture save to fall into enemy hands and become a total loss. In the event it was something of a miracle that, after flying a few last-minute patrols over heavily laden Allied shipping making a final dash for the open sea, it was able to gather its pilots and Hurricanes together for the flight back to England.

The squadron commander did not lead the unit on the last stage of its withdrawal from France to Tangmere, on the Sussex coast. He was in no position to do so. As the rest of the pilots took to the air, he was still lying prostrate beside the flight hut. A sparkle of humour was to be found in the note which was left pinned to his battledress: 'When you surface, you'll find a serviceable Hurricane expecting to be flown home. Try vector 030° for the English coast. Then turn right for Tangmere.'

The CO was a French Canadian who had earlier been lifted out of the remoteness of Training Command in Canada and pitchforked into the hot seat at the head of 242. The appointment owed something to politics. It was close to being a fatal mistake. But it cannot be laid at the door of the victim. Up to the time of taking over, he had had no operational experience whatever. He was thus quite unsuitable for the task. The responsibility lay squarely with Ottawa. It was a straightforward error of judgement, born of ignorance. In the circumstances, the result could hardly have avoided being devastating.

The rest of the unit was made up mainly of Canadians with short-service commissions in the Royal Air Force, with a leavening of English and others to fill the gaps. Its potential was unquestionable; but experienced and determined leadership would have been needed to realize it. Neither the CO nor the original flight commanders had been capable of providing it.

Leigh-Mallory had visited the squadron soon after its arrival at Coltishall, in East Anglia, from Tangmere. Having flown himself down from his headquarters at Watnall, near Nottingham, he went straight to the dispersal hut to see the pilots and ground crews. As he sat on a table in the crew room, his legs dangling back and forth under it, he listened intently – and with understanding – to the squadron's story.

The audience was impressive in its simplicity. It was the first contact the pilots had had in weeks with real live authority. In a few crisp, plain but sincere sentences, the group commander brought an unadorned message of encouragement and purpose. There had been precious little of that sort of leadership of late.

What he found had shocked him. There was no commanding officer. The so-called flight commanders had not been confirmed in their appointments and were tinged with the traumas of the past month. Stanley Turner, a Canadian in the Royal Air Force, who was to serve with lasting distinction during the next two years in the great battles for command of the daylight air over Britain, France and Malta, appeared on the face of it to be the senior officer present. But Stan Turner could be obstinate and rebellious if provoked. After being tested to the limit – and beyond – in France, he was close to being exasperated by 242's lot. Blunt and direct, he employed few words to express his rudimentary views.

It hadn't taken Leigh-Mallory half an hour to size things up. The paramount need was clear. A tough, experienced and spirited leader, who could fly aeroplanes and would command personal respect, must be found quickly to take over. He would require to have both the knowledge and perception to understand immediately what was needed and what changes should be made. He would then have to be given full authority to grip the squadron tight, drive the action through and mould the unit into a confident, coherent fighting machine. It would probably take a good man a fortnight to sort things out.

There wasn't a moment to lose in finding a new commander. But because 242 was a Canadian squadron in the Royal Air Force – not a home-bred squadron in the Royal Canadian Air Force – if an Englishman was to be appointed, his candidature would first have to be cleared through the various channels and eventually blessed by the Canadian government in London. It was no ordinary appointment.

By the time Leigh-Mallory had returned to his office at Watnall, his mind was made up. He was resolved that Bader was the man for 242.

As Douglas made his way by road to Coltishall, he was quite clear about the things he would look for first. The talk he had had with the AOC in his office a day or two before had prepared him for the challenge. But time was the problem. With the Germans now hard up against the Channel coast from northern Holland right down to the Brest peninsula and beyond, aerial attacks must soon begin. He might have a fortnight – no more – to get the squadron into shape and have a potent, disciplined force to lead in the air.

He was now thirty – old for a fighter pilot. By comparison with the pilots he had come to command, he was mature, set in his ways and very professional. He knew exactly what he wanted. And what he was determined to get. All his training and experience told him that the squadron must first be got right on the ground; the air would then follow. Like a new chief executive taking over a company, he looked at once at the key positions – the two flight commanders, the adjutant, the engineer officer and the senior NCOs; the rest (with a few changes) would fall readily into line.

He might not have picked Peter Macdonald to be his adjutant had he been starting from scratch. He had never met him before. Outwardly he was woolly, rather a mumbler and, let's face it, boozy. But Douglas saw beyond that. He had experience – worldly experience of commercial, industrial and political life. Born and educated in Canada, Macdonald had been an undergraduate at Cambridge in the early days of the First World War. Then, having served king and country against the Kaiser, and having established his connections with the Hudson Bay Company, he had entered the House of Commons in 1924 and, thereafter, made his home in England.

Sixteen years in parliament had given him status, influence and access to ministers. He knew his way along the corridors of power. As a serving officer he recognized how fine was the balance between his duties at Westminster and his responsibilities to his Service. The impression of a somewhat bumbling exterior cloaked a shrewd political judgement. Here was a formidable flight lieutenant who knew all about Canada and Canadians. His considerable private means were liberally bestowed upon the squadron.

In the event, Macdonald suited Bader's style of command well. He was a useful foil for some of his commanding officer's more extreme and precipitate actions; but his lot as an adjutant wasn't made any easier by Douglas's determination never to write letters to group or Command headquarters, nor to reply to official communications in writing. When an irate staff officer demanded an immediate reply to his letter of such and such a date, Bader would respond by signal or telephone. It compounded the adjutant's problems; but Macdonald's phlegmatic mien tended to allay pique. Opposite temperaments often breed unexpected affinites.

Bernard West, the engineer officer, or 'spanner', of 242, was the ideal senior NCO. Peacetime trained, and a sensible disciplinarian, he had started as an apprentice and knew all the tricks. Little escaped him. Douglas sensed that, whatever might be the aircraft state at the moment, given his support as commanding officer, Warrant Officer West would sort out the squadron's aeroplanes and ground crews. He felt instinctively he would be a linchpin, an indispensable prop upon which to build. A trusted 'spanner' was an essential prerequisite of a successful unit.

As for Mr West (Bader always insisted on the prefix which was a warrant officer's proper due), he had seen plenty of commanding officers in his time; but he hadn't encountered one like this. Suddenly the shutters had been thrown back and windows and doors opened.

A supercharged injection of air was sweeping through the squadron. He wondered, for a moment, where it all might lead.

He felt himself drawn to the new CO. He might be a difficult character, but he was a professional officer and Cranwell trained. His respect for a senior NCO was transparent in his trust. His ability to fly aeroplanes and fight in them without legs of his own made him an exceptional being. But 'Knocker' West's work was done on the ground and, as he had already learnt, his relationship with a squadron commander had to be based on total understanding and regard or it was nothing. It was Bader's attitude and Service credentials which provoked the confidence, not so much his extraordinary physical endeavours.

One thing West sensed at the start. If he didn't get 242's aircraft strength and serviceability 'right on the top line, Mr West', and keep it there, there would be trouble; plenty of trouble. He would be an exacting and uncompromising commander; of that he had no doubt. But he was a bit older than the others and far more experienced. With that sort of background, he was ready to chuck in his lot 250 per cent behind the CO. Anyway, someone was going to have to sort things out and establish morale.

It was no fault of the engineer officer that the serviceability of the squadron's aircraft, as Bader took over, was anything but 'on the top line'. There were eighteen brand-new Hurricane 1s on the strength, with their three-bladed, constant-speed airscrews, but no spare parts and no proper sets of tools to work with. When Bernard West reported this to the CO, the reaction was exactly as he had anticipated – complete eruption. The upshot was the instant dispatch of the now-famous signal to group headquarters with a copy to Fighter Command: '242 Squadron now operational as regards pilots but non-operational, repeat, non-operational as regards equipment.' The effect was not hard to predict.

A practised squadron commander delegates full responsibility to his two flight commanders and leaves the administration of their flights to them. It is one of the first ingredients of a successful command. Responsibility and trust have to be dispensed. If they aren't, there is usually a mess.

Bader had seen the way to do it a decade before, in 23 Squadron at Kenley, under Woollett and Day. Flight commanders in peacetime were given much authority and power, far more than they tended to be offered in war when the squadron commander had to shoulder the overall operational burden. But, to Douglas's trained mind, the principle remained inviolate. For unruffled, consummate command there must be delegation of responsibility. In the Shell Company they had called it line management. Stephenson and Mermagen had employed it in 19 and Treble-Two.

Within a couple of days he had decided that two new flight commanders must be brought in from outside – immediately. There was too much recent 'history' to use the material which was already there. He did not question the ability of men like Turner, Grassick and McKnight; it was just that he saw a new, untarnished start was needed.

Like a freshly appointed managing director telling his chairman his wishes, Bader informed Leigh-Mallory of his decision that two new men be appointed at once. He asked that one might be Eric Ball, from 19 Squadron, with whom he had served under Geoffrey Stephenson. The AOC was ready for the request and acquiesced immediately. Then George Powell-Sheddon was proposed for the other vacancy. He would be available forthwith. He hadn't flown operationally against the enemy but, like Douglas, he was older than the others, a Cranwell graduate and thoroughly professional. An Englishman, with the conventional background of a peacetime serving officer, he would add balance and discipline to the squadron. Besides, with his arresting stutter, he was something of a card. A fighter squadron needed a 'character'.

Bader was satisfied that, in Powell-Sheddon and Ball, he would have a pair of officers ready to back up his lead and help him to drive his changes through. Moreover, Canadians, like their other Commonwealth and Empire partners, responded to the right quality of English leadership. (If it was of the wrong kind, they, and the Australians, were the first to see to it that they got it changed; they had several methods of doing it.)

The nucleus of the squadron was now established. Bader, Powell-Sheddon, Ball, Macdonald and West – this was the foundation upon which the unit's fortunes would primarily rest.

The strident signal about 242's lack of equipment which he had earlier made to group headquarters, copies to Command, and which had landed him, a few days later, in the C-in-C's office, gave the lie to some of the more bizarre descriptions which have since been painted of his relationship with Hugh Dowding (Air Chief Marshal Sir Hugh – later Lord – Dowding), known throughout the Service by his nickname, 'Stuffy'. Forty years on, the true circumstances of the incident are of interest, for they reveal, in three separate respects, much about the two men's highly publicized characters.

First, it confirmed Douglas's sometimes dramatic penchant for spurning the usual channels and going straight to the top. The effects were familiar. An infuriated member of the C-in-C's staff at Fighter Command slamming down the telephone; a hostile report from an underling; dark mutterings about the total unplayability of the officer commanding 242 Squadron; the inevitable interview with the headmaster. And Bader, dodging the pitfalls, getting his way – and his spares – to the astonished delight of his engineer officer and the chagrin of the 'usual channels' between him and Command. Dowding, on the other hand, and contrary to the popular version, reacted quite differently to his squadron commander's known 'irregularities'. He was prepared to listen before he formed a judgement. Then he came down heavily on Bader's side and struck ruthlessly and without delay.

Second, faced with the crunch – and let there be no doubt about it, for an *acting* squadron leader, in the *first* week of his *first* command, to be sent for by the commander-in-chief (not the group commander, remember) *was* an ordeal – Douglas clung to one governing thought. 'Instinctively,' he recalls, 'I remembered my Cranwell training. It came to my aid now. It was the base on which I rested my case and my confidence.'

He began humbly but then he stood his ground. He regretted very much that the C-in-C should have been so troubled when he had so many other problems to deal with. There had been a clear difference of opinion between *two officers of equal rank*. He had spoken his mind as he had a right to do because the officer concerned didn't understand the problem and did not seem to accept that there could be one. Beyond that, as tempers flared, the individual had suggested that the C-in-C either was, or would be, very annoyed. Douglas said he couldn't be sure of the exact words that had been used.

'I doubted very much, sir, whether this really could be the case if you had been given the facts.'

The suggestion was, of course, rubbish. Dowding had received the report, which he showed to Douglas, but he had expressed no opinion upon it.

Third, when 'the officer of equal rank' was then sent for and, in front of Bader, confirmed that the squadron commander's version of their telephone conversation was correct – including the reference to the C-in-C's annoyance – Dowding's reaction was decisive.

'The whole purpose of these headquarters', he said to the unfortunate individual, 'is to sustain the squadrons in the field and keep them flying. I must ask you, therefore, to leave this headquarters within forty-eight hours.'

For sheer decisiveness of action, Douglas had never before seen anything like it. It was a stunner.

After the luckless officer had withdrawn and certain residual measures had been taken, Air Vice-Marshal Nicholl (Air Vice-Marshal Sir H. R. Nicholl) was then summoned and asked to solve 242's equipment problem at Coltishall. 'Daddy' Nicholl had run the Rugby football for the Royal Air Force when Douglas was playing stand-off half for the Service. They were old friends of widely differing age and seniority.

With the matter closed, Dowding allowed himself a smile. It was the first time that Douglas had ever seen the C-in-C smile. 'You'll stay for lunch, Bader?' The invitation was rhetorical and intended to be friendly and warming. 'But, first, we might perhaps go down and have a look at the Ops Room. If you haven't already seen it, it might possibly interest you.'

'And there they were . . . all the Windmill girls in their WAAF uniforms, and not much else underneath, sitting round the Ops Room table, polishing their finger nails.'

Bader now applied all his skills and flair to pulling the squadron together in the air. It was a relentless, dynamic application. The effect was dramatic and deep.

Denis Crowley-Milling (Air Marshal Sir Denis Crowley-Milling) was a twenty-one-year-old pilot officer in 242 at the time – and very junior. After school at Malvern, he had been apprenticed to Rolls Royce before the war and had joined the Volunteer Reserve in 1937. He had survived the French holocaust. Like others, he had grown up overnight and now was mature beyond his years. Short, fair-haired, fresh and good-looking, he had an aptitude for flying aeroplanes and an intellect which searched for knowledge. Young though he was, he had assimilated quickly the lessons which the fighting in France had brought.

He remembers vividly the impact the new squadron commander

made upon the pilots. Apart from his own flying and his leadership in the air, it was the age gap between him and the young members of the squadron which set him apart. It was a sort of head-of-the-school/new-boy divide. He seemed to be on a pedestal and quite remote. He communicated with the squadron all the time – in the air, on the ground, on duty and off it; but it didn't stop the young pilots holding him in real awe. He was on a different plane altogether. In a word, he was god.

No one ever thought to question his authority or challenge his tactics; nor did the younger ones risk stepping out of line. Behind all the ribaldry, laughter and bravado, there lay a martial discipline. The Canadians, who were not given readily to accept the rule book, recognized pretty quickly that there was one voice which now counted in 242 – and it wasn't theirs.

Yet, despite the strictures, morale in the squadron began to mount like the temperature in the noonday sun. Pride and loyalty and the demand for flying excellence were the key. There wasn't another squadron in Fighter Command like 242. The rest were also-rans. They left off where 242 started. Such was now the talk. Whatever the justification for it, the effect of this attitude was electric both on the squadron and its competitors. The more confident and 'superior' the unit became, the less the others could take it. It was the signal for Bader to add a dash or two of paraffin to the fire. He delighted in ribbing neighbouring squadrons – and their commanders – and provoking retaliation. The suggestion that it was 242 first, last and all the time riled the rest. But it worked wonders for the Canadians' aggressive spirit. Coming from a guy without any legs gave it an extra twist.

There was a bit of General Montgomery in Squadron Leader Bader around this time. Few armies in the Second World War developed such a blatant pride in their being as the British Eighth Army did, under Montgomery, in the Western Desert in 1942. 'There can be only one result. Together we will hit the enemy for "six" out of North Africa. . . .' Bader's approach and methods were not dissimilar; nor was his success. That kind of swashbuckling, piratical boldness thrives on advance and gains. It cannot countenance failure or withdrawal.

Two immediate demands were placed upon the pilots. From them, there could be no escape. As few in the squadron had more than 200 hours flying in their log-books at the time, the effect was sharp and positive. Each man was exhorted to get in the habit of chucking his aircraft about the sky. Stand it on its tail; fly it upside down; twist it about on its fore-and-aft axis; loop it, spin it, roll it off the top, do anything – but don't go about flying straight and level. There was another thing. Practise combat. Get on the other man's tail and stay there – *stay there*: never let him out of your sights. If he goes through the most violent evasive manoeuvres, stick there; never allow him to shake you off. Cling to him. Down, round, underneath, upside down, over the top, skidding one way then the other, spinning off. . . . Keep your grip on him.

The ability to thrive on aerial contortions was an essential part of a fighter pilot's make-up. There must be absolute mastery over the aircraft. There could be no question of being timid or hesitant with an aeroplane, of worrying about falling out of the sky or getting in some unnatural attitude. Every man must know the extremes of his aircraft. All this had to be practised and repeated and practised again until it became second nature.

There was one man in 242, when Douglas arrived, who had never slow-rolled, let alone spun, a Hurricane before. It could hardly be credited. For him it was quite an awakening. Even for the rest, who were not given to such stability, the regimen came as a rude and revealing disturbance. Hurricane Bader blew one or two of them irrevocably off course. They did not return to the fold.

He made the squadron go through as many manoeuvres as he could *together*. One aim was to make the pilots feel that they were as one, not a dozen individualists. The other was to instil tightness, discipline and control into the flying. Putting ten or twelve aeroplanes in line astern, he would loop the lot in formation. It was all right for those in front; for those at the back it was a tortuous exercise. Crowley-Milling was usually in the last aircraft; his seniority in the squadron normally ensured it. It was the hell of a job, he recalls, for Pilot Officer Prune at the rear to get over the top of the loop without losing too much speed and falling out of it. It was an unsettling experience. Pilots didn't take much to falling about out of control. If one of them failed to make it and plumeted earthwards like a crumpled high pheasant, hit right up in the neck, Douglas would put the squadron through it again; and again. The further back you were the less chance you usually had of succeeding. It came as a great relief to Tail-End Charlie, by now soaked through with perspiration, when the leader elected to switch to some easier exercise.

It was all part of the accepted routine in those first days of power. He wanted the squadron to have cohesion in the air; he gave expression to his wish by insisting that its formation flying be very tight. Bader tended to fly 242 tighter than the rest, even up to the moment of opening an attack on a cluster of bombers. It was a fundamental part of his drill. It wasn't until he took over the wing at Tangmere in 1941, and the sweeps started over northern France, that he opened things out and adopted altogether looser tactics, with pairs and fours of aircraft flying, with plenty of space between them, in line abreast. By then, the circumstances were quite different; so was his approach. But, for the moment, vics of three aircraft – really tight vics of three, keeping close station – was the order.

The log-book doesn't lie. Between 27 June and 3 July – eight days – he had 242 up nine times for squadron formations; 10 hours and 20 gruelling minutes of it. There was no more demanding form of flying for pilots with a couple of hundred hours under their belt – no matter how 'operational' they thought they might be. It required an exceptional output of concentration, and it was hardly the kind of work most calculated to commend itself to a bunch of Canadians, pulverized by the fiasco in France.

And yet, as with so much discipline, it worked wonders for spirit, confidence and bearing. Bader's First Hundred Days were packed, of necessity, into a fortnight. Their impact was breathtaking, the effect decisive. But instead of the German attacks starting almost at once, six weeks were to elapse, up to the end of August, before the rigours of the Battle of Britain embraced 12 Group on a major scale and involved its squadrons in the climax of the conflict. As we shall see, there was a reason for the group's partial exclusion – a contentious, nagging, gnawing reason which wasn't removed until the great battle was moving to its September crescendo; and then its removal became shrouded in controversy and argument, most of which rested upon misunderstanding, ignorance, a lack of cohesion and, much later, fiction.

For 242 Squadron, the intervening respite was, as things turned out, providential. It gave Bader the time to transform the unit on the ground and in the air. It amounted to an exceptional act of leadership, as significant in its smaller and limited way as the breathing space Montgomery used between assuming command of the Eighth Army in the desert and the Alamein offensive. 242 was now a finely drilled entity, strong, spirited and immensely aggressive. The pugnacity and resolve of its commanding officer fitted nicely into its mood.

*

It was a curious paradox that Douglas's first two personal victories with the squadron should have come during this period of relative operational quiet and in a way which was the antithesis of the collective principles he was preaching. Each was achieved when he was flying alone, without his disciples around him.

The early morning of 11 July was just his meat. Cloud base was down to 500 or 600 feet, with mist and drizzle covering much of East Anglia. Forward visibility varied between 2000 and 3000 yards. It was a stinker of a day, no use at all for squadron flying. In fact, no one was airborne.

The Coltishall controller called Bader on the Operations line at 0700. A plot had just appeared on the table, believed to be a single enemy aircraft, flying north up the Norfolk coast, from a point east of Yarmouth, towards Cromer. Its height was around 1000 feet. He wondered if the weather was good enough to put up a section from 242 to have a look.

'No,' said Douglas at once, 'but I'll go myself and have a look. I won't hang about. If I see nothing I'll come straight back. It's worth a try.'

As a patient wildfowler, with a feel for a dirty morning, is prepared to hide out on the marshes for an hour or so and await the morning flight, so Bader was ready to rough the elements on the off chance of sighting the enemy's early reconnaissance.

Staying right down on the deck until he was out to sea, 242's CO was encouraged to find the cloud base up to nearly 1000 feet over the water. Turning north up the coast, he could see small likelihood of the enemy flying a sortie below cloud in such conditions. But fortune sometimes favours the persistent. Suddenly, 400 or 500 yards ahead he caught a glimpse through the mist of a twin-engined aircraft also heading north; its stringbean-thin form told him it was a Dornier 17. The rear gunner confirmed his identification with a warning burst of fire.

'He who gets in close shoots them down.' Douglas remembered the old adage. At 250 yards, and then 200, he made full use of the rock-steady platform which the Hurricane offered. Two good bursts with his eight .303 machine guns, as the aircraft turned sharply and climbed, was all he had time to get in before the Dornier found sanctuary in cloud. Back at base, he reported his encounter to Operations, complimenting the controller on an accurate piece of plotting but regretting that the outcome had not produced more definite results.

A few minutes after putting down the receiver, the controller called back. A lookout post on the coast had just come through to say a Do 17 was down in the sea off Cromer. The time tallied precisely with the engagement. The hunch of the wildfowler had found its fair reward.

Five weeks or so later, on 21 August, there was a repeat of the solo performance in circumstances not dissimilar from the first. Hits were secured on another Dornier 17 which Douglas's good eyes had picked out above the overcast; the enemy had dived into cloud without any results being seen. Then the Observer Corps rallied to his side. A Do 17 had crashed into the sea at the given time of the interception. Further investigation had shown there were no survivors.

Another significant interlude now intervened. As a prelude to the so-called 'Big Wing' controversy which was soon to follow, its timing was specially interesting – even prophetically so. Some will dismiss it as routine; others, knowing rather better, will class it as foresight. Crowley-Milling, who was a witness at first hand to the episode, has no doubt that it showed, then, the way his squadron commander's mind was working and that, again, like Montgomery in the desert, Bader was several strides ahead of the game.

It was probably fortuitous that 66 Squadron, commanded now by Douglas's friend, Rupert Leigh, should also have been based at Coltishall. In this period of quiet, and in a purely local and free-enterprise initiative, without prompting from anyone, the two squadron commanders began flying a series of wing practices – 66 with its Spitfire 1s, and 242 with its Hurricanes. It was an unsung rehearsal for what was, within a few weeks, going to be blown up and magnified into some new and astonishing development in military aviation. What followed was, in fact, nothing more or less than a rational, tactical consequence of the course of the great battle which was developing for command of the daylight air. The concept of the Duxford wing found a derivation in four days' flying at Coltishall. Leigh was as enthusiastic an advocate of the exercise as Bader. Here were two, original and resourceful minds working in unison. There was nothing conventional or stereotyped about their approach to the tactical theme. None could say that it lacked imagination, flair, originality – or humour. The opponents said there was too much.

On 21 and 24 July, and again on 6 and 7 August, Bader and Leigh, off their own bat, spent 4 hours and 40 minutes flying the two squadrons together as a wing. There was nothing new about putting two or three squadrons together in the air as a wing; Keith Park, the 11 Group commander, had done it with his squadrons during the battle for France; Fighter Command was to do it endlessly during the next four years of war.

What was interesting about this exercise was its juxtaposition and timing, and the fact that two squadrons in Leigh-Mallory's 12 Group were flying together *as a wing in practice* over a month before Bader, with the group commander's full support, moulded 242, 310 and 19 squadrons together into a collective and interdependent entity and flew it as the Duxford wing. It was a premeditated act, not some precipitate stroke of expediency or opportunism.

Meanwhile, down in 11 Group, something was certainly stirring. The attacks which the Cabinet, the Chiefs of Staff, the Air Staff and Fighter Command had been expecting since Hitler's armies reached the Channel coast were now mounting daily; but they were principally confined, in strictly operational terms, to 11 Group's boundaries. Within them, the battle was really hotting up.

This was a massive area (see map on page 101). Under the aegis of Keith Park (Air Chief Marshal Sir Keith Park), it covered all the south-east of England, a fair slice of the south and, to the north-east, a sizeable chunk of the southern half of East Anglia. Beyond it to the west lay 10 Group, with Quintin Brand (Air Vice-Marshal Sir Quintin Brand) at its head, while northwards, up to the midlands and across to the east coast, 12 Group held sway. Over it, Trafford Leigh-Mallory, thumbs pushed through the two breast pockets of his tunic in characteristic stance, imposed his autocratic rule. Always disposed to listen to Bader's views on air tactics, as time went on L-M found another resilient adviser in Harry Broadhurst (Air Chief Marshal Sir Harry Broadhurst), the station commander at Wittering. Brooding there in his fortress 3 miles south of Stamford, and straining to lead his restless squadrons into the battle, Broadhurst was to develop into a brilliantly successful wartime tactician and fighter leader. He was thirty-five in 1940 and five years older than Bader. Flying aeroplanes, for him, was a natural and advanced art. He and Thelma Bader's first cousin, Teddy Donaldson, were probably the two best pre-war shots in the Royal Air Force, cornering, between them, the annual air-firing competition.

But Harry Broadhurst was much more than a fine pilot and leader.

117

He was a rugged, competent buccaneer who knew exactly what he was about and where, the Lord willing, he intended to go. Ambition was a spur. He and Douglas had several similarities. Neither was an easy man and each was strongly assertive. Both were controversial figures and always prepared to swim against the current to sustain a personal conviction. As a pair of officers, they were outstanding by any test. With 'Sailor' Malan, the South African commander of 74 Squadron and, later, the highly distinguished leader of the Biggin Hill wing, they possessed the three most resourceful brains among the senior pilots in Fighter Command. As the war wore on, they were joined on this élite pedestal by Johnnie Johnson (Air Vice-Marshal J. E. Johnson), a protégé of Bader who, by 1943, had become the unchallenged prince among the Air Force's current wing leaders.

Where Leigh-Mallory was undeniably lucky was in having, available to hand in 12 Group, two men of the calibre of Broadhurst and Bader to offer their distinctive views. Being older and widely experienced, each was intellectually capable of standing back and taking a broader and more detached sight of the battle as it developed. They lent support to L-M's somewhat heretical view that those who were actually doing the fighting in the air might, now and then, be able to contribute a mite to the tactical thinking of those who passed their days on the ground.

Whereas Park, and 11 Group, confronting the enemy only a few miles away in the Pas de Calais, were already absorbed with the mounting daily pressure of the Luftwaffe, Leigh-Mallory, Bader and Broadhurst, positioned further north and less committed, could paint on a broader canvas. They were able to see things in wider perspective and make use of the benefits of 'think time'.

As for 242 Squadron, the circumstances which had conspired, since Douglas took over, to give it 'drill time' were now rapidly changing. Still at Coltishall, it was right up on its toes and ready to go. Châteaudun, Le Mans and Nantes were place names which had long since passed into history.

10
Matinée performance

For the cast of 242, the curtain call for the Friday matinée came earlier than usual. The additional notice was unexpected and welcome. Up till then the warnings had been unnecessarily long delayed. It was unsettling having to go on stage in a rush.

Douglas Bader, playing the lead, had complained about the timing. At last his plea had been heard. Park's controller had given his opposite number at 12 Group sufficient warning to allow 242 to get airborne, gain altitude and be tactically placed to strike, before the raid came in.

The squadron had moved down to Duxford from Coltishall earlier in the day to be nearer the battle. Now it was being controlled from the local Operations Room and, in particular, by Wing Commander A. B. Woodhall (Group Captain A. B. Woodhall), the station commander. A well-tried First World War pilot, with a resourceful and tactical mind, Woodhall was to become the star among the Royal Air Force's wartime fighter controllers. Within two years, he had transferred to the great air battle for Malta the lessons he was learning in the struggle for command of British and French skies. Profiting from his association with Bader, he was developing a genius for this exacting and responsible role.

As the squadron formed up round its leader, Woodhall's deep and measured voice spelt out the instructions. They were short and concise. Fly vector 190° for North Weald, height 15,000 feet – or, in the operational jargon of the hour, 'angels 15'. It appeared that 11 Group's important sector airfield, on the north-eastern periphery of London, was likely to be the target. The enemy, with some seventy-plus aircraft involved, looked bent on attacking in strength.

It took 242 Squadron 15 minutes to get the height and be in the critical area. Positioning was now the key. No good, Bader knew, just to sit up over the top of North Weald at angels 15 – which was what 11 Group wanted – waiting for the onslaught. That was no way to defend a target. No matter what the theorists on the ground might say, no leader in his senses would try to protect, from directly above, a pocket handkerchief in a field 15,000 or 20,000 feet below.

Yet Bader was surprisingly charitable about the fallacy of such rigid, rule book thinking. 'We were learning. . . . We were all learning. That was the point.' As he jockeyed for advantage, the catch-lines kept echoing in his mind:

> He who has the height controls the battle.
> He who has the sun achieves surprise.
> He who gets in close shoots them down.

Wasn't that, after all, the enemy's concept? If North Weald was to be the target, thought Douglas, it was ten to one the attackers would make their run in from the west, with the sun at their back. He resolved, therefore, to make the instructions he was receiving from the ground his ally, not his master.

Working 15 or 20 miles round to the west of the raiders, he climbed another 3000 or 4000 feet above the given altitude. He had enough time to do it.

The positioning was just right. As the gaggle of bombers, with its Me 110 escort, turned into the target from the west, 242, with all the tactical advantage, came in out of the sun fast and hard, cutting into the attacking force before it had time to realize what had hit it. It was a classical 'bounce'. The interception that fighter leaders dream about. The sort of thing which occurs once in fifty sorties. Everyone got in among the Dorniers or 110s. Turner, Crowley-Milling, McKnight, Ball and Bader himself all registered kills; some collected more than one.

Douglas would have been entitled to give this matinée performance a rave notice in his log-book; but he played it cool, preferring to confine himself, with Sherlock Holmes and Dr Watson, 'rigidly to facts and figures'. The record could speak for itself:

August 30th Hurricane D 1 hour, 30 minutes. Intercepted 100 E/A [enemy aircraft] with Squadron. Shot down 12. Self 2 Me 110s.

A deadpan rider, written on the opposite page, expanded the detail:

Met about 100 E/A bombers at 15,000 feet *just west of Enfield* [author's italics]. Was up-sun and above them. Dived the whole squadron into attack from above and behind. Squadron destroyed 12 E/A for loss of none. No bullet holes in any aeroplane.

'Just west of Enfield' was significant. It pinpointed exactly the area of the engagement as being some 15–20 miles *up-sun* of the target – quite a different position from the one the 11 Group controller was trying to get 242 into. Bader saw that, if he followed the instructions and sat over the top of North Weald at 15,000, the squadron would be down-sun of the impending attack and at the same level, an appalling tactical position.

Six months later, with all the knowledge which had been gained in the interim, not even an inexperienced squadron commander, leading his pilots for the first time, would wittingly have allowed himself to be directed into such a situation. So Douglas led where others were in due time to follow. 'Heresy!' they cried. But nothing would deflect him from his conviction.

In a few lethal moments all Bader's long-held beliefs had been confirmed. What he had expected to be the case was now proved beyond doubt. The findings were incontrovertible.

The job of the ground controller was plain. He must put his flock in the vicinity of the enemy, passing on to the leader every scrap of information which radar can provide. In a word, he must paint a picture. Then it is up to the wing, squadron, flight or section commander to make the best of it. He must be free to act and exploit whatever opportunity is there.

The officer commanding 242 Squadron, and the controller, Duxford, were at one with this thinking. They had no difficulty in convincing the AOC of its sense. 11 Group, however, masters in their own domain, would not accept it. Argument followed. Yet, within a year, all had fallen into line. It had become standard practice in Fighter Command. Once again, Bader was ahead of the game.

The Enfield interception had pressed another signal thought strikingly upon Douglas's mind. The operation would have been doubly successful if, instead of a single squadron, *three, flying in touch as a wing*, had been available. Leigh-Mallory saw the force of the contention. Given the right calibre of leadership, there was little difference, as events were to show, between operating one squadron and working two or three – or more – together. It was a tactic tailored to 12 Group's geographical circumstances. Bader and Broadhurst could have taken it in their stride.

But Douglas and Broady also knew that, while wings could readily be operated from Duxford lying 40 or 50 miles behind the front line, the extreme pressures prevailing in 11 Group ruled them out. They said so at the time. It was a different ball game altogether. There, time and the proximity of the enemy were always the problem. Stations like Biggin Hill, Kenley, Hornchurch, Gravesend, Manston and Hawkinge, which lay within spitting distance of the enemy across the Straits, were constantly under attack before the squadrons could gain sufficient height to mount an effective defence. It was a tortuous business feeling that you would probably be bounced on the climb by an attacking force of superior strength. The conditions were suitable only for smaller formations – for squadrons, flights and sections, not wings. It was a case of improvising, of exploiting such opportunities as were there and, generally, making the best of each day's hazards.

Keith Park played this unfavourable hand with singular deftness and skill. Bader has consistently contended that, in so doing, it was the tall, spare, whipcord-tight commander of 11 Group who was the real victor of the Battle of Britain – not Hugh Dowding, Leigh-Mallory or anyone else lurking unseen in the back rooms. Erect, handsome and invariably smartly dressed and groomed, Park was cast in the mould of other granite-hard New Zealanders who, in two world wars, had left the sanctuary of their native land to fight for king and empire.

Like Leigh-Mallory – and, indeed, Dowding himself – he was no easy character. Unyielding, self-willed and decisive, he was an individualist with a flamboyant style of his own. He was hugely experienced. As an NCO in the first New Zealand Expeditionary Force, he had roughed it as a gunner in the hideous fighting at Gallipoli and on the Somme. He had been dreadfully wounded. Classed thereafter as unfit for all further military service, he had contrived a transfer to the Royal Flying Corps where there appeared to be – conveniently – no trace of his medical records. By 1917, he was a major commanding 48 Squadron, with its Bristol fighters, on the western front. For his toils, he collected two Military Crosses, a Distinguished Flying Cross and, from the French, a Croix de Guerre – not a bad day's work for one who was unfit to serve, let alone fly aeroplanes.

Fortune then smiled on Park's future. A hard worker, he was one of a group of able and successful young officers whom Sir Hugh (later Lord) Trenchard, then Chief of the Air Staff, had picked out to send to the Staff College. With him on the same course were two of the most astute minds in the Royal Air Force, Peter Portal and Sholto Douglas.

As the country moved on towards the Second World War, he had been a natural for the post of Senior Air Staff Officer at Fighter Command under Dowding. And when, later, with the Battle of France over, the immensely proficient Strath Evill was available to succeed him, he was tailor-made to take over 11 Group for the contest which was opening.

He was a thoroughbred in the job of defending south-east England against the Luftwaffe; but he was possessive to a point about the area of his responsibility.

Standing back in 12 Group, they saw things differently. At Duxford, Wittering and Watnall, away from the daily press of battle, they could put the picture in perspective. In their detached fastness, a grand design was emerging.

As the conflict rose to its final September climax, efforts, as we shall see, were made to implement the concept. It was never, however, to be put to the touch in the form that Bader had conceived – and Leigh-Mallory was vigorously advocating. After the virtuoso engagement of 30 August, Park, through his controllers, and by a calculated act of deliberate policy, saw to it that the 12 Group squadrons were neither allowed the chance, nor called off the ground in time, to enable expression to be given to the specific plan.

It was a crushing indictment of Hugh Dowding's capability as a battle – *battle* – C-in-C that he would not, or could not, bring himself to call the two group commanders together, resolve the issues which divided them and dictate from his Command headquarters the tactics which were to be followed. Instead, differences were allowed to smoulder on unchecked as controversy was fuelled and inflamed. Casualties were suffered unnecessarily in the air at the very moment when the pilot shortage in Fighter Command was threatening Britain's chances of survival.

Fate prevented Leigh-Mallory, who died with his wife in an air crash at Grenoble, in France, in 1944, from telling his version of the story. Nor, with the sole exception of Peter Townsend (Group Captain P. W. Townsend), has anyone – Robert Wright, Len Deighton, Johnnie Johnson, Al Deere, Johnny Kent, Derek Wood and Derek Dempster or any of the others who have set themselves up as so-called 'authorities' on the great 11 Group versus 12 Group, 'Big Wing' controversy of the Battle of Britain – ever troubled to discuss the issues in depth with Bader before placing their own construction on events in which, by their own definition, he was a leading actor.

Advantage, however, accrues to the biographer, for it is only now, more than forty years on, after suffering in public silence an interim of misrepresentation, and worse, that Bader is ready for the case to be deployed. In this way, he believes, the cause of his old AOC may also be served.

11
Fatal misjudgement

I put the question to Adolf Galland in the garden of Withers Farm, Sir Douglas and Lady Bader's country home at Marlston, in Berkshire, a few miles from Newbury. My wife and I, and Germany's best-known fighter leader of the Second World War, were staying the weekend.

It was 7 September 1980. The autumn sun was shining down, warm and strong, out of a sky of dusty powder blue. The fields, recently harvested, rolled away across the valley and up the hill to the trees beyond. The English countryside, quiet and still, was at peace with the world.

Forty years ago, on this very day, the German High Command, with Hitler and Goering pressing down upon it, had, in a fatal blunder, switched the direction of its attack from Fighter Command and the Essex and Kentish airfields to London and other major cities. The decision, politically quite as much as militarily motivated, was an undisguised consequence of Bomber Command's attacks on Berlin and the heart of the Third Reich. To appease their own population, the Nazi leaders had been stung into retaliation. The precipitate deviation of aim was to cost Germany the Battle of Britain and, with the invasion of Russia which followed, eventually the whole war.

'Tell me, Dolfo,' I asked (it was Douglas's nickname for this dark, heavily built and dignified man), 'why did your High Command allow itself to be diverted from the attacks upon our airfields in September 1940, when it just about had the battle "made"? Looking back, now, it seems an incredible misjudgement.'

Galland, with his suave courtesy and impressively good manners, threw up his hands and lifted his big round eyes to the heavens. A shrug of his broad shoulders and a slow shake of the head made an answer superfluous.

125

Until 7 September 1940, the Luftwaffe's bombardment had followed a clear-cut, systematic, military sequence. It bore the hallmark of Teuton precision, planning and courage. During the first month of the onslaught against Britain, from early July to the first days of August, the offensive had been directed aaainst convoys and shipping in the Channel, and coastal targets. Then, like some menacing, creeping artillery barrage, the sights had been raised and the attacks moved relentlessly forward against the whole gamut of Fighter Command's south-eastern (11 Group) complex, the radar installations and communications, the airfields, the aircraft and the pilots.

The purpose behind the plan was plain. Until the fighter arm of the Royal Air Force had been destroyed, or weakened into impotence, both on the ground and in the air, Britain could not be brought to its knees and an invasion mounted. This second phase, which had lasted a further month from the beginning of August until early September, had absorbed virtually the total weight of the Luftwaffe's daylight attacks of which 11 Group had borne the brunt. Operating under an umbrella of enemy activity, Keith Park's squadrons had performed prodigious feats. A critical development had, however, now intervened.

The steady flow of Spitfires and Hurricanes which Lord Beaverbrook, with extraordinary zeal and drive, was prising out of the factories into the squadrons, was not being matched by the supply of pilots. This, and not aircraft, had now become the paramount concern. With death, injury and battle fatigue, the wastage had taken its toll. Another month – even a fortnight – of the August attrition and the end of the game would be in sight.

It was at this agonizing juncture, when all hung tenuously in the balance, that the enemy, doing 'everything by starts, and nothing long', turned away and altered course. For Churchill's War Cabinet, it came like a blessed shift in the wind in some hard-fought, eighteenth-century engagement at sea.

As the direction of the attack veered away from the crucial military targets and on to London and the centres of population, Leigh-Mallory at headquarters, Bader at Duxford and Broadhurst at Wittering, with their fresh, razor-sharp wings of squadrons, gathered themselves to enter the wider and weightier battle which was opening. Like General de Gaulle, twenty years later, biding his time at Colombey-les-Deux-Églises and awaiting the call to Paris, they were sure their moment was coming.

*

With the Germans' change of plan, Bader was now wholly convinced of the course to follow. Used in the right way, and professionally led, the Duxford and Wittering wings, dovetailing together, were ideally placed to succour their hard-pressed comrades to the south without weakening the security of the midlands' industrial belt or the protection of the airfields north of the Thames.

Bader had thought the tactics through and discussed them with his AOC. They were at one with the concept. The principles were simple to comprehend.

It was 88 miles from the Pas de Calais, where the big enemy formations assembled, to the Thames estuary. Having reached 17,000 feet, the Ju 88s, Dorniers and Heinkels were joined by the short-range Messerschmitt 109 fighter escort and supporting elements. Once in position, the attacking force moved off across the Channel for London and surrounding targets.

The run in to the goal mouth was one of some 30–40 minutes. It meant that the 109s, which without their extra drop (fuel) tanks had an endurance of no more than 1½ hours, were fighting close to the extremity of their operational radius. They had little time to hang around and mix it. Galland has stressed again and again the constraints which the unfavourable endurance factor placed on the Luftwaffe's fighters actively engaged over England.

It was most noticeable when the German High Command was writing the operational orders for the massed bombing raids. There was then an insistence that the 109s should maintain close contact with the bombers, weaving and manoeuvring above and to the side of their charges in an attempt to keep position. It was a constrictive role and heavy on fuel.

Leaders like Galland and Moelders knew these to be quite the wrong tactics to employ for the high-flying, wide-ranging, speedy 109s. It was sacrilege to fly these beautiful aircraft in such a role. Galland, however, like Bader, played things his way. A wing leader must have freedom of action in the air, whether he be German or British. It is fundamental to the principles of air fighting, offensive or defensive. The *Kommodore* of Jagdgeschwader 26 and the commander of the Duxford wing were at one on the point. Practice dictated it.

So Douglas's plan for the 12 Group wing was positive, practical and pretty pugnacious. He saw it as being complementary to Keith Park's use of the 11 Group squadrons and as a means of buying them the precious time they lacked to gain height and position in the face of the incoming raids. It rested, like all his air tactics, on a few plain and clear tenets.

It required, first, that the wing should be called off the ground as soon as the radar had begun to show that the Germans were building up in strength over the Pas de Calais and that a major raid was imminent. With this kind of warning, the Duxford squadrons could have been at 20,000 feet over the estuary (with the Spitfires 4000 or 5000 feet above) by the time the attacking force was setting course across the Channel.

Another 15 minutes on a south-easterly course and the wing would be in position, well forward over East Kent, covering a broad area bounded by Canterbury, Ashford, Dungeness and Dover, with all the height and freedom to manoeuvre into a good, tactical, attacking position as the first enemy formations crossed the coast. The wing leader and the 12 Group squadron commanders would then have had *control of a battle of their own seeking* – the overriding requirement for a successful defensive action.

With the Spitfire squadrons engaging the free-ranging 109s high up, the Hurricanes, with a 3000-feet height advantage, would have made first contact with the bombers, coming in fast in an attempt to break up the main formations. Meanwhile, the 11 Group squadrons, knowing that the Duxford wing would be bearing the brunt of the attack, would have been airborne from their bases as the 12 Group force moved down from the estuary to the advanced patrol area. In this way they would have gained more than their customary time and room for manoeuvre. The chances of achieving priceless height and position before they were obliged to engage the enemy would have been immeasurably enhanced; and confidence would have flowed from knowing that the attackers had received some rough punishment before the Kenley, Biggin, West Malling, Gravesend, Hornchurch and North Weald squadrons moved in.

They could well have found, for a change, splintered formations of bombers and groups of deranged fighters to deal with. There would also have been the added stimulus of knowing that the 109 pilots, operating at full throttle in the early combats, would already be casting anxious glances at their lowering fuel levels. In a word, 11 Group might well then have confronted an enemy whose determination to press on to the primary target had been agreeably punctured. In this way, too, a significant tourniquet might have been applied to the alarming drain of squadron pilots.

Two years later, in the autumn of 1942, Keith Park, then the

AOC, Malta, used this forward interception plan with devastating effect in the last phase of the desperate defence of the island. The circumstances were virtually identical. Sending his squadrons and wings, often led by Thelma Bader's first cousin, Arthur Donaldson, across the Straits and sometimes as far as the Sicilian mainland, he met the enemy's attacks head on. It was the lethal left hook which finally shattered Kesselring's jaw.

There was, however, in Douglas's mind one governing prerequisite for the success of the plan. Control of the defence against the massed raids must come from the centre, from the headquarters of Fighter Command at Stanmore. There, the commander-in-chief had the whole scene in panorama before him. The map on the Operations table at Bentley Priory, unlike 11 Group's at Uxbridge which covered little more than its own area and a slice of the Pas de Calais and northern France, embraced the broad mass of the country – 10, 11 and 12 Groups, and so on. It offered a spread of the whole Command as well as of London and the other major cities and ports. All the necessary technical systems, and details of squadron strengths and locations, were to hand. There wasn't a valid reason why the defence couldn't be marshalled and conducted from this central point.

With the switch in the attacks from the airfields to London and the principal cities, the Germans' all-out September offensive had changed a group task into a Command responsibility almost overnight. It should, in Douglas's view, have been controlled from Command headquarters, under the aegis of the C-in-C, working through the groups. In this way there would have been cohesion and co-ordination – with no room for factious and fractious relations between the AOCs at Watnall and Uxbridge. He uses, as an analogy, General Montgomery's command of the Eighth Army in the Western Desert in 1942. Montgomery exercised authoritative and effective overall control of the successive engagements, dispensing his orders through the corps commanders. The mastery and conduct of the battle was his.

Hugh Dowding did not, however, see the need for comprehensive Command control until the third and last phase was too far spent. By then, the differences between Park and Leigh-Mallory, which should have been recognized and quashed at source long before they had had a chance to fester, had taken hold. With two such incompatible personalities they were not to be quelled without determined intervention.

One incident exposes the nature – and effect – of the independent character of the tactical direction Dowding was prepared to tolerate.

As the September convulsions raged on, Bader, leading the Dux-ford wing of four squadrons, 242, 310, 64 and 19, had just completed an uneventful lunchtime patrol in the Gravesend and Thames estuary area. After an hour of it, Woodhall, at Duxford, had told him to return – an exhortation which, like many others he received from the ground, the wing leader was not at once disposed to accept.

'I'll just have one more swing round, Woody,' he said 'and then come back.' It was characteristic of the fairly free, opportunist hand which he liked to play when there was no immediate 'trade' (enemy aircraft) about.

With that, Douglas took the wing into a wide, sweeping left-hand turn, southwards towards the Channel. Over Dover, with a measure of height in hand, he spotted several loose sections of Me 109s below. Working round into the sun, he dived the wing at speed into the attack, leaving a top cover to guard against retaliation from above. With his first burst, Bader got a 'flamer'. Cottoning on to the tail of a second 109, he left it smoking heavily with a dead 'stick' at 10,000 feet between Dover and Ramsgate, just to seaward of his favourite golfing corner of East Kent, with its three famous championship courses, Deal, St George's and Prince's. It was a textbook 'bounce', with 242 claiming six destroyed in the action for the loss of one pilot.

The wing dropped in at Gravesend to refuel. Within minutes of touching down, a message was received from Park at his headquarters at Uxbridge complaining that the 12 Group wing had been 'poaching on 11 Group's preserves'. Good for the AOC, the pilots thought. Nice of him to introduce a bit of humour by way of offering his congratulations.

Not a bit of it. Back at Duxford, Bader was dumbfounded to hear from Leigh-Mallory that Park had already registered a strong com-plaint. The squadrons couldn't believe it. It did nothing for the relationships between the two AOCs. The gamekeeper, out on his rounds of the estate, had caught the 'culprits' red-handed, nicking His Grace's birds.

The exchange, which had, of course, completely bypassed Dowding, set the Duxford wing by its ears. The knives were out. It made Leigh-Mallory and Bader more determined than ever to urge a fair trial of their 12 Group plan. With every day and every engagement which passed, their conviction grew that it would be the one really effective way of aiding Park's forces. Astonishingly, the C-in-C never called a meeting to discuss the various points of view.

Denied the chance to exploit the concept, the Duxford wing, with Broadhurst and the Wittering squadrons providing rock-solid back-up, now made the most of the few opportunities which came its way. Between its actual performance and the astonishing interpretations which latter-day commentators like Deighton, Wright and others have placed upon it there exists a fascinating and hitherto unchallenged divide.

12
Month of destiny

REALITY VERSUS FICTION

The Duxford wing, with Bader at its head, flew six major sorties during the September daylight offensive. On the 15th of the month, the day the battle rose to its crescendo, two operations were flown. Five squadrons were engaged on both occasions, 242, 302 (Polish) and 310 (Czech), each with Hurricanes, and 19 and 611 with their Spitfires.

Douglas always led with his own squadron, 242. He was still an *acting* squadron leader. There were no designated 'wing commanders flying' in Fighter Command during the Battle of Britain. The appointment was established, on Leigh-Mallory's recommendation, in the spring of 1941. By then L-M had taken over 11 Group, and Bader and Sailor Malan were his first two choices as wing leaders. Now, however, there was no doubt about Douglas being the preferred officer to bring the squadrons together. By training, ability, experience and personality, he was a natural. Because he was older and more mature than the others, no one could envisage anyone else leading while he was available.

Normally the wing consisted of the basic three squadrons – 242, stationed at Coltishall, 310 at Duxford, with Douglas Blackwood in command, and 19, at Duxford's satellite airfield, Fowlmere, with Sandy Lane in charge. Three squadrons (sometimes two) were to become the accepted complement for a wing in Fighter Command for the rest of the war. Wings were the staple recipe for most fighter operations, squadrons the ingredients.

With all the units operating on the same RT (radio telephone) frequency, the wing leader could keep constantly in touch with the other squadron commanders. All pilots could hear the comments and the orders. An assured RT manner, like a distinctive and relaxed voice on sound radio, was an important advantage in a fighter leader in war. Bader's personality came readily across in the transmissions. He talked a lot in the air, more than his counterparts in other squadrons. Crowley-Milling remembers it as one of the features of his leading. It was part of his style and quite uninhibited. It helped morale in those early, pulsating days. It was comforting for the younger and less experienced squadron members to hear a confident, breezy and jocular voice keeping up a fairly arrogant commentary, especially if the going was rough and the odds uneven.

Later on, when the squadrons of 10, 11 and 12 Groups were operating daily as wings on offensive operations over France and the Low Countries, economy of speech over the RT became a prime part of the pilots' fighting discipline. The channel had to be kept open for the leader and emergencies.

The conversations between the Duxford wing leader, in the air, and Woodhall, controlling on the ground, were broadcast in the local Operations Room where the Women's Auxiliary Air Force plotters sat round the table. Bader's graphic and totally unembarrassed language was a good deal rawer and richer than most of them were normally accustomed to. It got so rare on occasions that Woody felt obliged to switch the speaker off. Douglas thought this a pity. He felt pretty sure the girls enjoyed it. It stimulated thought and enlivened the day.

'Hello, Douglas,' the controller called to him one time, 'there's some trade for you on your left. Angels 15. You should see them below you.'

'Woody,' retorted Bader, 'my eyes are hanging down like a pair of dog's balls and I can't see a bloody thing.'

Thelma, now living near the airfield at Coltishall, from whence 242 moved down to Duxford most days, returning late in the evening, affected a rather prim and correct approach to all this banter when the pilots told her about it. A smile of mock resignation and a shrug showed that she knew there was nothing that anyone could do. Her husband's conversation had long since ceased to surprise her. The more staid the company and the stiffer the atmosphere, the more colourful and bizarre it was apt to become. Now and then she would put her foot down and that normally stopped it; but she didn't put it to the touch too often. Her judgement was too acute for that.

It was, of course, the ability of a leader to communicate freely and distinctly with his pilots in the air which enabled a gaggle of squadrons to be worked comfortably together. To Douglas, it made no difference whether he was leading two, three, four or five squadrons. The drill and the various dispositions were worked out on the ground so that each unit knew its role. A word now and then in the air was all that was necessary to maintain direction and, with it, cohesion. There was little to it with a competent and comprehensive leader.

Yet friction, attributed to 11 Group by modern authors, has fuelled the belief that a wing was a clumsy and unwieldy thing, a sort of Gulliver-like vehicle borrowed from Brobdingnag. The impression is given that it would have taken half a dozen pantechnicons to move 242, 310 and 19 from Duxford down to Kent. Such a concept has no affinity with reality. The wing became an agile, easily manoeuvred device of modern war.

Douglas Bader has always kept an uncluttered, unfettered mind. He can cut a fast swathe through a forest of irrelevant detail. This is one of his attributes; but it also rubs people up and makes them bristle. A straight line, by definition, is the shortest distance between two points. That is the path he habitually likes to tread. Convoluted digressions are not for him. If you read his prose, the English is forthright and economical, with short, simple words being given preference. There's no wrapping his thoughts up in a parcel which has to be undone before the reader can get at his meaning. Everything is put out on the slate.

It was much the same with his direction of the Duxford wing. His orders, like his concept, were basic, elementary, direct and clear. Everyone, down to the most junior pilot, understood what he was supposed to be doing. If he failed to do it, that was, of course, another matter. But he couldn't say in mitigation that he didn't know or hadn't been told.

The format in the air was rudimentary. It was consistently the same. Tactics rested on principles which didn't change. They could be tailored to suit the opportunities. If it was to be a three-squadron operation and enough warning had been given, Douglas would take the Hurricanes of 242 and 310 to 20,000 feet, their best operating height. The Spitfires of 19 would be positioned 4000 or 5000 feet above. While the Spitfires, with their superior performance at altitude, would take care (if that is the phrase) of the high-flying Messerschmitt 109s, the Hurricanes would address themselves to the bombers which usually came in at around 16,000 or 17,000 feet. If there was no significant fighter cover to contend with, the Spitfires would come down on the bombers after the Hurricanes had had a stab at breaking them up.

That was the theory; but it didn't always work out with the intended precision. Too often 11 Group called the Duxford wing off the ground too late for fair expression to be given to its purpose. In any case, the daily fare was pretty uninviting. Guarding 11 Group's northern airfields wasn't much of a main dish.

The drill was reduced to a simple, basic procedure. When it was a three-squadron mission, the two Hurricane squadrons, with Bader and 242 leading, would take off straight across Duxford's grass airfield in vics of three aircraft together and then at once start climbing on a southerly heading. As they gained height, 310 would slip easily into position, up-sun and a little above the leading squadron. The Spitfires of 19 took off simultaneously from nearby Fowlmere and gradually edged into place on the climb, taking up station well above and down-sun of the Hurricanes. It became a well-tried and repetitive process which could instantly accommodate an additional Hurricane and Spitfire squadron without fuss.

There was never any question of the wing leader orbiting the airfield to let the other squadrons 'cut the corners' and form up. Douglas never hurried the climb as an inexperienced and harrassed leader was apt to do. He took the wing up steadily at 140 m.p.h. and around 1200 feet a minute. At that even rate he could keep the squadrons together and bring them *en bloc* into the sensitive area. The aim was always to concentrate the force before an attack – provided sufficient time had been allowed by 11 Group to do so.

It took, on average, 4–6 minutes to get the Duxford wing airborne and on course for the climb to battle height – 4 minutes at best and 6 at worst. It never – repeat, never – took the wing 'seventeen minutes to leave the ground and another twenty to form up and set course from base'. Len Deighton ('that imaginative writer of fiction', as Bader describes him) has made the statement,[1] quoting 'the great fighter ace, "Johnnie" Johnson,' as his source. Whatever its derivation, the assertion is false and based on fantasy or hearsay. Johnson is a lifelong friend of Bader. The wise old owls among us who led wings with him in Fighter Command in 1943, and saw him at first hand operating with his Canadians, would class him, with Douglas, Sailor Malan and the wonderfully versatile American, Don Blakeslee,

1. Len Deighton, *The Battle of Britain* (Jonathan Cape, 1980).

as one of the four great Allied wing leaders of the war. However, Johnnie never flew operationally with the Duxford wing in the Battle of Britain. After a few restless days with 19 Squadron at Fowlmere in August 1940, he moved on to 616. By then the unit had been shot to pieces in 11 Group, pulled out of the line and sent first to Norfolk and eventually to Lincolnshire to rest and regroup. Moreover, he was plagued at the time by the recurrence of an old shoulder injury. When he had recovered and started flying with Bader in the Tangmere wing it was 1941. The fictitious 'incident' has thus been taken at second hand for neither Deighton nor Johnson has ever verified the story with Douglas.

In much the same context, it must be said that at no time during late August or September 1940 did it take the Duxford wing 55 minutes to reach Sheerness in the Thames estuary in the manner that the AOC, 11 Group, is alleged to have suggested.

Bader, with his methodical, clear-cut mind, had the times and the distances tightly buttoned up. For the accuracy of the record they must be set down. It was 47 miles from Duxford to Tilbury on the Thames, to the east of London. He had invariably reached this point, with the Hurricane squadrons up at 20,000 feet, within 18–19 minutes of setting course. It was a repetitive piece of regular, strict time-keeping which was only varied at the whim of the 11 Group controller. If the wing was deliberately held back and unable to gain the required altitude, it was brought into play with both hands tied. Then, it was a matter of fighting a corner and making the best of a deplorable job. It was one of the hazards of September 1940.

9 September was the day that would have gladdened the heart of the old First World War maestro, Mannock. It was a capital example of the advantages which accrue from giving a wing leader freedom to act and manoeuvre – or, if it's not given, from a leader seizing the initiative himself and taking commanding control of the interception.

Woodhall, fed up with continually having to pass on the 11 Group controller's rigid diktat, introduced a freer, interrogatory instruction.

'Hello, Douglas' – the deep and quietingly friendly voice was already familiar even to the most junior pilot in the wing – 'will you patrol North Weald to Hornchurch at angels 18? There's some trade approaching.'

It was between 1700 and 1750 hours on this hazy autumn afternoon. The sun was beginning to lose height in the western sky. It was a playback of the matinée performance of the Enfield interception ten days before. By the time the curtain went up on the act, with sixty to seventy Dornier 215s and another hundred or so fighters in attendance, Bader had pushed the wing up a further, precautionary 2000 feet above 11 Group's given altitude and taken it far to the west and south of the patrol line, bringing it round in a wide, right-handed sweep over London, leaving the reservoirs at Staines, and what would now be Heathrow, at its back.

With the wing attacking out of the western sun, combat was joined, in the laconic phraseology of 12 Group's official report (120/S.5011/1/Int. of 17 September 1940), 'over the south-west suburbs of London', with the 'enemy being driven off to the south-east having scattered their bombs'. A significant rider was added. 'The leader of the wing considered that at least 20 further bombers could have been shot down if additional fighters had been available to renew the attack after the bomber formation had been broken up.'

The reference in Bader's log-book was a good deal more pungent.

Patrolled London with wing. Intercepted E/A bombers and fighters south of Thames. Wing destroyed 20 E/A. 242 Squadron got 11. I got the leader – a Do 215 – in flames. P/O Sclanders killed. Sergeant Lonsdale baled out, OK. 2 Hurricanes of 310 collided. 1 pilot OK, baled out.

It is of interest that 12 Group's formal account credited the wing with 21 destroyed, one more than the leader's assessment. But Bader has never been much moved by the discrepancies in claims, believing that, in the press of battle, with the adrenalin running and the mind alight with myriad fast-moving impressions, with mounting closing speeds, and sometimes with two or three aircraft attacking the same target, there will always be duplications – German as well as British and American.

There was, in fact, greater variation in the Luftwaffe's claims than in the Royal Air Force's. During the period 10 July–31 October, i.e. for most of the Battle of Britain, the British claimed 2698 aircraft destroyed. The Luftwaffe said after the war, however, that the true figure was 1733. The Germans, for their part, contended that, during the same three-month spell, the Luftwaffe accounted for 3058 aircraft destroyed. The British ledger, on the other hand, showed our losses to be no more than 915.

On balance, Goering's pilots seemed to have had the edge on us in the numbers game. The ratio of their claims was around three for every single aircraft actually destroyed, while ours worked out a little more accurately – at around three claimed for every two actually downed.

Bader tends to make light of all the variations, believing that propaganda may well come into it. 'Who cares, anyway? We won, didn't we?'

On 18 September, nine days after the Staines encounter, there was another spirited engagement. For Douglas, it took on the characteristics of a fine game of open, attacking aerial Rugby, with the Duxford wing running the ball all over the London sky. It might have been fashioned for his style of opportunist, creative play.

The fixture was joined just south of the estuary and, this time, there were five squadrons in the 12 Group team, 611 (Spitfires) and 302 (the Poles with their Hurricanes) being added to 242, 310 and 19.

The details don't matter; the outcome does. Douglas covered it in a customarily brief, staccato note in his log-book:

...Wing ... caught large bomber formation [it was unescorted] south of the Estuary at about 1730. We were at 20,000 [feet] under 10/10ths cloud. E/A at 18,000. Wing destroyed 30 + 6 probable + 2 damaged. E/A numbered about 40–50. Personal score 1 Ju 88 and 1 Do 17. No casualties in squadron or wing. 11 [destroyed] to 242.

The wing's engagements between 7 and 27 September, with Bader leading each time, had vindicated Leigh-Mallory's contention. Taking only enemy aircraft claimed as destroyed – i.e. *excluding* those probably destroyed and damaged – the total was 135. Against this, 7 pilots had been killed. 135 to 7: it was quite a contribution to the month's victory.

And when, to all this, is added the backing-up role played by the Wittering wing of squadrons which, between 1 September and 30 November, flew thirteen operational sorties over Park's airfields, it becomes increasingly difficult to understand how history will be able to do other than to endorse the tactical concept which stands in the names of Leigh-Mallory, Bader and Broadhurst.

What historians will also have to take account of are the effects of Dowding's decision to stand back and let Park fight the battle for him from 11 Group. One result was to prevent the Duxford wing from ever being used in the manner which Bader believed was right for it. This, in turn, had one serious and regrettable by-product.

The loss of 11 Group's pilots – the most critical aspect of the struggle – was higher than it need have been. Had the commander-in-chief taken charge, understood the 12 Group thesis and then directed the battle as a Command enterprise, controlled from Stanmore, rather than a Group operation handled from Uxbridge, the rate of mortality would have been significantly lessened.

It is a harsh reflection, but the debit is there in the account.

IT WASN'T ONLY BADER . . .

Sir Denis Crowley-Milling, who, in an enduring Service career, rose from being an accomplished wartime fighter leader to a distinguished senior commander in peace, and eventually, on retirement, to the direction of the Royal Air Force's Benevolent Fund, retains some immovable impressions of the Duxford days. They are important to the true record, for his is a mind which eschews histrionics and instead analyses, dissects, weighs and reflects before striking a balance. He has the advantage of having been a witness to all Bader's operations with the wing.

As a junior pilot officer in 242, Crowley-Milling was of the same vintage as others in the Service who were later to set themselves up, understandably, as authorities on the tactical and strategic conduct of the great air battle of 1940. But a young officer in his early twenties, fully occupied with the daily rough and tumble, and often flying number 2 to a demanding CO or flight commander, saw things through different eyes from those of the experienced wing leader of thirty. In the air, he had little time for anything save sticking to his section leader and preserving his own skin. In those days of combat, it was every man to his own destiny – particularly the ones who flew on the flanks or at the back. Not for them the detached, broadly based view. The present was the thing, and what was going to happen tomorrow and the day after. Thinking long was not one of their preoccupations.

Thus Crowley-Milling recalls that, in September 1940, as a junior pilot flying beside Bader (and sticking there at *all* costs), he had no sense of taking part in the Battle of Britain. No one had. That was to come later. 'We just thought we were working much harder than usual, that's all.' There was another thing:

Douglas flew the squadron very tight right into an attack. There was too much to do, too much to think about to be frightened. There wasn't much chance to look round. Keeping station was the problem. It required your 100 per cent attention. And only God was there to help you if you didn't conform.

Crowley-Milling's counterpart in 11 Group, flying with his squadron, didn't know what Bader and the Duxford wing were up to; and neither, for the most part, did Park's squadron commanders. They were wholly occupied doing their jobs. But that didn't stop them, afterwards, from putting their own construction on the tactics of 12 Group and giving other narrators the benefit of their advice. Authors seldom lack 'advice' when it is one side versus the other – and it is the preferred side which is obtaining the benefit of an 'authoritative' opinion. The fact is that few, if any, of the leaders flying operationally in 11 Group in September 1940 knew what Bader's plan was. The versions that were propagated were inaccurate, distorted and biased. It was quite understandable in the circumstances.

It was not possible, however, to hide the impressions which the overstretched pilots to the south had formed of the presence of their northern neighbours. The personal contacts between the squadrons in 11 Group and those at Duxford left no doubt whatever on one point. They welcomed the sight of the so-called 12 Group 'Balbo' a curious term, detested by Dowding but coined by the Air Ministry after Marshal Italo Balbo, a famous Italian aviator, famed for his pre-war exploits, not least his leading of large formations of aircraft. The aerial phalanx spelt out its message of solidarity and support. By a converse token, the 12 Group pilots recoiled from hearing of the mounting losses among their friends in 11 Group. They longed to be able to give them more effective support.

But Bader wasn't the only one who was champing about and badgering Woodhall to press the Uxbridge controller to get the Dux-ford wing off the ground in enough time to take on Goering's raids on London. All the pilots, the junior ones as much as their senior comrades, were fretting at the treatment. The feeling was abroad that the wing was being held back, whereas, given its head, it could have been matching the odds with 11 Group.

'We used to sit there in the sun strapped into the cockpit of our Hurricanes for an hour or an hour and a half, waiting for the signal to go.' Crowley-Milling's impression was common to the wing. ' "Stand by. They're building up over the Pas de Calais" was the message we used to get from Ops and then we'd wait and wait while Douglas pitched into Woody telling him to ask 11 Group to let us take off. The answer was usually the same. "You must wait until 11 Group call for you." '

It was a provoking business for the air officer commanding, just as it was for the Duxford wing. But, contrary to what has been said by others, no one in the wing – and certainly not Douglas – ever heard Leigh-Mallory criticize Park on this, or any other, account. 'Air Vice-Marshal Park has got his own problems' was as far as Bader or any of the other squadron commanders, voicing their misgivings about 11 Group's 'reluctance' to get them off the ground, ever heard L-M go.

Broadhurst, like Bader, was, by now, unusually experienced. He was already firmly on course for the Service heights which he was ulti-mately to attain. He had first led the Wittering wing on 19 June with 229 Squadron, five days before Douglas took over 242 at Coltishall. He was quickly to become a committed adherent of the wing principle – used in the right circumstances, in the right way and at the right time. His was a fertile, tactical brain.

Paradoxically, two years later, at the time of the ill-starred Dieppe raid across the Channel, he was to offer Leigh-Mallory contrary advice. Slipping over the Straits in a Spitfire borrowed from Horn-church, he saw the Germans' Focke-Wulf 190s (fighters and fighter-bombers) coming in down-sun in pairs, from 18,000 feet, diving clean through Fighter Command's protective wing screen to bomb and strafe the Allies' ships and beach-head, before sneaking off inland at zero feet.

As soon as he had landed back at Biggin Hill, he telephoned Leigh-Mallory and told him that, in this situation, wings weren't flexible enough. Pairs of Spitfires should be detached and put up-sun above the FW 190s to catch them before they started to dive. L-M didn't like it. 'Broady' suddenly became 'Broadhurst'. Dammit, this was heresy. But the AOC, as ever, was ready to listen to experienced advice. The operational instructions were changed. The tactics worked. The pairs saw off the 190s and the squadrons and wings had a field day with the escorted bombers over the beach-head when they came in later in the action. 'Broadhurst' had once again given way to 'Broady' by the time the Hornchurch station commander was back in his mess in the evening and L-M was on the line offering thanks.

Broadhurst knew, just as Bader knew, that wings weren't the answer to every situation. Resilience, flexibility and opportunism must always be the key. Indeed, he has never, publicly, allowed his undeniable authority as an air tactician to strengthen the case of one side or the other in the continuing Park versus Leigh-Mallory saga. Rather has he preferred to take his stance on the unexceptionable premiss that each could have been right – depending upon the phase and circumstances of the battle.

It was exactly the posture which Strath Evill, Dowding's Senior Air Staff Officer throughout the battle, adopted in a reflective minute written on 25 September 1940, as the climax of the fighting was passing. Evill, with the outstandingly able Theodore McEvoy (Air Chief Marshal Sir Theodore McEvoy), possessed the fairest and most perceptive mind to be found on the Air Staff at Stanmore in five years of war.

The strongest impression left in my mind [author's italics] is the absolute necessity for flexibility in our tactical methods. It is quite useless to argue whether wing formations are or are not desirable, both statements are equally true under different conditions. . . . We must be careful not to be too rigid in our conclusions. . . .

No one at Duxford, however, in September 1940, when the massed raids on London were escalating to their peak, was in any doubt whatever that, at that special moment, wings were the answer to 12 Group's role in supporting their southern comrades.

THE DUXFORD CORDON

There was a significant – and important – difference in Trafford Leigh-Mallory's attitude to the Wittering and Duxford wings. At Wittering the comings and goings of the squadrons maintained an even flow. No sooner had a unit been refitted, rested and resharpened than it was dispatched back to 11 Group and the battle. Almost as it took off, a time-expired, exhausted and largely decimated counterpart would be touching down to take its place. There was scarcely a squadron in Fighter Command which hadn't been through the 11 Group cauldron at some point in the contest. Some had faced it more than once. It was an unrelenting turnover.

Things were treated differently, however, at Duxford. Here, Leigh-Mallory was resolute against change. If he was prepared to see Broadhurst and Wittering being used as a catalyst, no one was going to put the Duxford wing – and Bader – to similar purpose. Around

242, 310 and 19 he threw an iron cordon. Here were three highly trained, practised and well-led squadrons, blended and shaped into an aggressive whole. Why, then, after so much had been put into it, weaken it by breaking up the elements and dispersing them merely to plug a few leaks elsewhere? This was L-M's *corps d'élite*. Nothing and no one was going to be allowed to disturb it.

13
Private member's right

In 1945, nearly five years after the Battle of Britain, Peter Macdonald, 242 Squadron's old adjutant and still Member for the Isle of Wight, invited Denis Crowley-Milling to lunch in the House of Commons.

'If you don't mind,' he said, 'don't refer to me here as "Boozy Mac"; they might not appreciate it.'

Said more seriously than Peter's political friends would have allowed, the plea was understandable. Nicknames in the Royal Air Force were personal, transient things. They seldom conveyed to the outside world the same impression of friendly endearment which their Service authors intended for them.

The appellation 'Boozy Mac' had owed more to the former adjutant's natural, and disarming, tendency to slur his words than to any undue intemperance of habit. Indeed, Peter Macdonald was, mentally, a good deal sharper than most of his squadron had probably realized. He had been sixteen years a member of parliament when the Battle of Britain was fought. The experience had, inevitably, invested him with a discerning political judgement. He was well aware of his rights and responsibilities – and the power which went with them.

Access to ministers in wartime went hand in hand with his duties to his constituents, who were constantly in the firing line, and to the nation. All the same, as a flight lieutenant, and a junior officer, he had understood keenly the procedures and disciplines of the Service. The balance between his loyalties to the Royal Air Force and to the House of Commons and to the electorate who put him there was very fine. It was a conflict which many serving officers who were also members of parliament had had to reconcile in wartime. Political muscle had to be used sparingly.

Macdonald, who was close to Bader, was sensitive to the problems of the Duxford wing, the difficulties between the groups, the effects of the antipathy of the two AOCs to one another and Dowding's unwillingness to step in. He saw, daily, with his own eyes the frustrations of his commanding officer and the pilots' growing irritation at 11 Group's reluctance to call the wing off the ground in good time.

I well remember him telling me, when we were colleagues in the House of Commons in the 1950s, how he had despaired in those days of anything being done. 'It seemed hopeless,' he said, throwing up his hands in resigned reflection. But there was no doubt that he saw then where his responsibilities lay. The daylight battle might be tailing off, but who could say that the enemy wouldn't strike again – and soon? The usual Service channels had seemed deaf to Leigh-Mallory's and Bader's protests. Park's bleats about 12 Group 'poaching' on his estate were endemic of the malaise.

If there were blocks at the top of the Command – or on the way to the summit – nothing short of a political initiative would remove them. It was then that Peter decided to act, telling no one in the Service, not his own CO, nor the station commander at Duxford, nor the AOC. He had his private member's right to see ministers. He was convinced that, in the circumstances, that was where his duty lay. It required courage as a serving officer to pursue this course.

Macdonald first saw Harold Balfour (Lord Balfour of Inchrye), the Under-Secretary of State. One of the two political heads of the Service, with an exceptionally distinguished record as a young fighter pilot in the First World War, Balfour was an able and approachable minister. He was well versed in the political rough and tumble and a good House of Commons man. But he was also steeped in Service lore and a friend of the Royal Air Force. He cared about its traditions.

With his peacetime connections with civil aviation, he had kept up his flying between the wars. When Neville Chamberlain appointed him to the Air Ministry in 1938, he was then the only *active* pilot on the Air Council. He caused some professional blushes when problems blew up over the airworthiness of an elementary training aircraft. Some claimed it to be dangerous for beginners. Balfour decided to fly the aeroplane himself. He spun it to the left and to the right, stalled it, aerobatted it and gave it every chance to kick. He found it to be harmless. All that was required were a few amendments to the pilots' handling instructions. It became a friendly workhorse for the Service for years.

Macdonald got no change out of the Under-Secretary, who refused at once to discuss Service matters with a junior officer, irrespective of his membership of the House of Commons. Balfour has recalled the incident: 'He then asked if I would arrange for him to see Churchill. I replied that I would do no such thing but that as an MP he had a right to ask to see the Prime Minister.' [1]

Churchill, as Prime Minister and Minister of Defence, agreed to see Macdonald. With his massive parliamentary experience, and his enduring deference to the rights of private members, he may well have felt, in this special instance, that the traditions of the House of Commons should take precedence over the disciplines of the Service. To the end of his days, he guarded jealously the interests of back-benchers, even if they might be inimical to the purpose of his government.

The interview was to touch off a series of immediate and searching inquiries into the whole gamut of arguments surrounding the operational control of the Duxford wing in the context of the battle. Churchill, as Minister of Defence, had an overall responsibility to be informed of the circumstances. The impact and implications of his instant interest were to rebound and reverberate around the Service, and outside, for weeks, months, years and decades to come.

Because of Peter Macdonald's relationship with Bader and, therefore, with the family, I came to know him well during our years in the House. As an old parliamentary hand, he was generous with his advice to a new member. He had picked up his full share of wisdom along the way.

Of his intervention with Churchill in the autumn of 1940, he had, I remember, two further observations to make:

1. That, so far as he was aware, only two people ever knew at the time of his intention to see the Prime Minister – Harold Balfour, who neither assisted nor resisted the approach, and Churchill's private secretary with whom the meeting was arranged.

2. That, for Service reasons, he made a deliberate point of saying nothing to Bader, Woodhall or to Leigh-Mallory of his political move.

Confirmation of Macdonald's understanding and approach came, subsequently, in a curious way. When Douglas Bader was reading the first proofs of *Reach for the Sky*, he found to his surprise that Paul Brickhill had referred to a meeting between Macdonald and Chur-

1. Harold Balfour, *Wings over Westminster* (Hutchinson, 1973).

chill. With the author then in Australia, Douglas immediately tele-phoned William Collins, the head of the firm which was publishing the work.

'Billy,' he said, 'this must come out. It's untrue. You must promise me that the reference will be removed.' Collins at once deferred to the plea.

Some years, and several editions, later, Douglas happened, by chance, to pick up a recent copy of the book. He was astonished to see that the reference had been reinstated. It ran as follows:

In the House of Commons one day, he [Macdonald] had spoken . . . with the Under-Secretary of State for Air, who had suggested he see the Prime Minister. Macdonald had an hour and a half with Churchill who was gruff at first, but then thawed, and next day began sending for various group commanders.[1]

Incensed, Bader berated the publishers, recounting his earlier con-versation with Billy Collins, and claiming that he had no knowledge whatever that any such meeting had taken place. The statement was, therefore, he believed, untrue. In any case, he said, the Prime Minister would not have been sending for group commanders; the C-in-C, perhaps, but not AOCs. No one at Collins seemed to know how the reference had been infiltrated back into the text.

There could well be a simple explanation. Brickhill, having earlier prised the story out of Macdonald, had no doubt as to its strength. With the passage of time, and with the so-called 'Big Wing' contro-versy beginning publicly to boil up, he had decided to stick to his guns and run the piece in subsequent editions. It was not until later still, when he was discussing these events privately with Harold Balfour, that Bader learned at first hand that Macdonald's meeting with Churchill had actually taken place. The adjutant's rectitude in withholding knowledge of his actions from his commanding officer had been proved.

Some fifteen years on, there was a touching sequel to this historic meeting. 1954 was giving way to 1955 and Sir Winston, then eighty and nearing the end of his second administration, was on the point of handing over the leadership of the Tory Party to Eden.

Reach for the Sky had quite recently been published. Bader wanted to give Churchill a personal, signed copy. In it he had written a brief

1. Paul Brickhill, *Reach for the Sky* (Collins, 1954).

inscription: 'To the Architect of Victory, from one of The Few'. Macdonald, having then passed his thirtieth year as a member of parliament, had set up the meeting with the Prime Minister in his room in the House of Commons.

After passing a box of cigars across the table to Douglas and Peter, Churchill reflected for a few moments upon the great battle. Then, picking up the book and looking again at the inscription, he beamed his puckish thanks at the donor and held out a hand of gratitude. 'I must warn you,' he said, 'I might retaliate.'

14

One meeting

On 17 October 1940, a famous conference took place in the Air Council Room at the Air Ministry. All sorts of spurious interpretations were subsequently to be placed upon it. The day before, Leigh-Mallory telephoned Bader to ask him to go with him. 'I'd like you to come with me,' he said, 'but I'm not sure that I will necessarily be able to get you into the meeting; we must see.'

All the principal members of the Air Staff were there other than their head, Cyril Newall (Marshal of the Royal Force Sir Cyril Newall), who was away ill. Portal, who was to succeed Newall almost at once and become an outstandingly successful Chief of the Air Staff for the remainder of the war, took his place. Sholto Douglas, the Deputy Chief of the Air Staff, who, within weeks, was to take over from Dowding at Stanmore, presided.

The batting order, which has often been misquoted, was impressive in its content. The official minutes set it out in detail:

Present:

Air Vice-Marshall W. S. Douglas	D.C.A.S.
Air Chief Marshal Sir Hugh C. T. Dowding	A.O.C.-in-C. Fighter Command.
Air Marshal Sir Charles F. A. Portal	
Air Marshal Sir Philip P. B. Joubert de la Ferté	A.C.A.S.(R).
Air Vice-Marshal K. R. Park	A.O.C. No. 11 Group.
Air Vice-Marshal Sir C. J. Q. Brand	A.O.C. No. 10 Group.
Air Vice-Marshal T. L. Leigh-Mallory	A.O.C. No. 12 Group.
Air Commodore J. C. Slessor	D. of Plans.
Air Commodore D. F. Stevenson	D.H.O.
Air Commodore O. G. W. G. Lywood	P.D.D. of Signals.
Group Captain H. G. Crowe	A.D.A.T.
Squadron Leader D. R. S. Bader	O.C. 242 Squadron.
Wing Commander T. N. McEvoy	
Mr J. S. Orme.	

The purpose of the meeting, which has sometimes wrongly been described as a post-mortem on the Battle of Britain and, as such, a sinister device, designed by the Air Ministry and its supporters to pave the way for Dowding's removal as the Commander-in-Chief of Fighter Command, was contained in its title. This disclosed it to be a discussion to consider 'Major Day Tactics in the Fighter Force'.

The Air Staff paper of 14 October, covering the agenda, and the minutes, confirming the outcome, leave no possible doubt about its intent. Far from its being a critique of the Battle of Britain and those who were primarily concerned with its conduct, its aim was to project thought forward to the challenging months to come and the tactics to be employed in the daylight air. Night was not excluded.

Vigorous and heavy as the enemy attacks have been against this country, we must have regard to the possibility that more determined, better organized and heavier attacks may be made in the spring of 1941, if not before. . . . It is necessary that the lessons we have learned should be applied generally to enable the fighter defence to operate at maximum efficiency. . . .

The note was quite explicit.

Bader's attendance at the meeting and the reasons alleged to be behind it have since been blown up and falsified in absurd and grotesque fashion. The suggestion has even been put about that he was being used, in all his innocence, as a weapon in a politically motivated manoeuvre intended to discredit those upon whom had rested the principal responsibility for fighting the battle. ('Think of it, old boy, an *acting* squadron leader being "used" among that lot. They have only just avoided saying that Squadron Leader Bader called the meeting.')

The prospect for, relatively, so junior an officer was disturbing. Douglas's unease was not helped by the indifferent and rather surprised manner of some of his seniors as they all gathered before the conference. 'There seemed to be a fair amount of 'morning, Bader . . . 'morning, Bader . . . 'morning, Bader, about as we assembled. I sat there unnerved and not liking it much.'

It was, however, comforting to be sitting next to Wing Commander McEvoy who, with the permanent official, J. S. Orme, in support, was taking the minutes. Douglas felt that 'Mac', with his sensitive mind, was sympathetic to his predicament. 'I well remember the scene – Sholto, in the chair; Portal, on his right; Stuffy Dowding, on his left, with Keith Park [11 Group], Leigh-Mallory [12 Group] and Brand [10 Group] beside him at the table.' It was Park's appearance which made its lasting mark upon Douglas's mind. 'He looked spent and drained and totally exhausted.'

Sholto Douglas asked Bader, at one point, for his views on leading and operating big formations. 'You are the one', he said, 'who has actually done it operationally.' It was a testing moment. The room seemed to go extra quiet.

'I did not speak for long. In spite of my embarrassment, I remember thinking that this would be the only time that a fighter pilot might ever be asked for his views by the Air Staff.'

In fact, Douglas stuck to a single, broad theme. 'You, gentlemen,' he recalls saying, 'learnt the lessons in the First World War. They are still the same today. Height, sun, position and strength in numbers – this is still what counts. It follows that to gain the tactical advantage we must be got off the ground in time to win it. Time and good warning is what we need more than anything.' He wasn't too sure, but he hoped he had managed to get his point across.

The minutes put his contribution in brief perspective. Out of some 2000 words, the record accorded him three lines: '16. Squadron Leader Bader said that from his practical experience time was the essence of the problem; if enough warning could be given to bring a large number of fighters into position there was no doubt they could get most effective results.' So much for the attempt to use Bader 'to spearhead the attack' on Dowding.[1]

Was Leigh-Mallory right to have taken Bader to the meeting? Some have criticized him and, indeed, imputed to him certain base motives for having done so.

Forty years on, with all the interim in which to change his mind, Lord Balfour still holds firmly to the opinion he originally formed. 'I knew nothing of the detail of the conference; this was an Air Staff matter. But, shocking as it may have seemed to protocol-minded senior air officers, I cannot find it so reprehensible that a breath of reality from someone who was doing the job was wafted into Air Staff circles.'

The point was well made. Indeed, those who later served on Sholto Douglas's and Leigh-Mallory's staffs will recall the insistence of each of the two Cs-in-C on having represented, at any major, tactical conference, the up-to-date, practical viewpoint of a currently operational

1. Len Deighton, *The Battle of Britain* (Jonathan Cape, 1980).

squadron commander or wing leader. If it wasn't available on the staff, then it had to be brought in from the groups outside.

In this special instance, some of us would, I think, have gone further. Far from criticizing Leigh-Mallory for taking Bader with him to the Air Ministry on 17 October, there would have been a strong counter-question to pose. Why, when modern day-to-day fighter tactics were under review, did not Park and Brand take a leaf out of AOC, 12 Group's book and bring an operational squadron commander apiece with them? Or, further, why did not Dowding himself insist, when the meeting was convened, on three senior and experienced squadron commanders being present?

A discussion of 'Major Day Tactics in the Fighter Force' could hardly have been invested with practical authority without a personal contribution from those who had themselves actually been leading in battle. It certainly wasn't going to be found among a group of senior First World War leaders, no matter how worthy, distinguished, experienced or imaginative, who had not recently had to shoulder the responsibility. Papers and opinions, taken from others and represented at second hand, make an unimpressive substitute.

And to claim that because Keith Park was in the commendable habit of flying himself about in his Hurricane, observing the south-eastern battle, he had it all at his own finger-tips, only compounds the misconception. The AOC, 11 Group, wasn't leading squadrons or wings in anger against the enemy; there were other equally exacting preoccupations to concern him.

Against this stance, however, has to be set the contrary school. None represented it with greater conviction and strength than Jack Slessor (Marshal of the Royal Air Force Sir John Slessor), who became a valued constituent of the author in Chiswick in the 1950s. Slessor, having commanded the Royal Air Force's Coastal Command with mounting success in the Battle of the Atlantic, rose, in the peace which followed, to be an intellectually able and decisive Chief of the Air Staff. Here was an officer of crisp, assertive views which he was never afraid to expose either verbally or by letter. He was vehement and unequivocal in his denunciation of Bader's presence at the 17 October meeting, which he had himself attended. 'It was amazing', he was to say in correspondence years later, 'that young Bader was allowed not only to attend such a high-level meeting but also to air his views on the tactics of 11 Group.'

This may well have been a majority view at the time among the Air Staff. But, in fairness to Douglas, it must be stated that he did not air his views on the tactics of 11 Group. This was just what he was determined to avoid doing. Instead, he dealt briefly with his thoughts on the tactics of aerial fighting generally, and the use of wings against large formations in particular.

Whether or not Leigh-Mallory was right, one conclusion can certainly be drawn. Had Bader not stood his tactical ground, and had his AOC not given him 100 per cent support, it is most unlikely that the two principal findings of the conference would have emerged. These were clearly set out in the minutes:

20. D.C.A.S. said he thought the views of the meeting could be summarized as follows:
    The employment of a large mass of fighters had great advantages, though it was not necessarily the complete solution to the problem of interception. In No. 11 Group, where the enemy was very close at hand, both the methods described by A.O.C. No. 11 Group and those of A.O.C. No. 12 Group could, on occasions, be used with forces from the two Groups co-operating.
21. The A.O.C.-in-C. said that it would be arranged for No. 12 Group 'wings' to participate freely in suitable operations over the 11 Group area. *He would be able to resolve any complications of control* [author's italics]. In reply to D.H.O., the C.-in-C. said that co-operation of this kind could, in the present circumstances, hardly be employed generally throughout the Command as similar conditions seldom arose elsewhere.

For Bader and his AOC, this was just about game, set and match. The two conclusions had fulfilled their best hopes.

But events were now moving on. New appointments in Fighter Command seemed inevitable and imminent. When they came, Bader regarded them, with no emotion or surprise, as being within the normal sequence and metamorphosis of war. The principal characters themselves, however, were to take a rather different view.

15

Ministerial intervention

Sir Archibald Sinclair visited Duxford in late October 1940, following the Air Ministry meeting and Peter Macdonald's earlier intervention with Churchill.

Quite apart from the Prime Minister's expressed interest, the Secretary of State gathered enough from his conversations with Woodhall and Bader, and the squadrons, to satisfy him that he should ask the Under-Secretary of State to pay a call without delay and make a detailed, on-the-spot, practical assessment of the points the wing leader and squadron commanders had raised. The ever-present 11 Group versus 12 Group controversy appeared to be a dominant topic. 'Sinclair had come away feeling there was a conflict of operational views between the two Groups which was felt acutely,' Lord Balfour was later to write.[1]

The Under-Secretary flew himself up to Duxford, set in the open Cambridgeshire countryside between Royston and Newmarket, on the morning of 2 November. The same evening, he sat down in his room in the Air Ministry and dictated what was to become known as the Duxford memorandum. The paper was finished and placed on the desks of the Secretary of State and of the Assistant and Deputy Chiefs of the Air Staff, when they walked into their offices the next morning. As a quick record, it was a model of its kind, succinct, pointed, factual. It was a good reporter's job.

Balfour had started his early working life, before commerce and industry claimed him, as a news reporter on Northcliffe's *Daily Mail*. There he had learnt, in a hard school, the tricks of presenting a story: of distinguishing the core of it, keeping the copy tight, eliminating

1. Harold Balfour, *Wings over Westminster* (Hutchinson, 1973).

the padding, and writing strictly to space. It was a fine education for
the tasks which were to come.

As 'one of them' from other days, the Under-Secretary of State had
a 'feel' for the pilots' mentality. He might not agree with their views
or demands, but he understood what they were after and why they
were asking. Alone among Churchill's wartime ministers, he was in
a position to form a judgement of the Duxford wing leader's strictures,
the other squadron commanders' contentions and the strength of the
12 Group case. Confidence and conviction march in step with
understanding and experience.

Squadron Leader Bader says that his flight commanders and pilots have
friends in . . . 11 Group. [They] are entirely sympathetic to the wing formation viewpoint . . . [and] are fine material, but as a result of constantly
having to meet enemy forces in superior numbers, are becoming unnecessarily shaken in their morale . . . while, of course, not succeeding in repelling
the enemy in a way that a large formation can do. . . .
  Given the Wing Formation, with the maximum advance information
. . . and reasonable time to get . . . height and position, he [Bader] says
. . . he is absolutely certain of taking enormous toll. . . .

Sholto Douglas sent Dowding a copy of Balfour's report the same
day as he read it, 3 November. His covering letter was typically
pungent and direct. After pointing a finger at the differences between
11 and 12 Groups 'which were so patent at the conference we held
on 17 October' and which, he said, had not yet been resolved, the
Deputy Chief of the Air Staff loosed off a formidable broadside:

It is important that . . . [the differences] should be resolved since it seems
to be leading to a good deal of bitterness not only between the two AOCs
but between the squadrons in the two Groups. This obviously cannot be
allowed to go on . . . and it is for you to put the matter right. . . .

The commander-in-chief, then the most senior serving officer in
the Royal Air Force, clearly wasn't going to sit down under that.
Having admitted, surprisingly readily, in his reply of 6 November,
that this was all causing 'so much friction and ill-feeling' that control
of combined operations between numbers 11 and 12 Groups must be
withdrawn from the group commanders and the orders issued
through his own Operations Room at Stanmore, Dowding then
turned his guns, first, on the Under-Secretary of State and, second,
on the Duxford wing leader:

There remains the question of the Under-Secretary of State listening to
accusations of a junior officer [Bader] against the Air Officer Commanding

another Group [Bader hadn't, in fact, *accused* Park], and putting them on paper with the pious hope that the officer will not get into trouble.

Balfour has been in the Service and ought to know better. . . . A good deal of the ill-feeling which has been engendered . . . has been directly due to young Bader [he was thirty, remember] who, whatever his other merits, suffers from an overdevelopment of the critical faculty. . . .

But the C-in-C, having disposed of Balfour, was by no means yet done with Squadron Leader Bader. After describing how the redirection of the Luftwaffe's attacks to the north and to the west of the country might now lead to a redeployment of the Fighter Force, he introduced an unexpected twist:

This might give an opportunity of moving young Bader to another station where he would be kept in better control. His amazing gallantry will protect him from disciplinary action *if it can possibly be avoided* [author's italics].

The pique was unmistakable. We must, however, remember that these exchanges were taking place in the immediate aftermath of probably the shortest and most concentrated, and certainly the most vital, air battle ever fought in British history. Dowding and Park, having shouldered the hideous operational responsibility, were now close to the end of their tethers. Nerves were strung so tight they could be 'pinged'. Calm and deliberate thought was not getting its head. Vinegar was stinging the wounds.

Making due allowance for all the stresses, one observation regarding ministerial intervention in the affairs of Fighter Command cannot be escaped. The constitutional aspect leaves no doubt whatever about its propriety.

Parliament is supreme – in war as in peace. Governments are answerable to parliament and draw their strength from it. Winston Churchill, as His Majesty King George VI's First Minister and Minister of Defence, was responsible, through his secretaries of state and other departmental ministers, to the elected body and thence to the crown and to the nation for the vigorous prosecution of the war.

The professional heads of the Services were (and are) responsible to ministers who represented them in parliament and gave them political teeth. The Secretary of State thus had every right – indeed, it was his duty – to visit Duxford in the autumn of 1940, talk to the pilots and their leaders and satisfy himself at first hand of the current operational position. His responsibility to parliament demanded that he should keep himself informed of progress in the conflict and, where necessary, pass that information on to the Prime Minister as Minister of Defence.

Exactly the same basic rights and responsibilities were vested in the Under-Secretary of State, working, as he was, in ready accord both under, and through, his political master. Both ministers were therefore discharging their constitutional right, as well as their duty to the Service, in undertaking a personal and individual canvass of the Duxford wing's problems. And Bader, and the other squadron commanders, for their part, were similarly justified in responding to His Majesty's ministers' questions and developing the answers. It was then for ministers to decide how the information should be used. In the case of Archie Sinclair and Harold Balfour, it would have been difficult to find a pair of ministers who were more punctilious in observing the balance between their political and Service functions. Their loyalty to the department they served was never doubted.

So when Balfour asked Douglas Bader on 2 November 1940, 'How is the wing doing?' its leader was quite in order in answering straightly, 'Quite well, sir, but I wish they would get us off the ground sooner,' and then giving the Under-Secretary of State chapter and verse.

The commander-in-chief's complaint to the Deputy Chief of the Air Staff cannot, therefore, on constitutional grounds, be sustained. Awkward and vexing it may well have been to have the Under-Secretary probing and prodding about for the truth; but this was a proper part of a Service minister's remit. There was no basis at all for contending that, by responding to the Secretary of State's orders, Balfour was, in some way, misusing his power or exceeding his brief. The aim was to win the war. Dowding, under heavy pressure, was mistaken in his interpretation of the constitutional position.

On 17 November the Chief of the Air Staff sent the Commander-in-Chief of Fighter Command a brief note. It was to be virtually the last shot in the continuing drama. 'My dear Dowding,' it began,

With reference to your recent correspondence with [Sholto] Douglas about a report made by Balfour after conversations with Woodhall and Bader, the Secretary of State has directed that no reproof should be offered to either of these two officers on account of the conversations referred to.

It was signed 'Yours sincerely, C. Portal'.

Within a few days of dispatching his brief acknowledgment – 'with reference to your letter . . . no reproof has been or will be offered by me to either Woodhall or Bader' – Dowding had handed over his command to Sholto Douglas and Park was shortly to go through the same process at 11 Group in favour of Leigh-Mallory.

And so ended, for the time being, a saga which, if the stern truth be faced, should never have been allowed to develop in the first place. It ought to have been recognized by the C-in-C and then immediately gripped and squashed, by whatever means he considered necessary, long before it had had the chance to start wafting outside the boundaries of Fighter Command and into the allergic precincts of the Air Ministry, 10 Downing Street and the Palace of Westminster.

16
Winners' enclosure

KEITH PARK

Douglas Bader never regarded the changes which took place in Fighter Command in the autumn of 1940 as being anything but an expected outcome of the ending of the battle. As pilots, squadron and wing leaders, tired after a period of stiff fighting, were pulled out of the line and sent off to training establishments and headquarters' staffs to rest, so he saw the changes at Stanmore and Uxbridge. They were part of the ebb and flow of war.

The conclusion of Dowding's and Park's remarkable reigns at Fighter Command and 11 Group, with all the attendant recriminations which followed, has been magnified to the point of absurdity. The record, often twisted, sometimes misquoted and occasionally ignored, is there to provide its answer.

The two cases are, of course, separate and different. Let us take that of the enigmatic Keith Park first. His direction of 11 Group in the five months from Dunkirk to the end of the heaviest fighting in the Battle of Britain was brilliant – nothing short of brilliant. All the tactical disadvantages were ranged against him; but, with the squadrons, ground crews, controllers, Ops Room staffs and radar operators rallying behind his lead, he won a major battle for control of the daylight air. Park was himself a skilled fighter pilot. He knew the principles and the tricks. History may well justly conclude that he possessed the most perceptive and versatile tactical brain of all the fighter commanders of the Second World War.

If his relationship with Leigh-Mallory and 12 Group fell well below the level of events, it was partly because Dowding permitted it and partly because his personality and L-M's were incompatible. It was twelve of one and a dozen of the other. But which great battle

commander, on land, sea or in the air, has been a cosy, accommodating, snug individual? Mostly they have been assertive, prickly,
unconventional and often rude.

What is difficult to explain in Park's case is his lingering belief that
somehow, in some way, men were prejudiced against him, that justice
wasn't done and that he – and Dowding – were innocent victims of
a Machiavellian manoeuvre. 'Old Sir Keith . . . used to talk with me
in the Officers' Club in Auckland and shake his head sadly at the
gross injustices of life. . . .' The words belong to James Sanders, the
fine New Zealand journalist and wartime reconnaissance and shipping strike pilot. They leave a dispiriting impression of greatness
being tormented in the twilight years. And yet, if an analysis is made,
they are mocked by the record.

When Bader saw the 11 Group commander at the meeting at the
Air Ministry on 17 October, he was shot through with strain and
fatigue. Who wouldn't have been in the face of such physical and
mental demands? Why, then, Douglas has persistently asked, was it
so wrong to give this distinguished, but temporarily spent, officer a
rest by putting him out to grass for a while, commanding a group in
Training Command and dispensing the benefits of his extensive experience and flair? His refusal to accept the offer of a job on the Air
Staff (the rejection was ill judged but understandable) had narrowed
sharply the scope of his employment. He had seen the Air Ministry
as a place of intrigue and plots which was not for him. Tiredness
makes an unreliable counsellor.

Within two years, and rested, fit again and recharged, he had been
sent out to Malta to take over from the redoubtable Hugh Pughe
Lloyd, who, with Woodhall, had fought another island battle in the
spring and summer of 1942 as critical in its relative way as the one
which the 11 Group commander had himself waged in the summer
and autumn of 1940. Park, by his courage, confidence and resource,
allied to an engaging arrogance which turned a deaf ear to the pleas
of the Governor to conserve, by all reasonable means, the island's
dwindling reserves of fuel, had won another exceptional victory. The
consequences of failure at that moment – just as they had been in
Lloyd's time – would have been disastrous to the Allied cause.

From then until the end of the war, there had been uninterrupted
success – promotion, higher commands, honours and accolades:
Commander-in-Chief, Middle East; Allied Air Commander, South-
East Asia. Then home to friendly, familiar, companionable New
Zealand. The NCO gunner who had slugged it out with the enemy

160

Right: Golf is his ally. Eight years after losing his legs, and six after taking up the game, Bader had holed Hoylake, one of Britain's best-known championship links, in 77 strokes. Here he is competing with the great South African, Bobby Locke (extreme right), four times British Open champion, in an amateur and professional tournament.

Below: Union of courage. In August 1941, Madame Hiècque sheltered Bader in her home in St Omer after he had baled out over northern France and escaped from hospital. A sentence of death for her action was commuted to life imprisonment. In 1964, the French authorities invested her, then aged eighty, with the Legion d'Honneur. Bader, present at the ceremony, was made an Honorary Citizen of St Omer the same day

Cranwell cadet, 1929. Aged nineteen, and already an exceptional games player, Bader had not yet lost his legs

A summit is reached. Squadron commander, aged thirty — four years older than Dowding thought it right for a fighter leader to be

After the victories — capture; St Omer, 1941. Bader was 'entertained' by his German counterpart, Adolf Galland, commander of the Luftwaffe's Jagdgeschwader 26, and other wing pilots

Deutsches
Kriminalpolizeiblatt
(Sonderausgabe)
Herausgegeben vom Reichskriminalpolizeiamt in Berlin

Erscheint täglich mit Ausschluß der Sonn- und Feiertage	Zu beziehen durch die Geschäftsstelle Berlin C 2, Werderscher Markt 5—6
15. Jahrgang	Berlin, den 3. August 1942	Nummer 4345 a

Nur für deutsche Behörden bestimmt!

A. Neuausschreibungen.

Entwichene kriegsgefangene Offiziere

Aus Stalag VIII B in Lamsdorf entwichene englische Fliegeroffiziere.
(Unter Bezugnahme auf Kis.-Nr. 12363 v. 2. 8. 42.)

In der Nacht zum 1. 8. 42 sind geflüchtet:

Bader, Douglas Robert Stewart, 21. 2. 10 London, Oberstleutnant, Kgf.-Nr. 3797 Oflag X C; Beschr.: 1,78 m, athlet. Gestalt, dklbra. Haare, voll. Gesicht, graubla. Augen, beide Beine amputiert; läuft mit 2 Prothesen gut, ohne Stock, jedoch auffallwiegender Gang; engl. Fliegeruniform, jetzt vermutl. Zivilkleidung;

Palmer, John Fletcher, 6. 9. 17 Lymen (Grafschaft Shesbire), Hauptmann, Kgf.-Nr. 525 Stalag Luft II; Beschr.: 1,80 m, schlank, blo. Haare, schm. Gesicht, ungleichmäßige vorsteh. Zähne, sichtb. Zahnlücke oben r., gr. Nase; graubla. Haare. Flieger uniform, jetzt vermutl. Zivilkleidung.

Beide sprechen angebl. gebr. Deutsch. B. u. P. sind hierunter abgebildet.

Verstärkte Fahndung, insbesondere Zugfahndung, ist sofort mit allen verfügbaren Kräften durchzuführen, da Festnahme äußerst wichtig! Grenzübertritt mit allen Mitteln verhindern!

553.   2. 8. 42.   RKPA Berlin — C 2.

Douglas Robert Stewart Bader
ist festzunehmen.

John Fletcher Palmer
ist festzunehmen.

Wanted! Legless man on the run. Historic leaflet, issued in August 1942 by the German police after Bader, Flight Lieutenant Johnny Palmer, the air gunner, and three others were attempting to escape from Lamsdorf, the prison camp near the German–Polish frontier

The Battle of Britain, 1940
From Monarch and Parliament to the
Officer Commanding No 242 (Canadian)
Fighter Squadron in the Royal Air Force. . . .
The all-star command cast in the Bader
Story

His Majesty King George VI with his First Minister

The Rt Hon. Winston Churchill
MP and the Rt Hon Sir
Archibald Sinclair MP,
Secretary of State for Air

Captain Harold Balfour MP,
Under-Secretary of State for Air

Air Chief Marshal Sir Cyril
Newall, Chief of the Air Staff

Air Vice-Marshal W. Sholto
Douglas, Deputy Chief of the
Air Staff

Air Chief Marshal Sir Hugh
Dowding,
Commander-in-Chief, Fighter
Command

Air Vice-Marshal Sir Douglas Evill, Senior Air Staff Officer, Fighter Command

Air Vice-Marshal K. R. Park, Air Officer Commanding, No 11 Group

Air Vice-Marshal T. L. Leigh-Mallory, Air Officer Commanding, No 12 Group

Wing Commander A. B. Woodhall, Station Commander, Duxford

Wing Commander H. Broadhurst, Station Commander, Wittering

Acting Squadron Leader D. R. S. Bader, Officer Commanding, No 242 (Canadian) Squadron, Royal Air Force

Flight Lieutenant P. D. Macdonald MP, Adjutant, No 242 (Canadian) Squadron, Royal Air Force

Bader leading 242 Squadron's Hurricanes,
August 1940

The height advantage that 11 and 12
Groups' pilots longed for − but seldom saw.
German photograph, taken from above, of
the Luftwaffe's bombers crossing Kent at
17,000 feet en route for London's docks.
September 1940

Opposite above: Duel of Eagles. Robert Taylor's
beautifully proportioned painting of pursuer
(Adolf Galland, Messerschmitt 109) and
pursued (Douglas Bader, Spitfire) over
northern France any fine spring or summer's
day, 1941
Opposite below: The chivalry which animates
the air. Forty years on, two outstanding and
opposing wing leaders of The Second World
War join forces and face the press. Adolf
Galland (left) and Douglas Bader at a
conference in Canada, 1980

Family distinction. Arthur Donaldson, Thelma
Bader's first cousin, was the youngest of three
remarkable Royal Air Force brothers, each of
whom won the DSO. He flew for a short while with
242. In a low-level attack against Morlaix airfield
in Brittany in 1941, flak burst in Arthur's cockpit,
ripping his helmet, puncturing his skull and
knocking him temporarily unconscious. He led
263 Squadron back to base across 120 miles of sea

Almost one of the family, too. Stan Turner of
Duxford, Tangmere and Malta, brilliant
Canadian in the Royal Air Force — and 242;
chosen disciple of Bader. Habitually
perverse, usually obstinate and utterly
dedicated, Turner's place in Canada's Hall
of Fame is assured

Victory and release. Reunited again after the long prison years, Douglas with Thelma and
Shaun, their thoroughbred golden retriever, at the Addisons' home at Ascot. Summer 1945

Return to the Shell Company, 1946

Bader flew Jimmy Doolittle (General James Doolittle), famed US leader of the Tokyo raid, round Europe and North Africa in a single-engine 130 HP Percival Proctor light aircraft, dispensing goodwill. Here, the two Shell representatives are pictured in Madrid

A few months later, with only minimal aids and a primitive radio in support, Douglas was landing the Proctor in the French Sahara, close to one of Shell's outlying exploration camps

Opposite above: For Douglas, Timbuktu had always been a place of mystery — until he flew there in 1951 with Bill Swerdloff (centre), Shell's Aviation Manager in West Africa and David Videan (right) of the company's Aviation Department in London

Opposite below: Chief Morning Bird Bader. Douglas after his induction as Honorary Chief of the Blood Indians and a member of the Kainai Chieftainship. Alberta, Canada, 1957

Left: Far East, Middle East, Europe and Africa, Douglas often took Thelma with him on his overseas flights for Shell

Below: There were duties to perform. Ghana 1960: Thelma presenting a certificate to a newly enrolled member of the Red Cross Society in Accra

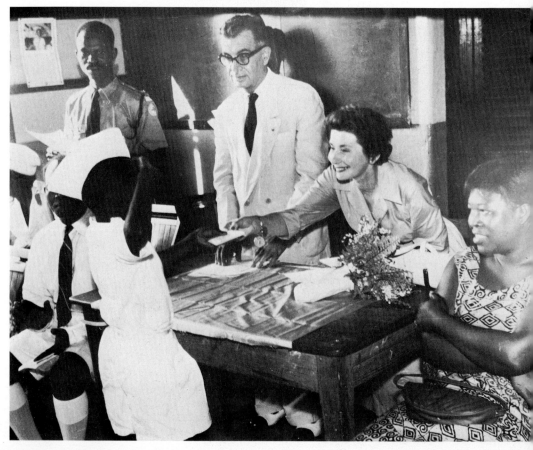

Service with a worldwide, multinational company

Opposite above: With John Loudon (Jonkheer J. H. Loudon), later to become an honorary British Knight and one of Shell's senior managing directors, at the world premiere of *Sound Barrier* at the Plaza, Piccadilly, 1952. For a while during his time as managing director of the Shell Aircraft Company, Bader reported to Loudon

Opposite below: The going was often rugged. During their 1957 visit to Canada Douglas and Thelma Bader sampled the remoteness of the Yukon. The helicopter was the familiar means of transport at Shell's Camp 102

After four years' flying with the trusted, single-engine Proctor, the company provided Douglas in 1950 with (among other aircraft) a Miles Gemini, with its two 120 HP Gypsy Major engines, for his travels

Fourteen years later, in 1964, the Gemini's place was taken by a Beach 95, Travelair, a beautifully stable aeroplane, complete with modern navigational aids. When Bader retired from Shell in 1969, aged fifty-nine, the company gave him the aircraft 'to preserve his customary mobility'

Thirty years earlier, the actress's legs in the foreground might well have disturbed their concentration. Douglas Bader with Peter Townsend (right) at Duxford during the making of the film, *The Battle of Britain*

Hardly a James Bond setting. Sean Connery and Douglas, in front of the most familiar clubhouse in the world, about to play a round on the Old Course at St Andrews

After The Lord Nelson, The Douglas Bader. When it came to finding a name for the new pub, built on the site of the old 11 Group airfield at Martlesham Heath, Suffolk, one-time home of Bader and 242 Squadron, it was to a teetotaller that the Brewers turned. Douglas pulled the first pint on 14 September 1979

Second marriage. On 3 January 1973, two years after the death of his first wife, Douglas married Joan Murray (née Hipkiss), daughter of the owner of a successful steel business in the Midlands

A proficient horsewoman, Joan Bader was one of the original volunteer supporters of Riding for the Disabled. Her work for the deprived and handicapped young complements the lead her husband gives to the disabled the world over. Here, during a visit to Perth in Western Australia, in 1978, Joan provides the evidence

In November 1980, nine months after celebrating his seventieth birthday, Sir Douglas took Lady Bader to visit the Ellis-Smiths, a South African family, living in Cape Town. He had promised to see Paul, aged three, whose legs had been amputated after an illness. 'There was the little boy,' said Douglas, 'running about all over the place on his artificial limbs, mobile as anything. He had never known what it was to walk on his own legs, that was the point.' With a young student friend of the family, Paul Ellis-Smith is here seen at home in Cape Town in very unusual pose with a hero

For Her Majesty Queen Elizabeth, the Queen Mother, the Royal Air Force has always reserved a special affection. Here, entering fully into the spirit of the evening, Her Majesty takes the floor with the former Duxford wing leader at the final Battle of Britain Ball at Bentley Priory, Fighter Command's wartime headquarters at Stanmore, 1973 at Gallipoli and on the Somme thirty years before – and had looked to be washed up and gone – had come a long way. Few had travelled further. It was a career that Bader came greatly to admire.

Douglas maintained his contact with Keith Park on and off during the closing years of the New Zealander's life. On his visits to Australia and New Zealand for the Shell Company, he would always try, if the opportunity offered, to make a point of calling or visiting his old comrade-in-arms. The personal respect was mutual; but neither ever raised with the other the tactical controversies of other days.

In 1974, not long after this accomplished leader had died, aged eighty-two, an undefeated champion of the air, a gesture, greatly appreciated in personal terms, was paid to Douglas. The Battle of Britain Fighter Pilots' Association invited him to give the address at Keith Park's memorial service, held at St Clement Danes.

When he received the invitation, Douglas insisted on ensuring that the decision to ask him had been unanimous. He would accept on no other basis. The old controversies surrounding 11 and 12 Groups had been fanned and inflamed with the publication, in 1969, of Robert Wright's work, *Dowding and the Battle of Britain*.[1] He felt the author had done a disservice both to his old commander-in-chief and to the Royal Air Force by some of his assertions. Wright had never consulted him over those areas of the manuscript in which he, Leigh-Mallory and 12 Group had figured. This was reflected in the narrative which, he believed, was slanted unfairly and sometimes inaccurately, not only against his AOC and himself, but also against the Air Staff, the Secretary of State and his Under-Secretary.

The chairman of the association, Air Commodore Donald Macdonell, the commanding officer of 64 Squadron during the battle, was able instantly to give the assurance he sought. 'Everyone wants you to do it,' he said. 'They are demanding that you do it. The wish is unanimous.'

Douglas was resolved that, in so far as he had the ability to choose them, the words he spoke to the packed congregation in the Royal Air Force's lovely church in the Strand should fit the memory of an officer who had served Britain in a moment of great need.[2]

1. Robert Wright, *Dowding and the Battle of Britain* (Macdonald, 1969).
2. The full text of the address is in Appendix C.

I first saw him in the mess at Northolt when I was a pilot officer in 1931. He stood there, tall, lean, upright, immaculate: every junior officer's idea of a fighting airman, this decorated wing commander. . . .

I last saw him . . . in 1969 in his house [in New Zealand]. He had just come in from sailing. He was wearing rope-soled, canvas shoes, shorts, a short-sleeved shirt; lean, bronzed, upright, immaculate. He carried his seventy-six years with disdain.

In between, there had been the glory: 'They were busy times, exhilarating times . . . with never a thought that we might lose the battle. Keith Park was one of us. We all shared the great experience.' In five or six, emotional, simple, plain-spoken minutes, Douglas had caught the character of the man with whom so many of his listeners had served.

There was a brief, yet spontaneous, epilogue to the address which cut an enduring mark upon Douglas's mind. At the Battle of Britain anniversary which followed at Bentley Priory, a former pilot stood up, unannounced. Hammering the table he brought the Few to order. In the surprised and wondering silence, he spoke for all: 'I'd like to say to Douglas Bader, on behalf of all of us, how much we thank him for what he said about Sir Keith at the service at St Clement Danes. He spoke for every one of us in the words he used.' The rumbling roar of acceptance came from a united room.

SIR HUGH DOWDING

Hugh Dowding's contribution to Britain's success in the autumn fighting of 1940 was in plain contrast to the public's conception of it.

Between taking up the challenge of Fighter Command in 1936 and the opening of the German offensive some four years later, the commander-in-chief had wrought the means of victory. His was an undemonstrative, low-key role, yet the attainment was dramatic. It is at least arguable whether there was another senior officer available in the Royal Air Force at the time who could have driven the work through with the same resolve, comprehension and acumen.

The features of the man – his attributes and shortcomings – offset one another in unusual balance. To his staff, the credits were quickly discernible. His seniority – he was fifty-four when he took over at Stanmore – and his unchallengeable devotion to the task; his absolute professionalism and his ability to distinguish between what was essential and what was merely desirable; a technical understanding which enabled him to anticipate the requirements of a radar reporting system and then relate it to the practical needs of an effective fighter defence; the patience and endurance which allowed him to build a bridge between the Air Staff at Fighter Command and scientists of the calibre of Henry Tizard and Robert Watson-Watt and maintain a ready exchange with them. His strategic sense and his faculty for recognizing the big issues and separating them from the small; his extraordinary moral courage and toughness which sustained him (with Cyril Newall's oft-forgotten support) in standing up to the weight of Winston Churchill's rhetoric and resisting the demands to commit more home-based fighter squadrons to the faltering Battle of France; the singleness of mind. And the golden heart that lay, often undiscovered, within this shy, withdrawn man.

And then, set against all this, his inability to accommodate himself easily with those in higher places in the Service and to compromise when something had to be conceded; the directness – and tartness – of his pen; the lack of sensitivity and tact and the absence of finesse in moulding his personal relations with authority; his formidable and unyielding determination to stand pat on an issue, not to budge an inch from it, and to be – well – just plain 'Stuffy'.

Douglas Bader got the balance between C-in-C and AOC exactly right in his St Clement Danes address: 'It is right and proper for me to say . . . something which I do not recall has been said before. . . . That great and vital air battle was controlled, directed and brought to a successful conclusion [by Keith Park]. . . . Had he failed, Stuffy Dowding's foresight, determination and achievement would have counted for nought.'

Dowding was a 'backroom' commander-in-chief. It was his style. He was not a battle commander, nor was he a war leader of the calibre or intellect of Portal, Harris, Tedder or Sholto Douglas. Frankly, he was never in that class. What he did was to prepare and organize Fighter Command for the supreme contest. It was in the four years from taking over in 1936 until the opening of the German aerial offensive in the late summer of 1940 that his real success lay. His introduction of the day-and-night radar systems, both ground-based and airborne, gave Britain the edge in this department. His stoicism in resisting Churchill's urgings to send additional British squadrons to prop up the collapsing French was paramount in pre-serving Britain's defensive strength. He saw that a greater and more critical air battle was to follow.

This was the true measure of Stuffy Dowding's imperishable achievement.

He faltered when he failed to take hold of 11 and 12 Groups – and their commanders – as the battle rolled forward to its all-embracing climax in September 1940 and became, manifestly, a Command and no longer solely a Group affair. Instead of seeing to it that all the resources and efforts of the two principal groups – and the rest – were co-ordinated and used to their utmost potential through his own central and overall direction, he stood back and left it to Park. One could not have envisaged Portal, Sholto Douglas or Harris playing it that way.

There are other aspects of the Dowding story which, in deference to the record, Douglas believes should be examined. They can be grouped together under two headings:

1 Dowding's treatment at the hands of the Air Ministry in the six years between 1936 and 1942 and the justification, or otherwise, of his complaints
2 The circumstances in which the leadership of Fighter Command came to be changed in November 1940, and the parts Churchill and Sinclair played in the episode

Except in the grotesquely distorted manner of his leaving Fighter Command, which is a separate issue, Dowding was subjected to treatment which no serving officer, least of all the most senior, should ever have been expected to endure. Harold Balfour, who, as Under-Secretary of State, was at the Air Ministry for much of four out of the six years of Dowding's discontent, was better placed than most to form an independent opinion. He has given his unequivocal judgement: 'The truth is that Dowding was shamefully served by successive Chiefs of the Air Staff over his personal career.' [1] No political hedging there. The facts would seem to justify the contention. Nevertheless, reading, now, all the intimate, and once secret, Service correspondence of those times, it is hard – in fact, impossible – to escape the conclusion that Dowding brought at least *some* of his misfortunes, possibly quite unconsciously, upon himself.

Taking the Air Staff's point of view first, there were, to be quite fair, certain factors which cannot be ignored. Contrary to the popular

1. Harold Balfour, *Wings Over Westminster* (Hutchinson, 1973).

image which the media assiduously promoted at successive post-war Battle of Britain anniversaries (the 'Father Figure', surrounded by the Few – his 'chicks' of other years), Hugh Dowding was not a widely loved Service character. He had crossed one or two important swords along the way. He had fallen out, sadly and unwisely, with one of the most respected and highly regarded Chiefs of the Air Staff, Sir John Salmon (Marshal of the Royal Air Force Sir John Salmon). He had no ear for politics, a science for which he had no special liking. With few exceptions, he wasn't much enamoured of politicians. Further, he was, in intellectual terms, a strangely untypical Wykhamist; Peter Portal, with a leavening of Christ Church to add to his Winchester years, was cast in a much more familiar mould. His was a signally superior brain.

Thus, as the time approached for Lord Swinton, politically the ablest and most influential Secretary of State the Service ever had, to decide on the man who should succeed Edward Ellington (Marshal of the Royal Air Force Sir Edward Ellington) as CAS in 1937, it was not to Dowding but to Cyril Newall that he turned. Nor was Dowding the alternative choice. The engaging and personally estimable – and clever – Chris Courtney (Air Chief Marshal Sir Christopher Courtney) was well ahead of him in the race.

Philip Swinton, one of the Tory Party's heavyweights in the Cabinet, was not persuaded, after taking his Service soundings, that Dowding, despite his seniority and experience, was CAS material at such a moment in British history. And when, instead, he was sent to Stanmore to command, it was not expected that he would remain in that appointment for more than two or three years. Retirement was already looming, and the intention was that Courtney should follow him at Fighter Command in 1939. Fate, however, was to order otherwise.

The spectre of war, and a traumatic flying accident at an inopportune moment, threw Courtney's blossoming prospects into disarray. The aircraft, a De Havilland 86, in which he, Kingsley Wood (the Secretary of State), Edward Campbell (the Secretary of State's Parliamentary Private Secretary), and Sholto Douglas had been travelling, lay on a Cumbrian hillside. There, too, lay the injured Courtney's expectation of leading Fighter Command in the Battle of Britain. Thus are men's fortunes changed. For Dowding, it was the touch of life. For the Air Council, the timing (it was 28 June 1939) could hardly have been more inconvenient.

That is the background; against it has to be seen, in all its undeniable and stark reality, the trail of incidents which had studded the C-in-C's recent career. He set them out in a letter to the Chief of the Air Staff, dated 7 July 1940, at the start of the opening phase of the Battle of Britain, with all the responsibilities which this was now bringing. It is a picture with which Douglas has much sympathy.[1]

'I should like you,' he wrote to Newall, 'to cast your eye down the following record.' The catalogue must be seen in detail.

Feb 8th 1937. Letter from Sir E. Ellington [Chief of the Air Staff]: 'It has been established . . . that an Officer of your rank will be employed as far as possible up to the age of 60' [i.e. for Dowding, 1942].

Aug 4th 1938. Letter from Air Council 'unable to offer you any employment in the RAF after the end of June 1939.'

Feb 23rd 1939. Paragraph in Evening Standard announcing my impending retirement and naming my successor.

Feb 24th 1939. You telephoned and told me that the Air Ministry proposed to reply that 'no change would be made during the present year'.

March 10th 1939. Interview with S of S at which you were present. Said I was not willing to extend service unless I had the confidence and support of the Air Council hitherto denied to me. Verbal assurance.

March 17th 1939. Reminder to S of S that I awaited an answer.

March 20th 1939. Letter from you asking me to defer my retirement till end of March, 1940.

March 30th 1940 [one day before date of retirement]. Request from you to defer retirement till July 14th 1940.

March 31st 1940. My reply accepting and asking who my successor would be. (No reply or acknowledgement received.)

July 5th 1940. Letter from you asking me to defer retirement till October 1940.

Apart from the question of discourtesy, which I do not want to stress, I must point out the lack of consideration involved in delaying a proposal of this nature until ten days before the date of my retirement. I have had four retiring dates given to me and now you are proposing a fifth. Before the war, as I told the S of S, I should have been glad enough to retire; now I am anxious to stay, because I feel there is no one else who will fight as I do when proposals are made which would reduce the Defence Forces of the Country below the extreme danger point.

I would therefore suggest that I should not be called on to retire otherwise than at my own request before the first retiring date given to me viz April 24th 1942, or the end of the war, whichever is the earlier.

To a rational man, it is almost inconceivable that the most senior serving officer in the Royal Air Force should have been given such ammunition to loose off at the professional head of his own Service.

1. Air 19/572, Secretary of State's file on Sir Hugh Dowding, AHB 1D/5/115.

Dowding, understandably, sprinkled a little salt on the open sore by sending a copy to the Secretary of State. A pointedly worded note in his own hand covered it.

Newall took six days to reply to the commander-in-chief. When he did respond, on 13 July, it was in firm terms which conceded little. Sinclair, on the other hand, with his usual courtesy, acknowledged the C-in-C's correspondence almost at once. Identifying himself openly with the decision to ask the C-in-C to retain his command 'until October', he added what turned out to be a prophetic rider: 'it was my wish that you should remain in command of our Fighter Squadrons, upon whose success in defeating the German attack upon our munition factories during the next three weeks, will almost certainly depend the issue of this war.' He concluded on a note of encouragement: 'I could give you no higher proof of my confidence in you and, although perhaps it seems superfluous, let me add the assurance of my full support.'

But Dowding couldn't resist a dig. A couple of days later, on 12 July, he came back with a singularly ill-judged reply to Sinclair, to whom, after all, he had only sent *a copy* of his letter to the Chief of the Air Staff. It was for Newall, not the Secretary of State, to respond. After going through the obvious pleasantries, the C-in-C added a barb to the tail: 'Since you have replied to my letter, I must assume that you take the view there is nothing in the facts which I have tabulated which calls for explanation or apology, and that I am to be placed on the Retired List at the end of October, 1940.' No secretary of state would stomach that.

When an answer eventually came from the Chief of the Air Staff, Dowding cared little for it. 'I realize', he wrote in his immediate reply to Newall of 14 July, '. . . that this is a matter upon which we cannot be expected to see eye to eye, and further discussion would be unprofitable.' A touch of asperity – even to the CAS – was seldom very far away. But there, for the time being, the matter was allowed to rest.

Meanwhile, as Douglas has pointed out, across the Straits of Dover, in the Pas de Calais and northern France, Goering's Luftwaffe was gathering for the great assault. Already the Germans were beginning to stab at Dowding's tenuously held Command.

The part that Churchill is alleged to have played in the Dowding affair has long puzzled Bader. He has never been prepared to accept the tale that the Prime Minister, as Minister of Defence, was not alerted to the circumstances by the Secretary of State. Nor, for that matter, has he ever believed the suggestion that in some way Churchill had 'got it in for Dowding' and wanted to be rid of him. The thought that the Prime Minister was displeased with him because he took a resolute stand on the issue of sending more fighters to prop up the Battle of France seemed totally out of accord with Churchill's respect for a man's mind.

Two statements by contemporary authors, well respected in their own fields, have, however, bothered him. The first belongs to Robert Wright. Writing with all the authority of a wartime personal assistant to the Commander-in-Chief of Fighter Command and, later, as confidant, personal friend and biographer, he is quite explicit in a question he posed in his book on Dowding:[1] 'If Winston Churchill kept the very tight control . . . over the senior appointments . . . how did it come about . . . that he knew nothing about Dowding being relieved of his command?'

The second is Len Deighton's.[2] By a curious paradox, it is a contradiction of the first.

It must be accepted that Churchill either acquiesced or even possibly prompted the sacking of Dowding. Fighter Command's Commander-in-Chief lacked the extrovert confidence and assurance that the Prime Minister liked to see in his commanders. . . . Churchill could behave with great brutality to those whom he decided were serving the war effort badly. Like Wavell, Dowding was a victim of the Prime Minister at his most callous. . . .

Thus the men who won the Battle of Britain suffered disgrace and ingratitude. . . .

The facts deride the contentions. Churchill gives the lie to them with his own pen. In two private and characteristically forthright letters to the Secretary of State, he leaves no doubt about his own feelings. The first was dated 10 July 1940,[3] *four and a half months, mark it, before Dowding was due to finish his tour of duty at Fighter Command and a month after the Battle of France.* 'My dear Archie,' it began,

I was very much taken aback the other night when you told me you had been considering removing Sir Hugh Dowding at the expiration of his present appointment, but that you had come to the conclusion that he might be allowed to stay on for another four months. Personally, I think he is one

1. Robert Wright, *Dowding and the Battle of Britain* (Macdonald, 1969).
2. Len Deighton, *Battle of Britain* (Jonathan Cape, 1980).
3. Enclosure 4A on Air 19/572, the Secretary of State's file on Sir Hugh Dowding, AHB 1D/5/115.

of the very best men you have got, and I say this having been in contact with him for about two years. I have greatly admired the whole of his work in the Fighter Command, and especially in resisting the clamour for numerous air raid warnings, and the immense pressure to dissipate the Fighter strength during the great French battle. In fact he has my full confidence.

I think it is a pity for an officer so gifted and so trusted to be working on such a short tenure as four months, and I hope you will consider whether it is not in the public interest that his appointment should be indefinitely prolonged while the war lasts.

This would not of course exclude his being moved to a higher position, if that were thought necessary. I am however much averse from making changes and putting in new men who will have to learn the work all over again, except when there is some proved failure or inadequacy.

The ending of the letter reflected Churchill's long friendship with Sinclair. It was signed 'Yours always, W.'

The Secretary of State took the first opportunity of discussing the letter with the Prime Minister. This came two days after it was written, on 12 July. Developing the arguments, Sinclair was able to persuade Churchill of the sense of not, for the present, looking beyond October; much could happen in the interim. He recorded a brief, manuscript note of action in red pencil in the margin of the Prime Minister's letter: 'Spoke W 12/7/40. He agreed that matters should rest at point reached in my letter to C-in-C [i.e. that Dowding should retain his command until October] and position could be considered afresh a month or more hence.'

The following evening, 13 July – it was a Saturday – the Prime Minister asked the C-in-C to dine with him at Chequers. It gave Hugh Dowding a convenient peg from which to dangle a neatly worded note to the Secretary of State, dated 14 July and written, again, in his own hand. It went marginally beyond the understanding that Sinclair had reached with the Prime Minister, but not materially so:

He [Churchill] was good enough to tell me that I had secured his confidence, and that he wished me to remain on the Active List for the time being, without any date for my retirement being fixed. He told me he had written to you on the subject.

A month passed before the Prime Minister returned to the matter in another private letter to Sinclair dated 10 August,[1] still well over

1. Enclosure 10A on Air 19/572, Secretary of State's file on Sir Hugh Dowding, AHB 1D/5/115.

three months in advance of the time when the Air Ministry had intended that the C-in-C should retire. By now, the German attacks on Keith Park's airfields were beginning to mount and the battle was entering its most lethal phase. Churchill came straight to the point:

I certainly understood from our conversation a month ago that you were going to give Dowding an indefinite war-time extension, and were going to do it at once. I cannot understand how any contrary impression could have arisen in your mind about my wishes. Let me however remove it at once, and urge you to take the step I have so long desired.

It is entirely wrong to keep an officer in the position of Commander-in-Chief, conducting hazardous operations from day to day, when he is dangling at the end of an expiring appointment. Such a situation is not fair to anyone, least of all to the nation. I can never be a party to it.

I do hope you will be able to set my mind at rest.

This *was*, however, a misinterpretation – deliberate or otherwise – of the understanding that Sinclair had reached with the Prime Minister in their conversation of 12 July which the Secretary of State had noted in manuscript on the Prime Minister's letter to him of 10 July. Churchill may well have thought at this juncture that it would be convenient to have rather more room for manoeuvre. If he did, it was, perhaps, a tactic with which he was not wholly unfamiliar.

Sinclair made the position clear to the Prime Minister when, with his customary good grace and manners, he responded two days later. The actual time limit for Dowding's retirement of October was, nevertheless, withdrawn, leaving him, as the Secretary of State put it to the Prime Minister, 'in exactly the same position as the other Commanders-in-Chief'.

September passed. A mighty battle was won. The daylight offensive tailed away. Nights became disturbed. The October meeting at the Air Ministry was put behind. The gaze was now fastened on the spring. It was time for the winners to unsaddle and leave the enclosure.

One question only remains to be posed and answered to complete Bader's search for the truth about the Dowding saga. It has caused continuing speculation.

When the moment came for the C-in-C to go in November 1940, is it really true that he was 'abruptly telephoned at Stanmore and asked to clear his desk within twenty-four hours', as Deighton tells us? [1] Wright had earlier given currency to the tale when he reported Dowding as saying: ' "I received a sudden telephone call . . . from the Secretary of State. . . . He told me I was to relinquish my Command immediately." '[2] Balfour has always refuted the story: 'sacked . . . at a moment's notice by the Secretary of State on the end of a telephone he [Dowding] certainly was not . . .'[3]

The new evidence overwhelmingly confirms the strength of the former Under-Secretary's assertion. The fact was that Sinclair called Dowding to his room in the Air Ministry on 13 November after discussing the matter with Churchill. After all that had gone on since July, it was in character for the Secretary of State to play things this way. Recording afterwards a note of the interview,[4] he told the C-in-C that it was proposed that he should lead a team of experts to the United States to press upon the Americans the facts of life about 'selecting, modifying and purchasing aircraft and air armament'. There were, in the USA, the note said, 'the finest production engineers in the world but they lacked war experience'. Beaverbrook, whose concern this was as Minister of Aircraft Production, 'desired [Dowding's] services'. The Secretary of State said he was proposing that the C-in-C's place at Stanmore should be taken by Sholto Douglas.

Churchill saw Dowding the next day, 14 November. He reinforced the Secretary of State's talk: 'I explained to him the importance of getting American war aviation developed on the right lines. . . . I wished him to undertake [the mission] in the public interest of which I was the judge. . . . I will give him a letter to the President. . . . Let me see his instructions, please, in draft form.'[5]

Two days later, on 16 November, with all, then, made ready, Sinclair telephoned Dowding at Stanmore to confirm the arrangements and the timing of the changes in command. The new Chief of the Air Staff, Portal, subsequently committed the substance of the conversation to paper.

So much for the tale that the C-in-C was fired by the Secretary of State on the end of a telephone – or, as Deighton would have us

1. Deighton, op. cit.
2. Wright, op. cit.
3. Balfour, op. cit.
4. Enclosure 13A on Air 19/572, Secretary of State's file on Sir Hugh Dowding, AHB 1D/5/115.
5. Enclosure 14A on Air 19/572, Secretary of State's file on Sir Hugh Dowding, AHB 1D/5/115.

believe, 'that Churchill either acquiesced in or even possibly prompted the sacking of Dowding'.[1]

The two final assignments which Dowding shouldered before his retirement in June 1942 – the leadership of the mission to the United States and, subsequently, the examination of the manpower, resources and establishments of the Royal Air Force in the United Kingdom were both failures. Never a diplomat, he was unsuited to both and should never have been invited to undertake them. It was only his sense of duty (and, in the case of the first, Churchill's insistence) which compelled him to accept the responsibility. The pity was that he didn't quit on the morrow of victory.

Should Hugh Dowding have been made a Marshal of the Royal Air Force? The background to the matter has often exercised Bader's mind.

King George VI stimulated the issue in a letter from his private secretary, Sir Alexander Hardinge, to the Secretary of State on 17 July 1942:

His Majesty wished me to raise with you the question of [Dowding] being promoted to Marshal of the Royal Air Force on retirement. . . .

. . . It has always seemed to [the King] that Dowding performed a really wonderful service . . . in creating and putting into practice, the defence system which proved so effective in the Battle of Britain.

None could have improved on the assessment. Buckingham Palace usually gets it right.

Sinclair gave his verdict to Hardinge on 21 July: 'I have reached the conclusion . . . there are certain objections to [Dowding's] promotion to Marshal of the Royal Air Force at the present time.'

Up to that moment only Chiefs of the Air Staff had been promoted to the Service's highest rank. Moreover, Dowding had already been 'retired' once – in the autumn of 1941. *At the time*, it looked to be the correct decision.

In 1945, a precedent was set when Sir Arthur Harris was made a Marshal after three unparalleled years at the head of Bomber Command. By then Sir Hugh Dowding had been given a peerage, an

1. Deighton, op. cit.

172

honour which, however, was denied to Harris. Douglas has always seen the compromise as a fairly rough form of justice.

Loyal to Stuffy to the end, Bader cornered Harold Macmillan one evening at Lancaster House during a reception on the twentieth anniversary of the Battle of Britain. The Tories had just won a resounding victory at the polls and Macmillan, confirmed by the will of the people as Prime Minister, was riding high.

'Some of us here, sir,' said Douglas, 'think that Lord Dowding should have been made a Marshal of the Royal Air Force. Is it too late now to do anything?'

The Prime Minister muttered something about having forgotten that Dowding wasn't a Marshal. 'I'll have a word with Jack Profumo,' he murmured. Profumo, then the alert and able Secretary of State for War, had no responsibility whatever for the Royal Air Force!

A few moments later, Jack passed Douglas, hurrying up the stairs. 'I can't stop,' he said, 'the PM wants to see me.'

'Don't worry, Jack,' teased Douglas, 'he's only going to ask you why Stuffy Dowding isn't a Marshal of the Royal Air Force!'

Lord Mountbatten was only a few paces away. Bader tried it on the Chief of the Defence Staff. 'Don't you think, sir, it might be possible to make Lord Dowding a Marshal of the Royal Air Force? Some of us think he was very badly treated.'

Mountbatten sidestepped the issue. 'I think you'll find there are establishment problems. You get it with Field Marshals and Admirals of the Fleet. When the list is full you can't make any more.'

It had, in fact, got nothing to do with it. There is no numerical establishment, as such, for Marshals of the Royal Air Force. The ultimate rank is reserved, nowadays, for Chiefs of the Air Staff and for an airman who hasn't been CAS but who may, because it's the Service's turn, become Chief of the Defence Staff. Still, it was probably as good as most of the answers about Stuffy Dowding.

17
The choice: Tangmere or Biggin?

It was December 1940. The pilots were idling the time away in the crewroom of 242 Squadron's dispersal hut at Martlesham Heath, the fighter station on Suffolk's east coast. Some were dozing; others were playing cards; a few, gazing into blankness, were unconsciously tapping out the rhythm of the current hit.

Winter had come early and several inches of snow lay on the ground. Flying was restricted to emergency scrambles. There was little going on by comparison with the tension and movement of the hectic September days. Boredom was now the foe. It was an unexpectedly inert atmosphere for the newly arrived supernumerary squadron leader from Flying Training Command to savour.

Arthur Donaldson, Thelma Bader's first cousin and the youngest of the three Royal Air Force brothers, tall, very fair and handsome, a most personable officer and successful with the girls, had just been posted to 242 from the Central Flying School at Upavon. There, in an advanced and sophisticated environment, he had become regarded as one of the most proficient of the staff instructors. He already had a substantial total of flying hours in his log-book. Now, having argued and badgered his way out of CFS, he had been sent to the squadron to gain operational experience, learn something about leading in the air, and possibly take over from Douglas when the time finally came.

Stan Turner, 'A' Flight commander, eyed the new arrival with a nice blend of indifference and disdain. 'Say, you play poker?'

Arthur, nobody's fool, hesitated. 'Yes,' he said, 'just.'

The Canadian pointed to a vacant seat at the table. 'Right, then, get your coat off and sit down there.'

'Within an hour,' reflected Donaldson, years afterwards, 'they had skinned me for a fiver – when a fiver was worth something. After that, I did rather better.'

Up to his arrival at Martlesham, he had felt out of things as an instructor. Teddy, his middle brother, had made a strong mark in the French battle, commanding 151 Squadron with its Hurricanes. He had collected the DSO in the process and had subsequently been sent off on an assignment to the United States. Jack, the eldest – Baldy, they tended to call him – the bell-wether of the flock, had perished earlier in the year, when the aircraft carrier *Glorious* was sunk off Norway by the German battle cruisers *Scharnhorst* and *Gneisenau.* He had been leading 263 Squadron, with its slow and obsolescent Gladiator biplanes, against the weight of the German forces, flying off the frozen lakes south of Narvik. His DSO had matched his deeds.

In the event, Arthur Donaldson did not take over 242 from Douglas. His manifest lack of operational experience in a squadron of such talents would have made his task unreasonably difficult. The evidence was plainly visible. One day, flying with the two battle-hardened warriors, Turner and Crowley-Milling, his section had intercepted a Ju 88. 'All I saw of the engagement', said Arthur, a transparently honest man, 'as I dropped further and further behind, was Stan and Crow belting into the 88 with everything they'd got until the aircraft disappeared into cloud. I never even got a squirt at it.'

Douglas had to tell the AOC, reluctantly, that, in his judgement, it would be most unwise for his wife's cousin to be given command of the squadron at this stage. It wasn't easy to say it of such a well-liked member of the family.

However, some weeks later, when 263, his eldest brother's old unit, was being re-formed and re-equipped with Westland Whirlwinds, Arthur was appointed to lead it. In its hazardous, low-level attack role, the squadron enjoyed considerable success. On the back of this operational achievement, he was subsequently posted to Malta under Keith Park. There, as the conspicuously skilful leader of the Takali wing, he was able to apply all the fighting principles he had learned from Bader at Martlesham nearly two years before.

In 1980, shortly before he died of a heart attack, having enriched the family name, he paid his former squadron commander a high compliment. 'Anything I ever learned about leading I picked up from Douglas in those few weeks at Martlesham in 1940 and 1941. He taught me everything I knew.'

He didn't always remember it. Hammering a Ju 88 one sunny autumn morning between Malta and Sicily, he inadvertently allowed an Me 109 to return the compliment. A cannon shell ripped into the side of the cockpit of his Spitfire, severing the last two fingers of his left hand as he gripped the throttle lever. Hit hard, also, in leg and foot, his emergency landing back at Takali was painful but faultless.

'Too bad,' they said to him afterwards, when eventually he was released from hospital, 'losing those two fingers.'

'Never mind,' he countered, giving full play to his roguish laugh, 'they're not the important ones!'

With Trafford Leigh-Mallory now firmly in control of 11 Group, the character of the fighter operations was transformed. Defence gave way to attack. For Bader's friend, Rupert Leigh, who had led 66 Squadron with signal distinction and aplomb in the summer and autumn battles, this was no new experience.

In the sombre quiet after Dunkirk, Fighter Command headquarters had hatched a most improbable plan to 'show the flag on the other side'. Designed to encourage the patriotic Dutch, it was an ill-thought-out operation.

66, based at Coltishall, were sent off with the Defiants, the rear-gun fighters, which, because of their surprise armament, had enjoyed a brief and never-to-be-repeated success against the enemy. The aim was to cross the southern North Sea, sweep in round the Hague, and come home. There would be no fuel to spare.

The Luftwaffe was waiting for them. In no time the sky was alive with Messerschmitts, Spitfires and Defiants fighting it out, with aircraft in varying degrees of disintegration plunging earthwards, smoking and flaming. Leigh's levity and wit, even in a crisis, were never far away. He switched on his RT to transmit, his voice unmistakable to the controller at Coltishall. 'It's absolutely extraordinary,' he said, '*it's just like the films!*' Here was a humour which never failed to appeal to Douglas, not least because it was usually tilted at authority.

Having left day fighting behind, Leigh later commanded 23, a Havoc squadron, engaged on night intruder missions over enemy territory, shadowing the Luftwaffe's airfields as the enemy's bombers returned from their nightly attacks against Britain. To add to the fun and sparkle, he put up a lighthearted suggestion to Fighter Command. Why not drop empty bottles of Guinness at night on the enemy? They possessed terrorizing properties 'just like whistling bombs'.

The proposal was taken seriously. Next day, two earnest and dedicated staff officers arrived at Ford, the night fighter airfield on the

Sussex coast, to investigate. Crates of empties from the mess were loaded into an aircraft and dropped from an altitude on some neighbouring waste land. The headquarters' representatives waited, agog, on the ground as the bottles rained down. There wasn't a sound.

Early in March 1941, Leigh-Mallory sent for Douglas to tell him that the commander-in-chief, Sholto Douglas, had agreed to establish the post of wing commander flying, at all the main sector stations. 'I'm making my appointments now', he said, 'and giving you first choice. Which would you prefer – Tangmere or Biggin? I shall let Sailor have the wing you refuse.'

Douglas picked Tangmere at once. There was a reason for it. He never wanted to have his pilots stationed near London. He had seen enough of that to be convinced of the distractions it caused. Fifty minutes from Biggin Hill to the Savoy after a hard day's fighting – and rather less getting back for dawn readiness the next day – wasn't the best recipe for a contest with the Luftwaffe's fighter squadrons from Wissand, Saint-Omer or Abbeville.

An auspicous note now appeared in his log-book, written, again, in the familiar hand: '18/3/41. Handed over command of 242 (Canadian) Squadron & posted to TANGMERE as wing commander.' As Bader took up station at Tangmere, 'Sailor' Malan, of whom he had become increasingly fond ('a dear chap, Sailor'), moved into Biggin. Between Fighter Command's two most illustrious leaders a good-natured and competitive rivalry was quickly built up.

18

'He was bloody marvellous'

Only exceptionally should officers over 26 years of age be posted to command fighter squadrons . . .

Sir Hugh Dowding, in his Battle of Britain Dispatch, set an upper age limit for squadron commanders. He did not, however, deal with wing leaders. There had been little experience to go on, and in any case the circumstances were different. When Douglas went to Tangmere he had just turned thirty-one. A full year's operations had matured him even further. He was now a dominant figure in the flying hierarchy of Fighter Command, assertive, confident and very set in his commanding ways.

He lost no time in establishing his authority over the three squadrons in the wing – 616, the South Yorkshire Auxiliary Squadron, with the Cranwell-trained Billy Burton in command; 610, the County of Chester's contribution to the Royal Auxiliary Air Force, commanded by Ken Holden, a Yorkshireman of solid worth and humour; and 145, formed at the start of the war, soon to be led with aggressive competence by Canada's Stan Turner. All were equipped at the start with Spitfire IIs.

Bader normally led with 616. It suited him and his leadership. Decimated in the fighting over Kent seven months before, it had re-formed under a new commander in the outer reaches of Lincolnshire, at Kirton-in-Lindsey. Burton, a sound and competent professional, with a firm discipline and an understanding of human nature, had arrived at the right moment. He was the man the squadron needed to pull it together.

He hit it off at once with Bader. Younger than the wing leader, with the bond of Cranwell to secure the relationship, he was well content for Douglas to lead with 616. He was smart enough to realize there was plenty for a squadron commander to learn from that kind of maturity and experience.

The choice was significant in another respect. Bader flew the wing in loose sections of four aircraft – two pairs flying together in line abreast. Positioned like the tips of the fingers of an outstretched hand, they called them 'finger fours'. Leading the pair on Douglas's right, and making up the four with the wing leader's pair, was the twenty-one-year-old Hugh Dundas, the Stowe-educated auxiliary who had joined the squadron just before the war. On Dundas's right, and flying usually as his number 2, was Johnnie Johnson, a piece of twenty-five-year-old granite from Melton Mowbray, in Leicestershire, a civil engineer by trade. On Bader's left was the rock-solid and dependable Alan Smith, the sergeant pilot from South Shields, in County Durham. He was the wing leader's customary number 2; but, if there had to be a stand-in, it was Jeff West, the New Zealander, who was to add spirit and ruggedness to 249 Squadron in the air battle for Malta a year later.

Within a couple of years, Dundas and Johnson had themselves become two of the Service's best-known and most successful wing leaders. When to them are added Stan Turner – who was to transform the flying in Malta – the aforementioned Arthur Donaldson and Alan Smith – who went from sergeant to a flight commander in North Africa in twenty-four months – and, then, of course, the ever-present Burton and Crowley-Milling, the question must at once be posed: what was it in Bader, and his leading, that enabled him, consciously or unconsciously, to stamp his model upon others?

The thought intrigues for it has an application far removed from the field of wartime flying. The same qualities were to become evident in later years with the inspiration he was to offer his fellow disabled the world over. ('If you've taken a lot out and been luckier than the rest, you must try to put it back; that's the point. You have a responsibility to replace what's been taken out and try to lend others a hand.' It's Bader's philosophy.)

'Cocky' Dundas, like Johnson and Smith, is as well placed as any to assess the features of his leadership. Between 24 March and 9 August 1941, the day Douglas baled out over France, he flew sixty-two consecutive sweeps or offensive operations with him against the enemy. The statistic is almost incredible until it is seen confirmed in the log-books – and until one realizes that the Tangmere wing often flew two, and sometimes three, sorties in a single day. Forty years on, with all the interim for reflection, and from his latter-day vantage point as managing director of the British Electric Traction Company, he is quite clear about it. His views are echoed by Alan Smith from the chair of Dawson International.

Dundas had known at first hand the traumas that 616 Squadron had had to endure in the Battle of Britain. He had himself been shot down early on in circumstances which would have unnerved most for good. Hit by a volley of cannon shells from an unseen 109 at 12,000 feet, when the squadron was bounced on the climb, it seemed to him as if the whole of the back of his Spitfire, from behind the cockpit up to and including the tail unit, had been taken clean away. The aircraft, or what remained of it, lost 11,000 feet while Cocky struggled to get out. When he had finally freed himself, his parachute opened instantly at 600 feet, just in time to break the fall before he hit the ground. On rejoining the squadron after a brief spell of hospital and convalescence, he found that Burton was prescribing just the right medicine. As a tonic to help it back to strength, the new commander would occasionally take the unit south to Duxford to operate with the Bader wing.

Dundas remembers vividly the first time he met Douglas. It was on one of these visits. The squadron was at Fowlmere, the Duxford satellite, waiting for a scramble. After his accident and short time off flying, he was feeling, understandably, anything but robust and aggressive. Such experiences, even at twenty-one, have devastating effects upon the nervous system. The wing leader suddenly appeared with the squadron commander at 616's dispersal point. This extraordinary figure, without any legs of his own and already decorated, stumped round the squadron talking to the pilots and the ground crews. The effect and the impression he left in those few minutes were painted instantly and for ever on the memory.

That, of course, is what leadership – real leadership – is supposed to be able to do. In Dundas's compelling phrase, Bader possessed the ability 'with knobs on'.

In the air, the attributes Douglas brought to his command were readily discernible to an acute and observant eye. They were, in a word, comprehensive. Day after day, he contrived to keep the wing together, to get it, without fuss, to the right point at the right time and in the right way. Cohesion and control were evident in every action. Once an engagement had been joined, there was little that even the most accomplished commander could do; it became a question of making the best of it and sticking, if possible, to pairs. But up to that point the Tangmere leader's mastery was all-embracing and consistent.

Bader was greatly admired in the wing. The pilots, from the junior to the most senior, looked up to him. They saw him as a quite exceptional person. Dundas, who became 'immensely fond of him', wrapped it up in a graphically plain sentence. 'He was bloody marvellous, that's all there was to it.'

Liddell Hart, in his dissertation on Marlborough, used an arresting phrase in conveying the qualities of the true leader: 'The power of commanding affection while communicating energy'. The description undoubtedly had an application for Douglas in his fighting days – at Tangmere in 1941 as much as anywhere.

'The power to command affection' was particularly noticeable in the evenings at the Bay House, the home which Thelma set up for Douglas at Aldwick, a short distance from the airfield and within a few miles of Bognor. There, when the wing had been stood down, a group of pilots would forgather – the junior ones as well as the more senior – with a crate of beer from the mess to replenish their weary bodies. Friendship and comradeship were to be found in abundance; and so was affection. Nor were energy and vitality ever far away.

The elements of leadership were there in those evenings. Thelma's sister, Jill, retains from them the memory of jollity, levity and spirit – and the sense of communion and sharing which came from facing, daily, common risks and dangers. The ethos was quite different from what it had been in the tautness, fatigue and stresses of the Battle of Britain.

As they gathered together, it wasn't long before they were immersed in the inevitable 'shop', with everyone contributing something – and the wing leader, of course, most of all. Tactics, encounters with the 109s, successes, 'shaky-do's', squadron and individual performances, the best height for their aircraft and the ability of the Luftwaffe to fight – the topics were diverse and perpetuating.

'It's no good,' Thelma would say to her sister, resigned to the familiar gossip as the pilots, responding to her husband's lead, really got down to it. 'It's no good, they're talking about "con rods"[1] again.'

Dundas's own time to lead came, a couple of years later, in Malta, when he had five squadrons under his command in 324 Wing. There,

---

1. Connecting rods: parts of the engine joining pistons and crankshaft.

in seven rough and continuous weeks' operations against the Luftwaffe over Sicily, his name was made. Through his screen of modesty it is possible to recognize the effect which his earlier experiences with Bader had had upon his own leading in those active Mediterranean days. 'I am quite sure that any success I may have had then was directly the result of what I had picked up flying with Douglas every day at Tangmere. I simply tried to do what he had done with us, that's all.'

It is when the records and careers of the outstanding officers who had learnt the trade under Bader at Coltishall, Duxford and Tangmere, in the fourteen months – no more – between June 1940 and August 1941 are examined that the true worth of his leadership – and his ability to pick subordinates – may be assessed.

It had a chain reaction, for those who had been apprenticed to him in this short but impressionable period were themselves able to impart their learning to others. I remember, as an example, what I was able to absorb of the skills of leading from flying with Stan Turner in Malta in the early spring days of 1942. He was then demonstrably exhausted, and greatly in need of a rest, but the hallmark of class shone brightly through his performances and lit the way for the rest of us to follow. A year later, the pupil turned master was deploying the same thesis that others might clutch the truth to their bosom and, in their turn, pass it on.

Bader's influence upon the air fighting of the Second World War, both in person and by proxy through his chosen disciples, was as profound as Mannock's had been in the earlier conflict. History may well declare it was his most telling contribution to victory.

The conferences of station and wing commanders which Leigh-Mallory used to call at his headquarters at Uxbridge after important offensive operations soon became a signal part of his style of tactical command. Consultation with his fighter leaders featured high among the first principles he established.

Theodore McEvoy, then the station commander at Northolt to the west of London, can still recall Douglas's forceful and occasionally abrasive interventions in the goodnatured ribaldry which used to break out among the leaders as soon as the AOC had left the room. In the 'mutinous murmurings' which followed one of the earliest meetings, one wing leader began to question the worth of the new offensive tactics, claiming that it was stupid for squadron aircraft to go on getting shot down over France with so little to show for it.

'Hell, old boy,' interjected Douglas, cutting the officer short, 'you can't just spend the rest of your life doing slow rolls over the aerodrome!'

His provocative comments were always available to score a point for Tangmere at the expense of one of the other wings or its commander.

There was the somewhat delicate occasion when Harry Broadhurst, the Hornchurch station master, leading the wing in place of its designated commander, had been heavily outnumbered by the 109s of JG 26 over the town of Lille, in northern France, at the extremity of the Spitfires' operational range. A ferocious battle had ensued. 'In the process of shooting down a 109 I became over-keen and was myself shot up, my number 2 having been shot down without my knowledge.'

Broadhurst had taken the brunt of the attack on his ample backside. As the shrapnel was subsequently being removed, an urgent call had come through to the hospital commanding him to attend the AOC's conference which was due to begin in an hour or two. He had made the journey to Uxbridge kneeling on the back seat of the car which was transporting him.

As I walked, somewhat late, down the gangway to my place, Douglas, with an evil grin, slapped me enthusiastically on the backside.

'Hello, hello,' he chortled, 'running away from the Hun again?'

I wasn't terribly pleased at the time, but eventually recognized it as one of Douglas's little jokes.

The summer of 1941 was now almost spent, and Bader, like other wing and squadron commanders in the group, had been on operations continuously for much of eighteen months.

'Sailor' Malan was one among the number. His leadership, first of 74 Squadron in the battle, and then of the Biggin wing, had kept him in the pit of the fighting. He had had a magnificent run, but he hadn't spared himself in all these strenuous months. He was now tired out; and knew it. In an act of great personal courage, he had made up his resolute and selfless mind to go off and have a private talk with Leigh-Mallory. He told the AOC quite straightly that he must have a rest. For the time being he was finished and couldn't take any more.

When personal example and discipline were uppermost in a leader's mind, it required quite exceptional strength of character to make such an admission. Much easier to say nothing, soldier on and risk the effects of his own fatigue upon those who were, daily, surrendering themselves into his trusted hands. L-M, the pilots' and, particularly, the wing and squadron leaders' AOC, took 'Sailor' off operations there and then. Within a matter of hours he had been dispatched on a rest.

The AOC sent for Bader immediately. Having told him in confidence of Sailor's request and how he had instantly granted it, he put the question bluntly to him: 'Don't you feel that you ought now to have a rest yourself? You have had a long spell of very active flying. I want you to tell me honestly. Would you like to take a breather now and then come back again when you are rested?'

Douglas was much moved by Leigh-Mallory's implied confidence and his patently sincere concern for his wellbeing. For all the outward, and often caricatured, tendency to stand on his dignity, L-M was a human officer who cared deeply about his pilots and their leaders.

'Thank you, sir,' he replied, 'but, if I could, I would like just to see the season out before being taken off.' It was like waiting for the end of the partridges and the pheasants before putting the guns away.

In less than a month, Bader was on his way to his first prison camp in Germany.

19

When it all went wrong

9 August 1941 was One of Those Days. A day when everything went wrong: when one irritant followed another; when anything Bader touched raised its head like a poisonous snake and hissed at him.

It started with his trusted number 2, Alan Smith. He was suffering from a heavy head cold and running a temperature. There were strict rules about not flying with the sinuses blocked. There could be danger in doing so in unpressurized aircraft. True, Jeff West was there to replace Smith and complete the four. And what a four! It was wonderfully accomplished: West, Bader, Dundas and Johnson – the Four Horsemen of the Apocalypse, the impregnable quadrilateral. All the same, strong as the section was, Smith, The Reliant, was absent.

Then Stan Turner, moaning, disgruntled, protesting, had recently been ordered to take himself and 145 away to Yorkshire for a rest. 41 Squadron, the replacement, with Elmer Gaunce, from Alberta, in command, was finding its feet. This day, uncharacteristically, it missed the rendezvous with 616 and 610 as course was set across the Channel.

Added to this, as the wing leader was taking off with his section, he saw his ASI[1] was dead and lifeless, with the needle registering zero. You can't lead a wing and get the speeds and the timing right if you don't know how fast you're going. So Douglas had handed over the lead to his number 3, the competent Dundas, now the commander of 'A' Flight in 616. He took it in his stride, guiding the wing to the nerve point. It was part of the drill to shoulder immediate responsibility.

Nor was the RT set in Bader's aeroplane transmitting or receiving as plainly as it should.

---

1. Airspeed indicator, an aerial speedometer.

It was One of Those Days – a day when, by the test of the wing leader's own operational strictures, he should probably himself have turned back. But Bader wasn't a 'turner-back'. He was a 'forcer-on'. In any case, the operation was commonplace – a target support mission with the bombers to Béthune, 20 miles south-west of Lille in northern France. There had been dozens of similar exercises since the spring. And this was August. It had become second nature like getting up in the morning, having breakfast, saying goodbye to the family and catching the 8.10 for the office. And, anyway, the season was almost over. Must finish the thing off properly.

The portents were hardly propitious.

The rest is history. The run-in to Béthune; the three loose sections of enemy 109s, 3000 feet below, approaching from the left front, pulling up and round very fast; Ken Holden, leading 610, sighting them first, a second or two before Douglas – and seconds in the air are precious, making, sometimes, the difference between success and failure.

Bader's own attack, for once – this once – went astray. The poise, the balance, the judgement, the timing, the positioning of the old Rugby half-back were missing. One pass, and now he was diving away deep before levelling off – in rare isolation – 30 miles inside France.

Johnson, having slid across to the left below the rest of the section, had been ripping into a 109 when, suddenly, a hail of cannon balls had passed his starboard wing as other fighters, working round from underneath into the attack, had let fly. The biter was getting bit.

But the wing leader, naked and unprotected, was now alone at 24,000 feet in the vastness of France's northern sky. 'If you get split up and find yourself on your own, don't hang about; clear off and dive like hell for home.' He had been drumming it into the pilots all the summer. This, however, was One of Those Days. Flouting his own discipline, Douglas went on. A chance sighting of three pairs of 109s in front; unseen, he picked off the rear aircraft of the centre pair before moving on to the unsuspecting leader.

'I was opening fire when I saw two 109s on my left turning towards me. . . . I then made my final mistake. . . . The rule is as old as air fighting: always turn towards your enemy. . . .' But two other Messerschmitts on his right, oblivious to what was happening, were still flying along straight and level,

. . . which was why I turned right towards them, intending to pass over the top ... or even behind them ... and then dive away ... home in the opposite direction.

The bad judgement which had dogged me the whole morning finally fixed me. I banked over right-handed and collided with the second 109. . . . If I had turned left towards the 109s coming at me there would have been no danger. . . .

I looked behind and there appeared to be nothing behind the cockpit. . . . It was time to leave.[1]

In an acutely observant piece of descriptive writing, Douglas brings back to life the final stages of his tortuous descent after freeing himself from the plummeting aircraft, and after his artificial right leg had been severed from its harness:

Suddenly the hammering noise ceased. . . . I pulled the parachute release and then I was floating in the sunshine above broken white cloud. . . . I heard an aeroplane just after I passed through the cloud. A Me 109 flew past.

The ground below was the farm and grazing land of northern France. A man wearing a peaked ... railway porter's cap and a blue smock, carrying on his shoulders a yoke to which were attached two buckets, was opening a gate between two grass fields. A woman with a scarf over her head was with him.

As he opened the gate, he noticed me about 800 feet above and in front of him. They both remained motionless, staring. I then realized that my appearance was a bit odd. My right leg was no longer with me ... the leather belt which attached it to my body had broken under the strain, and the leg, the Spitfire, and I had all parted company.

But the left leg was still there; these good French peasants were watching a chap arriving in a parachute with one leg, the other missing, and with a torn trouser flapping in the breeze. I felt rather embarrassed. The last 200 feet of a parachute descent were deceptive in those days. Even after the hectic ... last hour, indeed perhaps because of [it], I was actually enjoying this quiet drifting earthwards. It was so restful after the shattering noise which had preceded it. Then – bang – the ground leapt up at me.

When I became conscious a minute or so later, two German soldiers were bending over me removing my parachute harness. They carried me to a car and took me to the hospital in St Omer. A lousy day indeed.[2]

The wing sensed that something must have befallen its leader. The assured voice, directing, urging, enthusing, provoking, which had dominated the RT exchanges in every operation was silent. Johnson

1. Douglas Bader, *Fight for the Sky* (Sidgwick & Jackson, 1973).
2. Ibid.

and Crowley-Milling, who had grown accustomed during the summer to the ceaseless commentary, cursing one moment and praising the next, and all the time stimulating morale and spirit, felt instinctively that the strand which had linked the squadrons together and maintained the cohesion had snapped.

The rallying point was no longer there. In the unreal silence, something seemed to be missing from the wing's life. At a stroke, its personality had been cut away. There was concern and doubt where, before, there had been bravado, thrust and dominion.

Thelma never thought they would lay their hands on her husband. He was indestructible, inviolable. She could barely absorb the shock of knowing that he hadn't returned.

The reality wrapped itself round the Bay House like a cocoon. For five days and nights, comforted only by their closeness, the two sisters kept their vigil, yielding nothing to their belief that Douglas *must* still be alive. The pilots came round to the house. But they were more like brothers looking and looking for the dear old family dog which had, suddenly, disappeared than bulwarks in a crisis.

Then Woody broke the news. Douglas was safe and a prisoner. Limp with relief, Thelma and Jill thought about food for the first time, it seemed, for five days. That evening, Stokoe, the missing wing leader's faithful batman, crossed, unhesitatingly, the sacrosant line of demarcation between the family cooking and his normal Service duties. A dinner of special choice, revealing a standard of culinary skill and selection seldom witnessed in wartime, was placed on the table. Having served the main dish in a style that would have done credit to Jeeves, Stokoe silently withdrew.

Thelma could scarcely credit it. 'There,' she exclaimed, like one who knows she's been conned, 'and to think Stokoe has been telling us all this time he couldn't cook!'

The legacy which Bader bequeathed through his leadership funded Johnnie Johnson's rise to the summit of European air fighting in the next two years. Dogmatic, all-prevailing, direct and, like his mentor, enthusiastically aggressive, Johnnie took his place, with his Kenley wing of Canadians, alongside the US Eighth Air Force's Don Blakeslee, the insatiable leader of the renowned Fourth Fighter Group. Between the two of them, in 1943 and 1944, they bestrode the continent as none other among their distinguished contemporaries was ever quite able to do.

Johnson saw Bader as the nonpareil:

... the wing leader par excellence, the unrivalled tactician, the man who knew it all – and was able to teach it all.

He had one thing that none of the others possessed. He had the time – and the patience – to sit down with the pilots, the junior officers and the sergeant pilots, and talk with them about tactics. He made them feel they all mattered, the junior men as much as the seniors.

He was older than the rest of us, so he probably felt interested in teaching the younger ones; maybe he even felt he had a *responsibility* to take us in hand and show us what he knew. He communicated.

Often he would say at the end of a talk: 'come on, come up with me and I'll show you how you can get up the arse of a 109.' He gave us everything; he never got bored with it; he always seemed to be fresh. And yet, he may, at the end of his fighting, have been getting very tired. More tired than he probably thought at the time.

To be asked to fly with Douglas was like getting the nod from JC [Jesus Christ].

When he'd gone, some of us buttoned on the mantle he had specially cut out for us to wear. But the void was always there. It was never filled in my time. . . .

Plainspoken words of another maestro.

Thirty-nine years on, the wagging finger moved deliberately across the heavy, pliable face and the big, round, dark eyes. It settled lightly on the sealed lips as if to preserve a secret. Then, looking round to make sure no one was within earshot, Adolf Galland confided in his listener.

'There was no collision,' he said, 'there was no collision. Douglas was shot down that day in 1941.' The finger wagged again to safeguard the confidence.

To the biographer in search of the truth, the conviction with which the opinion was expressed so long after the incident occurred was impressive, the authority undoubted. The journalist's probing mind couldn't resist the question. 'Is it', I asked, 'that you really think Douglas could have mistaken the noise and effects of direct hits by 20 mm cannon shells from a 109 for the impact of a collision with another aircraft?'

The finger traversed the face again like a windscreen wiper. The big round eyes closed; the head shook slowly from side to side to negative the question. 'There was no collision. He was shot down.'

Bader will always think he hit the second 109 to his right as he banked and turned towards it. It is, for him, the only feasible explanation of the feeling that the whole of the rear part of his aeroplane had been taken away. At the same time, however, the observation must be made that this was the identical sensation which Hugh Dundas described when he was shot down by a 109 in the Battle of Britain. Others have said the same.

JG 26 – Adolf Galland's Jagdgeschwader, or fighter wing, of nine squadrons, based at Abbeville but deployed on other airfields northwards in the Pas de Calais – had been, with its leader, in the thick of the morning's action. It had lost six aircraft in the engagement. Wissant, the Saint-Omer satellite, lying between Calais and Boulogne, had been the centre of most of the activity.

The figure of German losses tallies closely with the victories which 616 (and the whole Tangmere wing) claimed to have scored that day – five 109s destroyed, including one to Douglas's guns, and two more probably destroyed but not confirmed. Against this the wing had lost two – Bader and a flight commander, 'Buck' Casson, Dundas' opposite number in the South Yorkshire squadron.

So what is the conclusion of the matter? Was Bader, unbeknown to him, shot down by a German marksman in a 109 or did he, as he believes, collide with another aircraft? Extensive searches by air force historians have so far failed to provide irrefutable proof one way or the other. The author's own interrogation of most of the principal British pilots who took part in the fateful operation has produced no unchallengeable evidence upon which judgement can fairly be made. One recent happening in Australia has, however, given fresh stimulus to the speculation.

At the end of March 1981, Douglas was visiting Sydney with his wife to open the Schofield Air Show. There, by chance, he was introduced to a former Luftwaffe fighter pilot, Max Meyer, who has long been domiciled in the Dominion. Customary pleasantries were exchanged, but no more.

The following day Bader was astonished to read in the press an account of an interview which Meyer had given to an Australian journalist. In it he claimed that he was the Messerschmitt 109 pilot who had shot down the Tangmere wing leader over Northern France in 1941. He said, among other things, that after the attack he had followed the Spitfire down until eventually he saw the pilot bale out and his parachute open. He had mentioned none of this to Douglas.

Back in England a new probe of the Luftwaffe's available records was begun. One entry in an operational log immediately caught the eye. Between 11.25 and 11.30 in the morning of 9 August 1941, a 109 pilot entitled Oberfeldwebel (roughly the equivalent of flight sergeant in the Royal Air Force) Meyer of No. 6 Staffel (squadron) in Galland's wing, JG 26, had been credited with the destruction of a Spitfire 'in the region of St Omer'. The record further showed that this victory had been followed by another fifteen minutes later. At 11.45, a Leutnant Kosse, from the same wing but from 5 Staffel, had claimed another Spitfire 'confirmed destroyed' in the Saint-Omer area. It was Kosse's eighth victory; Meyer's was his eleventh.

Can Meyer's recent statement, therefore, be correct? Was he, in fact, the man who picked off the Tangmere wing leader on that traumatic August morning with a volley of cannon shells which, to Bader, produced the sensation of a collision. And was Leutnant Kosse the conqueror of Buck Casson, the 616 flight commander who was also lost that day? The timing was certainly right, for Douglas's wing had been airborne from Tangmere at 10.40. Moreover, the fact that Meyer reported that he had followed his victim down until his parachute had opened, seems to have some affinity with Bader's own account of his descent. '... I was floating in the sunshine above broken, white cloud ... I heard an aeroplane just after I passed through cloud. A Me 109 flew past. ...'

Yet two questions stand out stark and unanswered. Why, if Bader's Spitfire did fall to Meyer's guns, has it taken forty years to be revealed? And why, if this is the fact, did not the Luftwaffe emblazon the victor's name in capital letters across the western sky? The shooting down of the Royal Air Force's famous legless wing commander by an unknown sergeant pilot must surely have been the red meat of which Joseph Goebbels's propaganda stories were made. Dolfo Galland's cautionary finger remained pressed to closed lips.

There is a postscript to add to this perplexing affair. Frank Wootton's painting of the incident, *The Bader Bale Out*, which the artist generously presented to the RAF Benevolent Fund in 1979 for subsequent disposal, has since been sold to the National Air and Space Museum in Washington, DC, for £6000. The proceeds are being used to support the fund's Duke of Kent School near Ewhurst, in Sussex, where priority is given to children whose fathers have died or been killed while serving with the Royal Air Force.

By how much will the value of the painting now be enhanced by the riddle in which its theme is wrapped?

20
Fleming scenario

There was magic in the name of Saint-Omer. To the pilots of Fighter Command, operating with the medium bombers over northern France in 1941, 1942 and 1943, the place stood for a galaxy of emotions – challenge, excitement, opportunity, apprehension and doubt.

In the earlier days of the European offensive, before the arrival of the United States Eighth Air Force, with its Fortresses and Liberators, and its long-range fighter escorts, it was a principal lair of the Me 109s and, later, the FW 190s. And of Adolf Galland and his men.

On the shows to Lille, 75 miles inland from the sea, Saint-Omer was the thorn in the Allies' side. It was the hurdle which had to be passed – and repassed – midway between coast and target. It stood there, vigilant, like a sentinel, guarding access and hindering exit. Tension was always eased when Saint-Omer was put behind.

For Bader, the old town had a special meaning. It was here that his father had been in hospital after being wounded in the First World War; and it was here, three years after the armistice, while he was working with the War Graves Commission, that he had died. Douglas was eleven when they buried him in the local cemetery.

Maybe it was the spirit of his father burning within him; more likely it was the recognition that once his injuries and pains had subsided, and he was fit enough to leave hospital, the Germans would bundle him off to the Fatherland, thus reducing to a tittle any rational hope of escape.

Whatever the reason for his impulse, the events which followed read more like fiction than the reality of modern war.

His exhortation to visiting German pilots to have the cockpit and

193

remains of his crashed Spitfire searched for his missing right leg. Its discovery, and the perfect repair that was made of it by the craftsmen at the nearby airfield; the similarly expert mending of the broken – and vital – leather belt by which his artificial limbs are secured from the waist. The utter incredulity of his captors that such a combatant should actually exist.

Douglas's planning of the means of escape while his damaged right stump was causing weakening pain; and, to this end, the courage of the French girl, Lucille de Becker, a servant in the hospital, in establishing the outside contact with the Hiècque family who were to come to mean so much in his life.

The chivalry of the air – in war as in peace – that cuts right across battle lines; and Adolf Galland's personal initiative in inviting his Royal Air Force counterpart to high tea in the pilots' local mess. His subsequent reprimand by Goering because of it. ('It was bad for me.')

And then, in the blackness of an August night, Bader's escape from the window of his hospital ward, shinning painfully – with artificial legs dangling – down the 'rope' of knotted sheets, stripped from the beds and tied securely together.

The prearranged rendezvous with the agent, smoking a cigarette for identification; the clatter and torture of the walk along rough, unlit, silent streets to the Hiècques' home, hard by the canal; the stump, without the usual covering sock to protect it, made red and raw with friction and effort.

And then, just as he was awaiting the arrival, later that day, of the Hiècques' son-in-law through whom liberation would come, his unforeseen betrayal by Hélène Lefèvre, a hospital worker, for whom, extraordinarily, he was afterwards to harbour no grudge, vindictiveness, or malice – indeed, only compassion, understanding and humanity. His inevitable discovery among the straw in the shed at the bottom of the garden; the girl, sitting uncomfortably in the car as they drove him away; and his thoughts, not so much for himself and his future, but for the fate of the Hiècques – and Lucille – accomplices in the plot that failed. (He was not to know until the war's end that sentences of death by firing squad were commuted to life in a German concentration camp.)

And then, again, to cap it all, the signal, sent by the Germans to the British, requesting a spare right leg for Bader and, with it, the offer of a free passage for a Lysander to land and deliver it; and the Royal Air Force's belligerent response in dropping it by parachute from a Blenheim over Saint-Omer while *en route*, with an attacking force, to a target deeper inland.

The sequence might have been the scenario from an Ian Fleming novel rather than the real-life endeavour of a disabled officer in modern war.

Douglas's was a personal and individual plan of escape of which he was the principal author. It owed nothing to the sophisticated assistance and planning of the French Underground network. The pity was that the escaper was not aware that, during his five days in hospital, the resource, ingenuity and clandestine courage of the Organization was already being applied to the concept of rescue by stretcher and then by simulated ambulance, driven and manned by intrepid sympathizers.

On 21 August, twelve days after his wing leader had taken leave of his Spitfire, Denis Crowley-Milling had been shot down over Saint-Omer on the way back from a bomber escort mission to Lille. With his customary precision and judgement, he had contrived to put his aircraft down, wheels up, in a small, open field.

Intent on escape, he had moved quickly away from the Spitfire the moment he had undone his straps and harness and destroyed the secret contents. Walking hard until dusk, he had evaded the searching German patrols. Eventually, by devious means, he had made contact with the Fillerin family whose work as secret agents in the Pas de Calais region, under cover of their successful farming activities, filled an epic page in the continuing struggle between Teuton and Gaul.

Having lain hidden by the Fillerins for a week at their farm, Denis was passed on to M. Didery, another Underground agent, whose shoe and horseshoe business in Saint-Omer gave him legitimate reason for free movement among the farming community in an area where Fighter Command was becoming increasingly aggressive.

As he sheltered in M. Didery's flat, he heard of the elaborate plan which the Organization, led and masterminded by the Belgian, Dr Albert Guérisse, alias Lieutenant Commander Patrick O'Leary, had been devising for Douglas's escape from hospital, his subsequent passage down 'The Line' to the south, the crossing of the Pyrenees into Spain, and the journey home.

Alas, before the plot could be given a chance to succeed, the illustrious 'parcel', as the Underground referred to each of their human cargoes, had made his own abortive break and was on his way – legless – to Germany via ambulance to Brussels and then by train to Frankfurt. Crowley-Milling had been flying the close escort with his squadron when the canister containing Bader's spare leg had been dropped by the Blenheim and seen to float earthwards. He now received the attention which would have been accorded to his former wing leader had he been removed from the hospital.

Travelling with forged papers and in disguised dress, he survived a breathtaking catalogue of incidents. He had boarded the Lille-bound train with Didery, slipping the station guards, thence to be taken to a 'safe' house occupied by the notorious Paul Cole, the Army NCO who had been left behind by the British Expeditionary Force after the evacuation from France.

Cole had quickly fallen on his smart and nimble feet. Living in Lille with a French mistress whose husband was a prisoner in Germany, he had offered his services to the Underground and become dedicated to the hazardous process of escorting escaping aircrew down 'The Line' to southern France, stopping *en route* at hiding places in Paris and Toulouse.

Crowley-Milling turned out to be one of Cole's most successful 'parcels'. After reaching Spain, and surviving the unpleasant effects of gross malnutrition in a Spanish gaol, his release had then been secured by the British authorities who, with little delay, had found a passage for him back to the United Kingdom. Taking only the time which was needed to regain fitness, he was soon back again on operations leading, first, a Typhoon squadron and then a wing, and finishing the war as another of Bader's highly decorated and accomplished protégés.

Cole's astonishing deviousness and resource were to prove his undoing. Some while after passing Denis across the Spanish frontier, the ex-NCO was one day confronted by his mistress's husband who had returned unexpectedly to Lille from Germany. Learning of his wife's unfaithfulness and the nature of her lover's activities, he lost no time in leaking the news to the Germans. The Gestapo could usually spot a useful man when they saw one. Dangling enticing terms before him, the German secret police quickly found that Cole's principles in no way inhibited him from switching his allegiance and revealing to them many of the details of the Underground's intricate system and network. The consequences of his defection in terms of human suffering, misery, sacrifice and mortality were hideous in their brutality.

After the Normandy landings and the victorious sweep of the Allied armies through France, the Low Countries and into Germany, the traitor could see that he was backing a loser. No trouble, now, to deviate again, this time to the Americans who had the added advantage of being the best paymasters in the business. For the price of an irresistible quantity of US dollars, he was once more ready to divulge the enemy's secrets.

Such duplicity could not last, undetected, for ever. When his luck finally ran out after he had been compromised by the love of a mistress, it was a French police bullet which felled him and sent him to join hands in death with the Devil.

By an ironical twist, it was to the unyielding Albert Guérisse, released now from the horrors of Dachau, that the French authorities turned for identification of Cole's body as it lay, like cod at the fishmonger's, on the cold slab of a Paris mortuary. The Belgian doctor, maimed, bruised, beaten and humiliated by his torturers – but still totally unbroken – had no difficulty in fulfilling the task.

It is interesting to reflect that, had Bader known that the old firm of Guérisse, Fillerin, Didery & Co. were plotting his removal from the hospital at Saint-Omer and had they succeeded in their purpose, it would almost certainly have been to the hands of Paul Cole, former British Army NCO, that this rather special 'parcel' would have been entrusted for safe passage down 'The Line'. They would have made an incongruous pair.

Twenty-three years later, in 1964, Thelma and Douglas Bader went back to Saint-Omer for a ceremony which was unique in Anglo-French relations. The interim had brought its agonies and rejoicings.

After the awful years of captivity, Douglas had already had his reunion with Lucille de Becker and the Hiècques, then just returned from Germany after their own long sojourn in prison. He had landed at the United States Air Force base at Merville and asked the colonel if he might have the use of a jeep and a driver to take him to Saint-Omer. The first call was at the *gendarmerie* where he inquired of the Hiècques' present whereabouts. The officer on duty perfunctorily asked the group captain his name.

'Bader – Douglas Bader.'

The gendarme looked up as if he wasn't sure that what he had heard was true. There was a split-second, quizzical, almost disbelieving silence. Then, suddenly, the room seemed to fill and erupt.

'Le colonel! . . . Ah! Le colonel! . . . Le colonel!'

197

Within minutes, they were all round at the Hiècques'; the same house, by the same canal. The emotion was uncontrolled. 'There we were,' said Douglas, recalling the meeting, 'all embracing and kissing, and everyone blubbing. Madame was blubbing; I was blubbing; the gendarmes were blubbing. . . .'

Nine years on, when Danny Angel was making the film of *Reach for the Sky*, he flew Thelma over to Saint-Omer for the day to see the little northern French town, the hospital and the Hiècques' house by the canal. Madame, unfortunately, was away, visiting friends in Lille.

But now, on this May day in 1964, another ten years later, and twenty-three since the Escape that failed, everyone was there. It was Madame Hiècque's eightieth birthday. On this anniversary, and on the arm of 'le colonel', she was invested by the French authorities with the Légion d'Honneur. On this day, too, 'le colonel' received the honorary citizenship of a town which will ever be enshrined within the Bader story.

21
Betrayal

Is there such a person as a 'bad' prisoner of war? Come to that, does the being exist who can fairly be termed a 'good' prisoner of war? If the answers are yes, then, somewhere in the paradox, an attempt must be made to describe what is meant by 'bad' and 'good'.

It is the constitutional duty of Her Majesty's Opposition in the House of Commons to oppose. By a similar token, it is cast in the mould of military lore that an officer or NCO who is captured has a duty to escape; or, at any rate, to try to. It is not part of his ingrained discipline to settle down, get broody and become a complacent, acquiescent, docile captive who gives his captors an untroubled run.

How easy it is to say it; yet how many are there, when it really comes to it, who have the qualities to try to live up to, let alone to fulfil, such ideals? Not many.

Billy Malcolm (Lieut Colonel A. W. A. Malcolm), the senior British officer in the camp, Oflag VI B, at Warburg, near Cassel, for part of the war, an officer for whom Douglas developed a fine regard, had an acute perception of a prisoner of war's mentality and performance. He reckoned that, of the officers under his aegis, 20 per cent or so were normally engaged, directly or indirectly, in some form of escapist plot, pursuit or exercise. It is probably a higher percentage than some would expect, but, then, much will always depend on leadership, example and environment.

If by being a 'bad' prisoner it is meant that a man is for ever scheming schemes of escape, stirring things up in the camp, provoking others into action, being difficult, challenging, being insistent for his 'rights', and usually giving officers and guards no peace, then Bader must at once be said to have been scholarship material.

If, on the other hand, a 'good' prisoner is regarded as being one who resigns himself quietly to his lot, recognizes he is there for the duration of the war and nestles down to learning a worthwhile trade or profession, playing the game by the rules and giving no trouble, then Douglas was at the bottom of the class. Plumb, dead, bottom. Mute acquiescence was not his form. His temperament could never have become attuned to it.

From the moment he shinned down the wall of the hospital in Saint-Omer, to that fresh and brisk spring day in Colditz – Oflag IV C – more than three and a half years later, when the place was overrun by the United States First Army and its inmates set free, he made himself – deliberately – as his colleagues have tended to have it, 'a plain, bloody nuisance to the Germans'. It is as well to be clear about it. He never intended that it should be otherwise.

After he had been frustrated in his second, and only other really serious, attempt at escape – from Stalag Luft VIII B, at Lamsdorf, in August 1942 – Bader was summoned before the commandant. Having listened in silence to the reprimand, which included being told that he had defiled the honour of an officer by trying to escape in a private soldier's uniform, he turned to the interpreter: 'Tell the commandant', he said, 'that I have only two things to say in reply. One, it is my duty to cause as much trouble as possible, and, two, I am proud to wear the uniform of a British private soldier.'

It was the same intransigent stance he had adopted, and stuck to, about saluting German officers. The Germans wanted the British to salute all their officers, irrespective of rank. They required a wing commander, for instance, to salute a captain. Bader would have none of it. 'I will salute officers of equal rank and above, and no one else.'

And when, after his fifth stop along the prison line, they told him, inevitably, that he was bound by train for Colditz, the prisoner of war's ultimate institution, he played it equally hard. Through the interpreter, he made his demands known. 'I shall expect to travel first class and be accompanied by a batman and an officer of equal rank.'

He suspected that the interpreter, who was clearly embarrassed at having to pass on a seemingly endless series of persistent requests, was probably a bit on his side. With the trace of a smile on his face, he relayed the commandant's response. 'He says he would be ready to meet all your points but he wants you to know he is the only officer here of equal rank. And he has got other things to do.'

Douglas felt that was one he could concede.

*

The criticism that Bader brought down on his head from some of his fellow prisoners of war was vehement and deep-seated. Some of it endures to this day. The belief was held – is still held – that he overplayed his hand at being, as they put it, 'the really difficult bugger in the camp', the one who was never happier than when he was 'Kraut-bashing' or 'Goon-baiting', the Royal Air Force officer who gave the impression to the less belligerent, but able-bodied, captives that if they weren't trying to escape, or seeking the means of doing so, or otherwise turning things upside down, they weren't doing their duty or had gone 'soft'; the extrovert exhibitionist who chucked snowballs unnecessarily at the German officers, whose persistent provocation of the Germans put them on the alert and, unwittingly, actually thwarted plans of escape; the wing commander whose schoolboy baiting of the enemy and 'futile' attempts at escape were a show and a charade which served only to make an intolerable life 'worse for the others than it need otherwise have been'. It's a rough indictment.

It is important, nevertheless, to say that, out of the six German establishments in which he was held during his imprisonment, there was only one where the criticism was not heard: Colditz, the menacing floodlit castle on high ground, jutting out into a river, the prison camp, 30 miles from Leipzig, from where Airey Neave escaped, but which very, very few others ever tried to leave. (There was no tunnelling at Colditz, unlike Stalag Luft III, at Sagan, the 'Wooden Horse' camp where Pat Ward-Thomas, the *Guardian* journalist, and others built a small golf course and manufactured their own golf balls and clubs; where Douglas was 'entertained' by the Germans for three months, until they became exasperated with his behaviour.) Colditz, the camp populated by 400 hard-liners, Polish, Dutch, British, Czech and French, the unyielding, troublesome ones, the *corps d'élite* of the Allied prisoners of war, the dedicated anti-Germans. The men who gathered within its feet-thick, impregnable walls were plumed with strikers' feathers. They were the marauders, the hawks, the eagles and falcons. The doves did not consort with such company.

Having once arrived there, on 18 August 1942, Bader knew that the chances of anyone, least of all himself, finding freedom again were virtually nil. Colditz was a cul-de-sac, the end of the road. And yet, in the two years and eight months he spent there until 15 April 1945, the morale and the spirit never flagged. It was always simmering away just below boiling point.

We were all together in Colditz. We combined together, that was the point. We were wholly anti-German and dedicated to it. Unlike the other camps, there were very few new arrivals, new recruits who had just been shot down, to bring in the news. We were, mostly, long-standing prisoners, united by the concept of escape, even if it couldn't be effective, and by the resolve to challenge. That was the reason for our being there and that's why we all combined so well.

He was not, as things go in prison, uncomfortable, and he had the unspeakable advantage of the comradeship of his stalwart friend Peter Dollar (Lieut Colonel Peter Dollar) to sustain his spirit. The walks which the Germans let them take together maintained physical shape and kept the stumps of his legs in tolerable condition.

Mental illness in Colditz, despite the isolation and lack of chance of escape, was rare to non-existent. 'It was almost unheard of; but if anyone ever went out of his mind, it was always because there had been a weakness there before; not because of anything that happened in Colditz.'

Repatriation was raised with Douglas while he was there and the chance offered to go before a Swiss Commission. He rejected it out of hand. Repatriated prisoners of war could not fight again. That would never do for him. And when eventually the Americans freed Colditz in mid-April 1945, while the European war was still being waged, he eschewed again – and totally – any suggestion of a hearing before the commission. 'I had not been wounded in war. I was never prepared to be repatriated.'

Bader's critics in the earlier camps were more frequently those who had already spent a year and more 'in the bag' as captives before he arrived. Some had been shot down in the first months of the war; others had been taken prisoner in 1940 at Calais or at the time of Dunkirk. They had settled down to their occupations and interests; with all Europe subjugated and crushed under the Nazi boot, the Germans were telling them that in no time they'd be home with their families.

When Douglas breezed in in the early autumn of 1941, he brought an entirely different message. The Battle of Britain had been won – resoundingly; Hitler had committed the most expensive blunder of his infamous career by attacking Russia; the United States was becoming more and more involved in support of the British cause. We couldn't now lose. He was convinced that we would win and said so.

The syndrome that he represented was at variance with what he found. The two, in a way, were incompatible – even irreconcilable. The older and more senior of the prisoners were, to say the least, sceptical. The younger among them were entranced with the re-markable apparition that had just entered. Here was someone whom they could take to and admire. If he, with his two tin pins, his rolling gait, his bravado and brashness, could stir things up in the camp, why shouldn't they? When he stomped about the place, setting the Germans by the ears, they thought it an engaging pastime and wanted to join in.

The divergent attitudes, and the potential fissures which could open, were plain to see. But Bader has always aroused intensely held, conflicting emotions – blind allegiance, devotion, support and faith, and, then again, controversy, debate, argument, intemperance and censure. There's seldom much middle ground; there certainly wasn't in the earlier prison years. Usually the balance was tilted, definitively, towards one side or the other.

Two features in those incongruous years were laid bare. The first, although few then would have understood it, left him denuded. It was probably the root cause of much of his restlessness. The second was a God-given blessing which acted as a shield against imprison-ment and the months of boredom.

Douglas, for his balance, needs to have authority, responsibility and command. There must be something and someone to look after – to tend, to mould, to harangue, to direct and, goodnaturedly, to castigate. Whether, as in the Service, it was a flight, a squadron, a wing or a sector, or, in civilian life, a fleet of aeroplanes or a company to run, made small difference: whatever and wherever it was he needed to have 'his show', 'his baby', something that he felt could be made better than its competitors. Whether it actually *became* superior to the rest was immaterial; what mattered was that he should *feel* that he had something he could lift above its counterparts elsewhere.

In prison, all this was missing. He was, in a sense, a bystander, a commentator, a critic of things over which he had little or no control. He was a freelance, beholden to few (certainly not to the Germans) but himself. It gave the effect of a sort of no-man's-land. It was unnatural. It wasn't his role. For those who really know Bader, it accounts for much of what was criticized.

The other attribute was to compensate for the rest. He could well have felt, after all that had gone before, that the Almighty had treated him scurvily. Having climbed back from disaster; having succeeded against all the odds; having confounded expectations; and, having conquered as few mortals could ever have done, then to be hurled down to the ground again, even into a prison cell, in a mocking, heartless gesture of retaliation, must surely have been enough to drench him in self-pity. But Bader has never seen things that way.

I have never thought of myself as a disabled person, as being different from ordinary people, or physically worse off than others.

I lost my legs as a result of an accident which was *my fault*. That's the point. If someone else had been responsible for it through being a silly clot, that would have been different. But it wasn't like that. It was *my fault*. I was to blame. So I've never had any regrets – except to miss the possible chance to play rugger for England. But even that was a transient thing.

I knew I had been responsible for it all and I had to learn to make do with what I'd got.

It was the rider that supplied the emphasis: 'I have never thought *backwards*. That is the point.'

The poet could not have found a more telling example to prove his theme:

> To mourn a mischief that is past and gone
> Is the next way to draw new mischief on.

Kenneth More tells a story which sketches in clear relief the intensity of some of the feelings that Douglas's performances in prison provoked.

In the middle and late 1950s, after his captivating portrayal of Bader in the film *Reach for the Sky,* he found invitations pouring in from Royal Air Force messes all over the country to pay visits for one function or another. He went to a Battle of Britain lunch at the station at Andover, a well-dressed affair, with the girls all got up in their best frocks and new hats. The CO sounded Kenny in the middle of it. 'I take it you'll be ready to say a few words? They'll all be expecting it.'

The reticent murmur of acceptance stimulated another question. 'Any idea at all what you'll talk about?'

'Well,' said Kenny, 'I thought, perhaps, they might enjoy a story or two about Douglas Bad—'

'Christ!' interjected the CO, before the sentence was finished. 'Don't mention that bastard's name in this mess.'

'What!' parried the guest of honour, rocked by the reaction. 'Do you mean . . . ?'

The CO, uninterested in the response, was picking out officers in the room. 'See him at the end of the table? He was in the "bag" with Bader. So was he . . . and he . . . and he. They kept losing their fucking Red Cross parcels because he was always trying to escape and annoying the Germans. Bloody silly.'

'And so', said Kenny, years afterwards, 'my speech went out of the window.'

Douglas knew better than anyone that once he was inside Germany the opportunity to get away could only be minimal. Even so, his attempt to escape with Johnny Palmer, the flight lieutenant air gunner, and three others from Stalag Luft VIII B, the large troop camp at Lamsdorf, in August 1942, was a serious, practical and carefully planned affair. But for a piece of unpredictable misfortune, it could well have succeeded.

Dressed as a private soldier, Bader, with Palmer and the other three escapists, had joined one of the working parties which the Germans used to send out, from the base camp, to the small cages in the region. By this means they had reached the hutted camp at Gleiwitz on the Polish frontier. Once they were across the border into Poland, an altogether new vista would open. Not too difficult then, they thought, to find help from the fervently patriotic Poles. Success beckoned.

At that moment, with hopes mounting on a flood tide, fate snarled at Bader a second time. Hélène had betrayed him, against all expectations, when he had almost got away in Saint-Omer. Now, in a 10,000-to-1 shot, a young Luftwaffe fighter pilot from Abbeville, in France, whose squadron had been mixing it all the summer with its rivals in the Tangmere wing, happened to be visiting Lamsdorf. He heard Bader was a prisoner in the local camp. Why not go round, he thought, and swop a few experiences with 'Herr Ving Commander'? The prospect for a fascinated, enthusiastically keen young officer must have seemed irresistible. There never would be another chance like it!

The guards facilitated his passage and directed him to the sick quarters, to the hut and to the room which Douglas was sharing with Johnny Palmer, who had damaged a foot when his aircraft had been shot down. In his disciplined way, the pilot knocked politely on the door. There was no reply. The room was empty. Where was 'Herr Ving Commander' and his companion? Greatly disappointed, he asked the guards if they were out. The alarm was raised.

The search traced its methodical way from one lead to another until, eventually, it settled on the working party up at Gleiwitz on the frontier. While the other three in the elusive quintet slipped over the border (one, ultimately, to secure his freedom, the other two to be recaptured and shot), Bader and Palmer were tracked down and brought back to Lamsdorf. But not before the German police had gone to the incredible length of circulating among their regional offices a leaflet revealing, in potted detail, the features of the two 'englische Fliegeroffiziere' for whom they had been energetically hunting. It is barely conceivable that, in all seriousness, they should have thought to circulate a confidential leaflet describing the physical characteristics of a *legless*, escaped prisoner of war! The enemy's security could hardly have had to stomach greater ignominy.

More than twenty years were to pass before Douglas saw a copy of this strange document. It was sent to him, without notice, by a former Belgian civilian prisoner who, at the time, was performing menial tasks in the Gestapo's offices in Leipzig. He had picked it up from a desk and hidden it away among his belongings. It contained a compliment which, in its most liberal translation, struck Bader's fancy. All those years on, it almost seemed to make frustrated escape worthwhile. 'Walks well without a stick.' They might have added that he has never used one in his life.

22
Decision

April in Paris, 1945; the late afternoon. An American airfield near the French capital, the headquarters base of a US Army Air Force communications network. DC 3s and other transport aircraft parked on the tarmac; continuous take-offs and landings; bustle and activity in support of the Allied armies now waging the last weeks of war. Douglas Bader, first away from Colditz, has just flown in in a small Beechcraft Expediter. With the formalities over, an aide takes him to the officers' mess. The commanding general, in informal greeting, holds out a hand of welcome and introduction: 'Doug, General Macdonald. We're sure glad to see you. There's a long-distance call waiting for you in the next room. Perhaps you would care to take it?'

It was Thelma and the first spoken exchange which the two had had for three and a half years. Douglas was stunned by the link-up. In a spontaneously warm and human stroke, the Americans had set up the connection. It might have been lifted from a Hollywood film set. The returning captive had never met the general or anyone else on the airfield before. They were all strangers to him. And yet, within an hour of his landing, they had located Thelma in the family home at Ascot, 25 miles or so from London, and called her to the telephone. In years of Anglo-American relations, Douglas was to enjoy many instances of the Americans' capacity for friendship; but none cut a deeper mark upon his mind than this first step in the act of reunion. It was all done without drama, as a mere item in the day's work – like getting one of the pilots to take a letter over to England with him and post it to Thelma.

Homecoming, for those who had had to endure long periods of separation, was often disturbing. There was a great need of quiet rehabilitation. For Bader, with the public gaze fastened upon him, the difficulties were compounded. The comparison made Colditz seem like a secluded European watering spa for the retired and the aged.

To feel, suddenly, the concentrated attention of the media after the isolation and immunity of the old medieval castle, was like facing the arc lights in a television studio. As an aircraft, caught in the beam of the searchlights on a moonless night, turns and twists and dives for the protective armour of darkness, so Douglas employed all the arts of manoeuvre to avoid the public glare.

Reporters, doing their duty for their newspapers, held the family home under seige, keeping up their round-the-clock vigil in anticipation of the legend's return. Thelma, anxious for her husband's well-being, gardened – and kept her balance and humour with the press.

'Here,' she said with a chuckle, handing a hoe to the newsmen who were hanging about the drive 'why not take this and come and do some weeding?'

After the two had been reunited, there was no question of an undisturbed, unmolested existence. The contrast with the life each had been living blared out at them like the music from a fairground on a summer's evening. Nothing, it seemed, could still the strident noise of the hurdy-gurdies. It was a taxing and exacting transition, the antithesis of what they had hoped for and needed.

For one of Bader's temperament, it was just the wrong kind of therapy after the prison years. Normally impatient and swift to react, the effect was to exacerbate his impatience and restlessness. In the mellow afterglow of later life, when the balm of achievement, recognition and acclaim has soothed the nerve-ends, and strife is diluted, it is easy to forget that this was a period of real difficulty. It was a time when Douglas was at his most sensitive and turbulent, even beyond his own customary habit.

In every outstanding career, there are the peaks and the troughs, the mountain tops and the cold, deep caverns lying down below. Life seldom walks an uninterrupted upward path. In the Bader years, the time in prison, and its aftermath, was the low ground over which greatness towered; the period when he was easily put out by small things of little consequence, when the familiar bonhomie, breeziness and guffaws could not always temper the irritability.

Dean Acheson, the United States' Secretary of State, had yet to utter his famous critique, 'Britain has lost an Empire but not yet found a role.' But there was probably something of this in Bader's life as war turned into peace and the civilian climb back began.

Meanwhile Thelma, with her balance and judgement, compre-
hended completely the vagaries of her husband. Her wisdom told her
when to be silent; when to persuade – and dissuade; when to support
– totally; when to be firm and when to yield; and when, simply, to
let things be. Her philosophy was in tune with the preacher's: 'To
everything there is a season, and a time to every purpose under the
heaven.'

For the returning son, there was now one purpose 'under the heaven'
which must quickly be fulfilled.

He had to decide where his future lay. Should it be with the Service
of his choice to which he was naturally drawn and for which he
would always reserve so much loyalty? Or should it rest once more
with the Shell Company with which he felt compelling ties? Or,
again, should it be, as Peter Macdonald was strongly urging, in
public life – partly in the House of Commons and partly in the
business field.

He did not, as some did in their lives, agonize over the alternatives.
He went, instead, straight to his conclusions with characteristic directness and zeal. And when he had made up his mind, he would
harbour no doubts, no second thoughts about whether he had acted
wisely; once a decision had been taken, that was the end of it.

He had, in fact, virtually made up his mind by the time he left
Colditz. One consideration had motivated him beyond all the rest.
Because of his legs, he would never be given an unrestricted medical
category in peacetime. He would not be able to serve in hot countries,
a necessary prerequisite of future command and promotion. The
stumps of his legs, with liberal daily applications of Johnson's baby
powder and knitted socks to protect them from chafing, could stand
short sojourns in great heat and humidity; but continuous service for
a couple of years would be out of the question; perspiration and
soreness – and worse – would, he knew, go hand in hand. A restricted
category would bar his way to the top. Unless he felt he had as good
a chance as the next man of reaching the summit, or something very
near it, he did not wish to stay.

There was, moreover, a subsidiary consideration. Leigh-Mallory
was dead – killed, with his wife, only months before in a disastrous
air crash in France. As the Allied Air Commander, and with his
wartime record and seniority, his power of influence over Douglas
and his destiny would have been very great in the next years. It helps

in the Service to have a senior and distinguished guardian angel watching over you. In L-M's mind, the successes at Duxford and Tangmere would never have been far away. They would have been there, like reminding signposts, pointing his protégé's way. Dermot Boyle, now the air officer commanding 11 Group, was as close to Douglas as anyone in the Service; and probably closer. But not even his clear-headed persuasion could deflect his subordinate from his resolve.

There remained the other two alternatives – a return to Shell or a new start in public life. Macdonald, a Tory knight by this time, and a man of considerable influence, was tugging hard at him to enter politics. A long-serving member and well placed to 'suggest and represent', Peter knew that the safe seat of Blackpool South was vacant and that, if Bader would offer himself, he was a certainty to secure the Conservative nomination.

Next door, in Blackpool North, Jack Roland Robinson, a wartime wing commander in the Royal Air Force, had been the sitting member since 1931. He put his weight behind Macdonald in an effort to coax Douglas to stand. Married to a Woolworth heiress, Jack Robinson was a personable and popular member of the Tory party, and dedicated to Churchill's leadership. With Robinson and Macdonald behind him, the way was open to a seat in the House of Commons for life.

Denis Crowley-Milling recalls an evening spent in Robinson's Hampstead home. Between the host and his parliamentary colleague the weight of all the arguments was invoked to turn Douglas towards their way of thinking. With his name, standing and ability, the prospects were limitless. . . .

Bader was not to be moved. The more he thought about it the less he wanted it. Highly decorated war heroes were, he felt, being used quite brazenly by the three political parties, not for their acumen and potential, but for their glamour and electoral appeal. He wasn't going to lay himself open to that kind of charge. There was, however, a more cogent, personal factor. The House of Commons did not hold for him the same appeal that it exercised over his contemporaries who had already decided to stand. He doubted whether his temperament and style would be suited to political life.

Beyond this, the Shell Company, to which he knew himself to be increasingly drawn, would not countenance a full-time member of the staff – director, executive, manager or anything else – combining his responsibilities with those of a member of parliament. It was the job or nothing. There was no middle way.

And so, having discarded the other options, Bader plumped again for Shell, the company which, thirteen years before, had been ready to take him on and give him a chance – aged twenty-three, legless and untrained – at £200 a year. It certainly wasn't the money that moved him. A restarting salary of £1250 a year was far below what other companies had offered him to join them. It went much deeper than that. For one thing, there was his innate loyalty to an organization which had stuck by him when the going was very rough, when the Service had been obliged to discard him.

But there was something more. He remembered again now the little incident when, soon after marrying Thelma, he found his finances were so stretched that he had had to ask the company if he could borrow £50. It was the reaction which had become riveted in his mind: 'How will you pay it back?' Not when or why or any of half a dozen other questions which might have been asked.

There was another compelling consideration. With Shell, he would be able to keep up his flying and maintain his interest in aviation. There would be a light aircraft ('I have always been a light aeroplane man') in which to fly himself – and sometimes Thelma – about the world. Flying would remain, for years to come, the one thing which, with his disability, he could still do better and more easily than anything else, even than driving a motor car. It was made for him, and he for it.

Bader had the inside of a year to play out before he retired a second time from the Service and rejoined Shell in St Helen's Court in the City. Richard Atcherley (Air Marshal Sir Richard Atcherley), 'Batchy' to the Royal Air Force, a Schneider Trophy pilot and one of the most brilliant of his generation, was commanding the Central Fighter Establishment at Tangmere. He and Douglas had been officers together in 23 Squadron at Kenley in 1930. Now an air commodore, he was able to offer the former Tangmere wing leader the job of running the Fighter Leaders' School arm of the establishment. It was a group captain's post.

It was, as things turned out, an unwittingly mistaken appointment. In the three and a half years that Bader had been away, the role of the fighter aircraft had broadened massively in character and extent, embracing ground attack and tactical support of various kinds in co-operation with the land forces. A new breed of highly decorated and widely experienced wing and squadron leaders had emerged.

These officers were exhausted after four years or so of almost continuous fighting in Europe, the desert and North Africa. They and Bader, who was freshly returned to flying, were far apart in their attitudes. *They* thought he was completely out of date; *he* thought they should get off their backsides and do more flying. It was a short-lived and unhappy time which Robb (Air Chief Marshal Sir James Robb), the C-in-C, quickly resolved by offering Douglas command of the North Weald sector of 11 Group, an area steeped in Fighter Command and Battle of Britain history. This was red meat to a former wing leader.

Before he left Tangmere, Bader had played a limited but widely publicized part in the general election of 1945. Invitations poured in from candidates all over the country asking him to speak in their support. After Churchill and a few other Cabinet ministers, he was the strongest draw of the campaign, appealing, as he did, to the voters as a whole, irrespective of party.

At the meetings he addressed for his friend, Henry Longhurst, in Acton, in West London, and for the author in West Fulham, half an hour from Westminster, the police insisted that the doors of the halls be closed well before the start. Outside the school where he spoke in Fulham, overflow crowds packed the playground hoping to catch a glimpse of the 'legless hero' as he arrived or left. Inside, a strong and colourful Royal Air Force contingent gave the group captain close, and much-needed, escort against a heckler who started bombarding the chair with repeated points of order as soon as Douglas rose to speak. Holding a copy of King's Regulations in one hand and stabbing an accusing forefinger at the speaker with the other, he launched into a series of interventions. He stopped the show.

'What I want to know', he asked, 'is what right has the speaker to be appearing on that platform tonight? It's forbidden in Army orders' ('he's in the Air Force, mate') 'for servicemen to take part in political meetings. How does he square that with King's Regulations?'

In the hullabaloo that followed, one fact became plain. The chairman knew nothing whatever about King's Regulations. It was questionable whether he had ever heard of them. Douglas eventually came to his rescue with a characteristically spirited retort. Amid rousing applause, he could just be heard saying: 'I don't know about

Army Council Instructions' ('you can say that again, brother'); 'I'm in the Royal Air Force' (prolonged cheering). 'But I can tell you I have had official permission to speak here tonight.'

The next day, as the headlines leapt out of the national newspapers – 'Bader howled down'; 'Bader on election "ops" ' – Whitehall issued stringent instructions about serving officers taking part in the election. But not before Bader had made another national mark.

North Weald was an agreeable valediction to his time in the Royal Air Force. Here, surrounded by fighter squadrons on familiar-sounding stations, and with old friends like Al Deere (Air Commodore A. C. Deere), the irrepressible New Zealander, and the Irishman, Tim Vigors, close at hand, he saw out the innings. It was a comfortable environment, exactly to his taste.

Nothing much more serious than the first post-war Battle of Britain fly-past was at stake. Then, on a day of poor weather and low cloud, Robb, the C-in-C, had turned to Boyle, the 11 Group commander, as they stood on the tarmac with Bader, awaiting zero hour for a decision. 'I think we must leave it to Group Captain Bader to decide whether to go or call it off.'

Douglas, knowing that the rest of the squadrons and wings would already be building up over East Anglia, getting themselves into position for the run in across London, gave his instant answer. 'We're on, sir.' With that, he hauled himself up on to the wing of his Spitfire, slung his leg over the side of the cockpit, fixed his straps and set the engine going.

As he taxied out for the take-off, with an all-star cast of actors packing in around him, he reflected that this would be the last time he would lead a great fighter formation in the Royal Air Force.

When the time came to leave, there was no remorse, no nostalgia, no 'sweet sorrow' in the parting. He had felt, deep down, in Colditz that he really should retire. 'It had become as clear as a bell to me that it was right to leave.'

The break, then, when it came, had been premeditated. It was clean and completely decisive. He did not allow himself so much as one last, lingering look over the shoulder. 'I have never thought *backwards*. That is the point.'

23

Second innings

Walter Hill was still managing the aviation department when Bader returned to Shell in July 1946 to begin his second stint with the company. Hill's business acumen and ability as a manager were undoubted. His record in building up the department from scratch and expanding it into a significant marketing enterprise proved it beyond question. He was precise, particular and acute. He picked his staff astutely, gathered around him men of diverse talents, and seldom made a mistake about personnel.

But Hill was a very difficult man. He did not endear himself to his colleagues, although none would deny his skills. He was possessive with his staff. Having once got a good man, he saw to it that he kept him and was loath to recommend him for higher things. It was an understandable weakness in his armoury. He could not be said to be the selectors' choice as the ideal manager for Bader. But he was an accomplished practitioner; work was his play.

Douglas's relationship with him took on something of a contested neutrality; but there is little doubt that Hill saw in his subordinate, even in the early days, a character of arresting colour. After the war, he knew very well he had in him an instrument by which the doors of the most secure business strongrooms could be unlocked. In the aviation department's area of interest, there were few men of influence whom Bader didn't know or, through trusted intermediaries, could not reach. Although, in those post-war times, he could be abrupt and intolerant, he possessed an individual appeal and renown which none in the company, let alone the aviation department, could rival. When he chose to use them, Douglas's winning ways were irresistible. Hill was smart enough to see it. Being himself cast in an opposite mould, he could readily discern the attractions. It stands greatly to his credit that he allowed Bader full rein, avoiding tying him to a specific appointment but rather letting him have his head, improvise and play things his way. It was a latitude of which the returned group captain took total advantage.

It was a benefit both to Hill and to Bader that Roy Snodgrass, having been released from the Army in the latter part of 1945, should have returned to the department in that year. He was well into the swim of the administrative chores by the time Douglas made his post-war entrance and opened his second innings with Shell.

The Bader–Snodgrass relationship, slow, initially, to flower because of the blatantly opposite characters of the two men, was, in later years, to become the axis around which some unpredictably bizarre events and incidents were to spin. It was to endure for the next twenty-three years until 1969, when Douglas, at the age of fifty-nine, retired from the organization and Snoddy stepped into his chair as the managing director of the group's aircraft company.

The association rested on a golden plinth. Snodgrass complemented to the letter his colleague's independent, nonconformist style. He had the humour which allowed him to accept phlegmatically Bader's rare and unprogrammed approach to the discharge of business. Nothing that his number 1 did – even the most unexpectedly wayward actions – ever disturbed him or threw him off balance. He was ready for anything, surprised by nothing. But, when the inevitable moments of hidden bafflement did arise, there was always an infectious preparedness to laugh at the latest departure from accepted custom and practice.

Snodgrass's accounts of their early overseas flights and visits would lack credibility if they were told by a less nakedly honest mind. The minute detail with which they are invested adds to the picturesqueness of the tales. The modesty of approach and the deliberate tendency to underplay only enriches the record. Jealousy and envy found no place in Snoddy's soul. If, in later years, his role became increasingly that of the minder of the shop, looking after the admin. and the paperwork, while Bader moved about and had his being abroad, he accepted it with equanimity and grace as his part of the deal. He appreciated that he was playing alongside a unique eccentric.

He possessed, moreover, the faculty to interpret the exigencies of Douglas's mind. He was one of the very few people (Crowley-Milling, outside Shell, was another) who could accommodate his opinionated directness and reflect a contrary view – and even influence him with it – without huffing and puffing, provoking argument and, quite possibly, encouraging rejection. If Snoddy took a decision in his colleague's absence, acted upon it, and then, on reflection, began to have second thoughts about its wisdom, Douglas would be vehement in his defence. 'No, you weren't mistaken,' he would say. 'In any case never admit a mistake; never say that you were wrong. Even if I disagreed with your policy and action, I would still back you 100 per cent.'

Bader's loyalty to those who worked with him, and for him, was as intense as his support of the company which employed him. He was the bull to end all bulls of Shell. There wasn't, in his eyes, another multinational company like it. The rest, by comparison, were selling platers – just like other people's wings and squadrons used to be in the Royal Air Force in wartime.

Bader's first ten or a dozen post-war years with the company made up a period of kaleidoscopic change – and intermittent frustration. His temperament demanded that the pace be forced. Pause was not for him. He wanted to push on to the next stage before the fruits of the last advance had been picked. Nor was his frustration mitigated by the speed of Shell's post-war build-up after the lacerations and convulsions of the global conflict. It was a hard-won and, at times, tortuous recovery. The financial pressures upon the company, in the United Kingdom and far outside, which the group's astonishing growth over the next four decades was to render incomprehensible in retrospect, were contained by the support of the banks. These were the ramparts and the bulwarks against which the currently adverse economic forces were pounding in vain. It is a long-forgotten period in the fight back, recovery and rise of a great multinational organization.

Two events in the earlier post-war years did something to quench Douglas's thirst for authority, responsibility and change.

His flying, on behalf of the company, across much of the world in the tiny single-engine Hunting Percival Proctor V, with its limited aids, cruising speed of 120 m.p.h. and duration of about five hours, became an enveloping interest. Occasionally Snodgrass went with him; more often it was Hugh Miller, the engineer, who took his skills with him into the Royal Navy in wartime; and now and then it was Thelma. Bader's responsibilities in those days were concerned primarily with the refuelling arrangements on the airfields, the design and provision of equipment – mobile and static – and the means by which customers' aeroplanes had the company's 'gravy' pumped into their tanks.

In the late summer of 1946, between 15 August and 16 September, Shell, in a well-conceived public-relations exercise, sent Bader and his friend Jimmy Doolittle (General James Doolittle), the United States' famed leader of the Tokyo raid, on a goodwill tour of Europe and North Africa – fertile country in the great Anglo-American theme. Why it elected that it should be done in the little Proctor is obscure. 'Rather fun, old boy, the "legless ass" ' (Douglas's mocking epithet for himself, taken from the French 'l'as britannique' – 'the British ace') 'and just about the best driver in America, planted in the passenger seat beside him, reading the map.' There was something curiously captivating and incongruous about these two remarkable and highly decorated Shell employees, sitting side by side in a diminutive single-engine 'pisser', with no aids worth speaking of, a rudimentary radio and fixed undercarriage protruding below, carrying the name and prestige of the company to a few of the capitals of Europe and the Near-Eastern Arab world.

The itinerary had a stirringly historic ring about it – Hanworth, Lympne, Le Touquet, Orly, Le Bourget, Lyon, Marseille, Nice, Rome, Cagliari, Tunis, Gabes, Tripoli, Benghazi, Tobruk, Cairo and then back again including Bone, Algiers, Oran, Tangier, Casablanca, Gibraltar, Lisbon, Madrid, Bordeaux and Paris. Against the last hop of an hour and a half from Paris to Lympne there appears in Bader's hand in his log-book a deadpan statement of flying fact: 'Exceptionally bad weather over the Channel.' It cloaks an anxious experience.

The route forecast from Le Bourget was poor, low cloud, raining, forward visibility barely 1000 yards. But, with the Proctor and its slow speeds and scope for manoeuvre, it was manageable. Doolittle, having now had fifty and more flying hours with Douglas, had sized up his worth and was quite happy to go. As they crossed the coast at Cap Gris-Nez, the conditions quickly got worse, with a lowering cloud base down to 200 or 300 feet over the water. Douglas spoke his thoughts to his distinguished passenger. 'It doesn't look too good, Jimmy. I think I'll just nip back to Le Touquet and get a check on what it's like across the Channel and over the other side.'

'Hell,' said the general, 'get yer belly down on the water.'

They crawled into Lympne to find a posse of pilots and aircraft waiting for the weather to lift to cross over to France. Doolittle played on their disbelief. 'What are you guys waiting for? We just came across, didn't we?'

With that, the two of them got into the Proctor, took off and made their confident way up the east–west railway line between Ashford and Tonbridge, the traditional bad-weather route that the old Imperial Airways pilots used to follow into Croydon. They called it the Iron Dog. Bader knew it by heart from other days. 'You take the second branch line to the right, straight up through the valley, and there's Croydon right ahead. We used to do it as pilot officers in Gamecocks at Kenley in 1930.'

Only a week elapsed before Snodgrass followed Doolittle into the passenger seat of the Proctor, sitting beside Douglas on an overseas trip. The Danes were holding an air display at Aalborg, 80 minutes' flying time away from Copenhagen. The Shell representatives in Denmark had suggested to Hill that the company should have a presence from London at the rally.

The weather could hardly have been worse. It was the usual recipe – low cloud, rain, poor visibility. Both at Hanworth, to the south-west of London, where the Proctor was kept and serviced, and at Lympne, the customs clearance point for the continent, the airfield controllers remonstrated vigorously against take-off. Undeterred, Douglas pressed on. Such was his confidence now in the air that, without ever taking undue risks – or risks which could not be carefully calculated – it required overwhelmingly adverse conditions to stop him if he had a will to go.

Conditions across the Channel were as bad as expected. Up through France, Belgium and into Holland, the story was the same; if anything, worse. Thirty-five years on, the detail and circumstances are still fixed, diamond sharp, in Snoddy's memory. 'As we flew on, north-east, Douglas circled each airfield that we passed, getting a check on the weather at the next one and making sure it was still open. It was like playing musical chairs. We must have orbited a dozen airfields before we reached northern Holland.'

Having made a couple of circuits of the airport at Groningen, 25 miles from the German frontier, Douglas decided to put down. After a brief stop and with the weather lifting a little, the Proctor was off again, heading north-east for the Danish capital. To the east, the light began to fade. Out came the Shell sunrise and sunset chart which, in the inter-war years, Snodgrass had been responsible for producing. 'I wasn't too sure,' he said, 'that Douglas quite knew how it worked!' A brief perusal confirmed that the blackness of night would soon be upon them. 130 miles to the east, just over an hour's flying time away, lay Hamburg. 'That's where we're going,' said Douglas, with characteristic decision.

As they circled the airfield, one red Verey light after another was fired from the control tower. 'When they had run out,' said Snoddy, 'they started switching the runway lights on and off. It was quite plain they didn't want us to land.'

Bader, however, was determined. Hamburg it was and Hamburg it was going to be for the night. As the Proctor touched down, the spray thrown up from the runway made the aircraft look like a speedboat. It was difficult to see in the darkness; but with so much water about Douglas wouldn't risk taxiing in without someone sitting on the tail to keep it down. 'Do you mind, Snoddy, getting out and jumping on the tail while I taxi in? I want to make sure we don't go up on our nose.'

Snodgrass, in a new suit, jumped down from the wing – and went up to his knees in a couple of feet of water. Protesting loudly, he dutifully mounted the tail. 'Of course,' he said, as he recalled the incident, 'as soon as Douglas opened the throttle to start taxiing, the propellor threw the whole lot over me!'

Drenched by the cascade, Snodgrass looked as if he had just been hauled out of a swimming pool fully clothed. Rude comments greeted them as they made their way to the control tower to check in. It was a Royal Air Force station. As they walked over to the main buildings, with members of the flying control staff in close attendance, Douglas caught sight of a purposeful but strangely familiar-looking group captain advancing towards them. 'Good God, Joe,' he said, letting out a volley of guffaws, 'fancy seeing you here.' It was Joe Cox (Air Vice-Marshal J. Cox), an 'old chum' from his first days in the Service. They had been at Duxford together in 1932, just after Douglas had lost his legs.

'Christ,' exclaimed the uniformed figure, 'it's you is it? I might have known!'

It was a lively evening in the mess.

It was the second turn of Fortune's wheel which set things moving up for Douglas, Snodgrass and Hugh Miller. Towards the end of the 1940s, Shell's now growing fleet of aeroplanes was brought under the aegis of the aviation department. These aircraft, some of which were owned by the company, some on charter to it or leased, were concerned primarily with supporting the exploration and production of oil. As such, they had hitherto been the responsibility of one or other of these two major divisions, neither of which knew much about aeroplanes.

It was a logical step for the department that possessed the aviation knowledge and expertise to keep a practised eye on the fleet. Not only did this development provide Bader with a wider responsibility; it also gave his colleague, Miller, further chance to demonstrate the versatility of his able engineering brain. His name began to appear more and more frequently in the passenger column of Douglas's log-book on the Proctor's overseas flights.

Miller hit it off easily with Bader. Like Snodgrass, he found he could manage his colleague's whimsical and capricious ways. Moreover, the knowledge and flair which had taken him to the rank of engineer commander in the Royal Navy, and to command of the important naval base at Fayid on the Suez Canal, had quickly won Douglas's confidence and respect. His disguised and often unintentional humour strengthened his obvious appeal.

On one of their trips together to the Middle East, they stopped off in Malta before setting out again on the next leg of the flight to Tripoli. While Bader was always ready, within reason, to stretch a sea crossing to the furthest, convenient landfall, Miller was vociferous in commending the virtues of the shortest route across the water. He had his own reservations about the infallibility of the moving parts of a single, 130 h.p. aero-engine.

Rather less than halfway across to Libya, with all of another hour's flying over the sea still to go, a message was picked up by the Proctor's modest radio. A ship was reported to be on fire and in distress to the north-east of their present position and at least another hundred miles further away from land. Miller reacted without hesitation to the report. 'We ought, certainly,' he said, 'to go and see whether we can give any help.' He had hardly got the words out before he realized what he had said. Biting his lip, he could barely credit his stupidity. Douglas never let him live it down. From then on it was always to be the longest route over the water.

Such is the unwavering strength of the mariner's discipline when it comes to a ship in distress at sea.

24

'Sahib, sahib, look, sahib!'

Douglas had 2016 flying hours in his log-book when, on 4 October 1948, he and Thelma, putting their trust in the single, Gipsy 6, 130 h.p. motor and God, set out from Croydon in the Proctor bound for the Far East. Batavia, in Java, was to be the last stop. After that, they would take a company-owned twin amphibian for the final hop across the Java Sea to Borneo. They planned to be away for just over a couple of months and be home again around 10 or 12 December, in time for the Christmas rounds.

It was much the same sort of trail as the great aerial pioneers like Alan Cobham, Amy Johnson, Jean Batten, Charles Scott, Jim Mollison and others had blazed no more than a decade or two ago to the accompaniment of banner headlines, an inch and a half deep, across the front pages of the world's press. There wasn't much that was different in 1948; rather more airfields and a limited, four-channel VHF radio carried in the aeroplane were probably the biggest changes – plus, of course, the fact that the pilot at the controls had no legs of his own.

Twenty years, almost to the month, had passed since that memorable autumn day at Cranwell, when, still with his own legs, Bader had climbed into the old Avro 504 with 'Pissy' Pearson for the first time and had been shown, without dramatics, the pure art of flying. His legs might now be artificial, but the skills and the feel in his hands were still there; so also was the flair and the judgement.

Bader had become an accomplished pilot. The 2016 flying hours in his log-book were 'real' hours – navigator-less, individual, light aeroplane and fighter hours. The total was amassed in single-engine and often quite primitive aircraft on numerous, relatively short flights, sometimes in 'forbidden' weather, with few aids, and with countless take-offs and powerless, no-motor landings. Unlike an airline, transport or bomber pilot's tally, it hadn't been notched up sitting, tediously, for hours on end, behind two or four thumping engines, with the automatic pilot plugged in and a crew of all the talents feeding data to the driver. The total, which was then a shade more than a third of the aggregate it was ultimately to reach, had been made up of raw, natural ingredients, stirred in together with the changing elements. This was the grammar of flying, the grammar of which Pearson had made Douglas master at the end of the 1920s, during their flights together over the flat fenlands of Lincolnshire.

Thelma, setting out on an 18,000-mile trip for the first time, had just the same unquestioning faith in his ability to manage an aeroplane as she had had, eight years before, in his wartime survival. Snodgrass once said: 'If I ever had to crash in an aircraft, I would want Douglas to be flying it.' Thelma understood little about it, but she knew enough to recognize that that went for her, too. On the whole, however, she thought it unlikely that it would ever quite come to that.

The log-book records the place names on the journey: Croydon, Deauville, Bordeaux, Marseille, Rome, Brindisi, Bari, Athens, Nicosia, Damascus, Baghdad, Basra, Bahrein, Sharjah, Jiwani, Karachi, Jodhpur, Delhi, Allahabad, Calcutta, Akyab, Rangoon, Mergui, Penang, Singapore, Batavia. Mostly, the stages were of $2^1/_2$–3 hours' duration, but, exceptionally, stages like Athens to Nicosia and the flight from Singapore to Batavia took 4–$4^1/_2$ hours.

Most of this was new air space for Bader, offering new things to learn. With flying, he had always thought there was but one school for knowledge, the school of experience – hard-won, proved, real experience. He turned to it again now when it came to facing, in the little Proctor, the monsoon in southern Burma on the run down to Rangoon from Calcutta. In these days of stratospheric flying in large airliners, miles up above what pilots call 'the weather', no one bothers about such things as monsoons. But in those times, when all the flying in a light aeroplane had to be done 'under the weather', they could mean the difference, literally, between disaster and survival.

Just as in his first years in the Service he had recurred to the theses of his heroes of the First World War, of Mannock and Ball, Bishop and McCudden, Richthofen and Boelke, so now he sought out in Calcutta one of the older and most tried pilots, a true academic of the local air, whose record since the 1930s, flying up and down the

Burma coastline to Rangoon, confirmed his worth. 'How', Douglas asked him, 'do you play the monsoon?'

The reply exposed a treasure chest of knowledge. 'Don't worry about the weight of rain. That will vary; sometimes there won't be any, at others it will be torrential. But you won't have difficulty following the coastline as the cloudbase seldom gets down below five hundred feet. Out of the rain, the base will lift to as much as a thousand to twelve hundred feet with good visibility under it.

'There are three kinds of raincloud you must watch for – white, black and brown. You must learn to distinguish between them. This is vital.

'White is just heavy rain and is no bother. Black, you will find, are the linc-squalls; they could be as much as fifteen miles long. Fly alongside and round them. It's too bumpy for comfort underneath them; they are narrow – sometimes only a few hundred yards wide.

'That leaves the brown raincloud. Avoid it. Whatever you do, give it a miss. Don't, in any circumstances, fly into it.'

The words of the sage stuck in Bader's mind like Mannock's first principles of air fighting. In twenty years of flying on and about the equator, on the Far-Eastern and African runs, he was never to forget them. Over and over again, he found their truth proved. But he never met the brown raincloud.

He was humble when it came to learning about the air.

Part of the appeal of flying – this rarefied form of light aeroplane flying – lies in its diversity and in its visual contact with the ground. Its attraction is in sharp contrast with the utter boredom of modern airline travel.

Some of the experiences were unforgettable. There was the run-in to Rangoon from 4000 to 5000 feet, across the unrelenting flatness of the Irrawaddy delta, with the evening sun still shining strongly behind. A dozen miles or so ahead of the Proctor was the great Shwedagon Pagoda, its magnificent dome caught by the angle of the setting sun, glinting its golden welcome to the approaching aircraft. Douglas and Thelma wondered if they had ever seen anything quite so beautiful in their lives.

But if flying with Shell had its attractions, it also had its occupational hazards. Bedtime on the first night in Rangoon, in the Burma Oil manager's old-fashioned, sprawling, colonial-style house, certainly provided a diversion.

Douglas, with his tin legs propped up, handily, beside the bed, had turned in, ready for sleep. He was tired after the flight down from Calcutta and Akyab. Thelma, having attended to the application of the usual galaxy of cosmetic lotions and creams, was just climbing into bed under the big mosquito net which reached, tent-like, almost to the ceiling.

Then Douglas spotted it out of the corner of his eye – 'a great, big spider, old boy, bigger than your hand, right up at the top of the net.' Like a 109 at 6 o'clock, 3000 feet above, it possessed all the advantages of height. Thelma, standing on the bed, brandishing a rolled newspaper, was too short to reach it. Douglas, with or without his legs, could make no worthwhile contribution to the engagement. He contented himself with encouraging his wife and offering advanced tactical advice. Irked by the attentions, the thing withdrew from sight.

Sleep didn't come easily. The vision of a tarantula, crawling about the pillows in the darkness, was an effective antidote. The matter was made the subject of an elaborate and highly flavoured report to their host at breakfast the next morning. 'There was a bloody great tarantula . . . stuck at the top of our net, looking at us. . . . And there was I, without my legs . . .'

The disinterested, throwaway response left no scope for retort. 'My dear chap, that's only an old house spider, quite harmless and friendly.'

The next night, when they went to bed, there it was again, poised at the top of the net, eyeing them. They accepted it with a doubting deference.

Some of the characters whom Douglas and Thelma encountered on this and, indeed, their other journeys were as colourful and compelling as the stories which surrounded them.

Jubb – that's how they referred to him, just plain Jubb – the Yorkshireman from Leeds, lived at Mergui, halfway down the coast between Rangoon and the Malayan township of Penang. His house was built on stilts with an outside wooden staircase leading up to the front door. Rugged, independent and blunt, Jubb might have been a Somerset Maugham character, a typical north-country Englishman who had 'gone out East' between the wars to make his way and amass some capital. With his 'bit of rubber' and 'bit of tea', he had moved north up to Calcutta when the Japanese overran Burma. Now, with things back to normal, he had re-established his lucrative business.

Douglas and Thelma made friends with him at once. He had just the sort of character that appealed to them, extrovert, opinionated and funny. They had come across him in an unlikely way.

After landing at Mergui about 11 o'clock one morning, they had asked the young Burmese customs officer, who sat, importantly, in his white suit in a little shed beside the airstrip, whether they could get a drink or a cup of coffee. 'Yes,' said U Tun Min eagerly, 'I will take you to Pop's house.'

With that they were driven off at speed in a jeep, with U Tun Min sitting proudly at the wheel. 'Pop's House' they took to be the local tavern. Their surmise was wrong. 'Pop's house' turned out to be Jubb's house; it was no more than a couple of miles from the strip, up a jungle trail.

There was no one at home when they drove up, As they waited on the verandah at the top of the staircase, a blue Buick pulled up outside leaving a ribbon of billowing dust along the track behind it. Out of it climbed this well-built Yorkshireman, in a grubby shirt and pair of equally grubby grey-flannel trousers. Hospitality was written across his bronzed face.

'Come in,' said Jubb. His accent was still just as broad as it was when he first left his native Leeds fifteen years ago. 'Winnie, Winnie,' he called, 'we've got company. Bring some bananas and tea.'

Within minutes, a beautiful half-caste Burmese girl, the offspring of Jubb and his Burmese wife, entered the room with exquisite grace and elegance, carrying a tray full of 'bananas and tea'. Winnie was U Tun Min's lovely fiancée – good reason for the young customs officer to want to take the new arrivals to 'Pop's house' for refreshment.

After a stay of 45 minutes, Jubb drove Douglas and Thelma back to the airstrip, pressing them to call in again on their return from Borneo. When, eventually, they did come back a month later, it was a disconsolate Jubb who greeted them. He was sitting in a chair with one leg up. Winnie had married U Tun Min a couple of days before, and her father had become a casualty in the prolonged celebrations which had followed the ceremony.

Thelma put a parting question to him as they prepared to leave. 'Have you', she asked, 'any relations still living in England?'

'Aye,' he said, 'I've a sister living i' Leeds. She's a stuffy old cow. The last time I were back a year or so ago, I knocked at t' door. She stared at me. Looked as if she weren't sure whether I'd just come owt o' jail or was getting ready to go back in.

'When I got back here, I decided to send her some brass. She wrote back askin' what she should spend it on. I said: "Get yerself a new bed or summat – and spend t' rest on vice." '

When they finally got back to England, Douglas and Thelma wrote to Miss Jubb. They said they had seen her brother at Mergui and that he wanted them to bring messages. A week passed and back came a 'frightfully stuffy', spinster's reply.

'Thank you for your letter,' it ran. 'I'm glad to hear about my brother. Yours sincerely . . .'

Douglas couldn't wait to get back to Mergui to show it to Jubb.

After spending ten days in Borneo, Douglas and Thelma set course from Java for home on 11 November. Apart from the call on Jubb, there was another incident which coloured the way.

To the south of Sharjah, in Oman, Douglas had one of the first of his many encounters with the disabled. These meetings were to become a feature of his Shell journeys across the world. Not only did they give him a great deal of personal satisfaction and joy, but they also confirmed in him the strength of the message he felt he could bring to those whose misfortune had been so similar to his own.

Within him there was now stirring a private crusade. He would never say anything about it – never *have* anything said about it if he could prevent it; but those who were closest to him could sense the spirit which was burning within. 'If you've been luckier than others', was all that he would say, 'and been able to get over the problems, you must try to put something back, to pass on one's experience. That's the point. Life is for giving, not always for taking.'

It was a theme which was to recur again and again: 'Life is for giving, not always for taking.' It directed his thinking and influenced many of his actions for his fellow disabled in the Shell years and beyond.

Among the Sultan of Oman's forces, there was a good leavening of stalwart Baluchis. Oman may have seemed remote to these levies but the pay was better than the average run in their native Baluchistan. Under British officers, these physically hard, smart and disciplined warriors made a notable contribution to the strength of the Sultan's army.

The local British commander, Colonel David Smiley, asked Doug-

226

las if he would come and see three of the Baluchis who had lost legs in the local operations, treading on mines or through some other misadventure. 'I've got one working as a clerk in the orderly room,' said the colonel, 'another is a tailor and the third is doing a job in the kitchen.'

Douglas was struck by the fineness of the men, their spirit and bearing. One of them had been provided with a very rudimentary artificial limb by some local relief organization. 'What happens to these men?' he asked. 'Do the War Office look after them? Do they get a pension?'

The answer was 'No' on both counts. The War Office would have no part of them. They were levies, raised and paid by the Sultan, and that was the end of it.

'Balls to that!' retorted Bader, resolved to do something for them if he could.

When he got back to London, he asked Dermot Boyle, who was then in charge of manning at the Air Ministry, if he could get the Army to do anything. The answer was the same; they weren't their responsibility. So off he went to see Fred Stephens, who was then on his way to becoming chairman of Shell. 'Can't the company do something for these poor chaps?' he urged. 'We're digging for oil down there and it wouldn't do any harm locally to be seen to be lending a hand.'

Shell were sympathetic. 'We'll help,' said Stephens, 'but we can't be seen to be setting up a Shell welfare service in the Oman. We'll pay for the limbs for these men but they'll have to come as a present from you. The company can't be seen to be involved.'

Bader's Royal Air Force friend, Sam Elworthy (Marshal of the Royal Air Force Sir S. C. Elworthy), who within a couple of decades was to rise to the pinnacle, first of the Service and then of the Defence Staff, carried responsibility for Aden at the time. Douglas asked him if his senior medical officer, the next time he was doing his rounds of the Gulf, would take plaster casts of the three Baluchis' stumps, mark up the measurements on the charts and send them back. The hospital at Roehampton would do the rest. Sir Miles Thomas (Lord Thomas), chairman, then, of BOAC, had promised to fly the legs out 'for free'.

It was some while before Bader was again in Muscat. A new British commander, Colonel Waterfield, had taken over. 'You must see these men and talk to them,' he said. 'They're cock-a-hoop over their limbs.' Douglas was pleased with what he saw.

'There they were, these marvellous chaps, absolutely thrilled to get decent legs. "Sahib, sahib," they said, "look, sahib, look!" and off they went round the room high-kicking like stormtroopers, delighted to be able to show off. They were tickled to bits with the limbs Roehampton had made them.'

It was a foretaste of what was to come. 'There are still people, all over the world, walking about on Shell legs. But no one ever hears about it.'

Douglas and Thelma reached Croydon from Marseille and Bordeaux in the middle of the afternoon of 11 December. Their arrival, midway between the 10th and the 12th of the month, was right on schedule. To complete, almost to the hour, the homeward journey of some 9000 miles, embracing twenty-three separate landings, eighteen overnight stops and 79 flying hours, in a 120 m.p.h. single-engine aeroplane with minimal navigational aids, demanded an unusually high degree of pre-flight planning.

For Bader, however, flying aeroplanes has always been a meticulous, finely tuned art, a science in which precision is paramount. But it has been more for him than that.

One evening about dinner time, soon after they arrived home, Thelma's sister telephoned her and asked if she could speak to Douglas. 'He won't be back for about an hour,' she said. 'He's gone night flying for fun.'

Fun – 'the fun of flying'; it's Douglas's phrase. For fifty years it has been a light of his life.

25
Shell's special mixture

The decade of the 1950s, like the spring of the year, brought Douglas Bader its perplexing extremes. Shafts of bright sunlight pierced the overcast and sent the shadows chasing one another across the land. In the second half of this fluctuating spell, Douglas began to feel again, for the first time since 1940 and 1941, the satisfying warmth of authority and responsibility on his back. Two events hastened the advent of summer.

In 1954, Bader's friends Ian and Billy Collins, the British Davis Cup tennis players, published, through the family firm, Paul Brickhill's *Reach for the Sky*, the Australian author's compellingly moving portrayal of Douglas's initial assault on the ice-face of adversity. A year later came the making and showing of Danny Angel's similarly successful film which took its title from the book. The release of the story, in book and film form, gripped a reading, and cinema-going, public.

Financially, Bader's gains from these exposures were vastly different from the wildly exaggerated guesses which circulated at the time. For his contribution to the material upon which Brickhill's story was based, Douglas received a single lump-sum payment of £10,000. Under the deal, he waived all rights to any share of the subsequent royalties from the book. He received nothing at all from the sale of the film rights of the manuscript, nor from the film's extensive run.

Few could have forecast at the time the extraordinary success of the written and celluloid versions of the saga. There were, indeed, good reasons then for finding a settlement which would rest upon a round-figure, all-embracing capital sum. Profiting from hindsight, and the subsequent course of history, there is little doubt that his interests would have been better served, and a fairer base found, had the agreement included a share of the continuing royalties of the works. But it didn't look like it at the time. It did not seem then to his advisers that this would be at all a prudent course. Whatever the arguments – and there were many – one thing cannot be denied. Without his achievement and his own matchless endeavours during the first half of his life, there would have been no fortunes to be made from tale or film.

The proceeds from the book contributed towards Douglas and Thelma's purchase of a small mews house off Queen's Gate, in South Kensington, a few minutes' walk from Hyde Park. This they renovated and furnished comfortably in a style which reflected Thelma's taste for colour, antique furniture and other fine pieces. Here they based their lives for the last fifteen of their thirty-seven years together, entertaining their friends at weekly dinner parties which were rumbustious and spirited affairs. Their variously assorted guests were drawn from every circle and sector of British life and from many parts of the world.

There was, however, much more to the by-products of the book than the undeniable enjoyment of material gain. The personal standing and eminence which resulted from the painting of his colourful saga lifted him, overnight, on to a hitherto unattained plateau on the mountainside. Up to then he was just a legend in the countries in which his exploits were known. Now, with the exception of the United States, where, for singularly obscure reasons, the film was not distributed, his fame spread from one hemisphere to another.

Public acclaim affects men in divergent ways. A few can cope with it without visible effect; they are the blessed minority for whom humility, good grace and manners are God-given assets. Advancement enhances their value. Their characters are embellished in the eyes of their fellow men. Far more, however, are changed by success and notoriety to a degree which, without their realizing it, deprives them of much of their pristine shine. Achievement and fame are not their allies; they become the symbols of immodesty – and the loss of the human and humble touch. It is not their fault. Their virtues are not strong enough to shoulder the climb. On the ascent, they lose their way and then their original identity. Many instances can be cited from public and private life. They are men and women to be pitied, not censured.

World cheers and applause made not a whit of difference to Bader. He continued to behave exactly as he had done before when he was no one – and heads didn't turn in the street. At times he would be unreasonably and unthinkingly difficult; at others he could charm a raging tiger to his side. In the family, and with his close friends and colleagues, he was just the same: preposterously dominant and assertive at one moment, and winning, generous, wonderfully engaging and loyal at another. If his friends got into difficulty, even through their own unwitting fault, he would stand four-square behind them and damn those who attempted to criticize them for their mistakes. Just as Dermot Boyle said of him at Cranwell, a quarter of a century before, he could be naughty without ever being disloyal. The fact was he remained – would always remain – a pilot officer in the Royal Air Force. He drove a motor car like one – very well and about 8 or 10 miles an hour too fast. With the international searchlight upon him, the paradox in him didn't change; he was unpredictable and, again, utterly dependable. He compelled others to follow.

The Bader who played on the world stage was no different from the Bader who had led 242 Squadron and the Duxford and Tangmere wings. He was a natural, spontaneous leader in either role. But he would lead *his* way, in *his* style and with *his* team. And to hell with the rest.

As he rose in the late 1950s, and beyond, to a crescendo of fame, there was, of course, always Thelma to hold the mirror before him:

> And, since you know you cannot see yourself
> So well as by reflection, I your glass
> Will modestly discover to yourself
> That of yourself which you yet know not of.

Sometimes the glass reflected powerful, objective and opposing views. Like stabilizers in a ship, she added balance and helped her husband to ride out the storms – and, now and then, if she thought it prudent, to seek calmer waters.

The second event which studded the later 1950s and was to colour brightly his remaining twelve years with Shell was the formation, within the group, of a subsidiary company with the specific, and exclusive, task of looking after the multinational's fleet of aeroplanes. Bader was appointed its first managing director, with Snodgrass as his number 2. His accession to the position supplied a personal need and, together with the publication of the book and the distribution of the film, was to create, in line with the crash at Woodley in 1931 and the scaling of the heights of the Battle of Britain, the third watershed in his life.

Shell now possessed a fleet of aeroplanes – chartered, leased or owned, and based over much of the world – which was as great, numerically, as that of the state-owned British Overseas Airways. For the first time since he had clattered into Leigh-Mallory's room at Watnall and, later, Uxbridge, and been given command, successively, of 242 and the Tangmere wing, he had his own show, his own progeny to influence, mould and shape. In personal terms, it was enormously satisfying; he felt that his life's training fitted him for the task. He knew very well that no one, among Shell's nearly-quarter of a million employees, could tell him anything he didn't already know about aeroplanes and how to fly and operate them.

In effect, Douglas, as managing director of the group's aircraft company, reported directly to the group chairman or a senior managing director. Whoever that was was also, effectively, chairman of Shell Aircraft Ltd. The stark truth was that, with his personality, independence and the latitude he had long enjoyed, it required a man of authority to manage him. He was now quite a fish to ride on the hook. Three men of power were his principal overlords during his time in executive office: Frederick Stephens; Jonkheer John Loudon, the Dutchman, who rose to be one of the most senior and highly regarded of Shell's international officers, a man of erudition and broad interests; and Sir David Barran. Stephens and Barran each became chairman of the British parent, Shell Transport and Trading, while Loudon was to join that exclusive circle of foreign nationals who have enjoyed the conferment of an honorary British knighthood. Eight years after stepping down as chairman of the group, Barran, who had reached the top via a managing directorship of Royal Dutch/Shell and the presidency of the Asiatic Petroleum Corporation of New York, was elected to the chair of the Midland Bank, a signal distinction.

Bader's masters were, thus, a high-powered lot. Their attitudes to him (but not their views of him), and to his style of management, differed noticeably. Between the comfortable, and relatively benign, approach of Stephens, and the altogether tighter and tougher stance of Barran, there was a wide divide. Balanced dexterously, and with perception, between the two was Loudon. His experience of the production of oil on the two American continents, and elsewhere, had made him aware of the requirement for a separate and supporting aircraft operation within the group. It was a concept of which his colleague and fellow managing director, Felix Guépin, was a leading advocate. Guépin was an important adherent to Douglas's cause.

232

Bader's transition from Shell's aviation department – and from Walter Hill's management of it – to the leadership of Shell Aircraft followed a characteristically unorthodox and uncharted course. It was not achieved quickly, nor in a single stride. Before the act was complete there were, in the interim, some interesting, and varied, hands to play.

The overseas journeys, and all the flying which went with them, first in the Proctor and then, from the beginning of 1951, in the more advanced Miles Gemini, with its two Gipsy Major 120 h.p. engines, served a need. They provided enjoyment and an almost continually changing scene. They were balm for an impatient mind.

But Douglas was now forty, and time was passing. The freedom he was being given suited his temperament and his lifestyle. The ability to fly himself about and traverse large areas of the earth's surface virtually at will could not fail to have its attractions. Moreover, the increasing opportunities which were now arising to express his strongly held and often controversial views, both through the diversity of his speaking engagements and his outspoken articles in the Sunday press, helped him to feel he was contributing to the national dialogue on some of the more pressing issues of the day: Britain's role in the Middle East; the need to maintain the nation's defensive strength; the importance of the country's aircraft industry and the wisdom of 'flying British'; strengthening ties with the 'old' Commonwealth; crime and punishment; and the usefulness or uselessness of the United Nations.

Enjoyable and stimulating though the life was, none of these activities brought him the real fulfilment he sought – and needed. Nor had his long-running relationship with Hill become more compatible with time; rather the reverse. The longer it endured, the more susceptible it became to the inevitable differences which are so often inseparable from business and office life. Their ways were the length of a runway apart. An earlier incident had demonstrated it unmistakably.

An aircraft of British South American Airways had been refuelled by Shell at Dakar, in West Africa, before taking off on the South Atlantic run. Through a series of most improbable, and yet understandable, mistakes, the 2000-gallon tanker which had been used to fill its tanks had itself had water, and not gasolene, pumped into it from the static installation. In the darkness, the water had, inadvertently, been transferred to the airliner.

Only a stroke of fortune had averted disaster. As the pilot started up the motors, the residue of fuel in the lines, which had been left there when the engines had previously been shut down, enabled them to fire normally; but as the aircraft began to taxi out to the runway for take-off, the water started to flow into the feed. Suddenly, and apparently quite inexplicably, all the motors spluttered to an ignominious stop.

When the trouble was discovered, immediate and justifiably vehement protests began to fly out of the office of BSAA's chief executive, Donald Bennett (Air Vice-Marshal D. C. T. Bennett), the wartime commander of Bomber Command's famous Pathfinder Force. The manager of Shell's aviation department was on the receiving end; it wouldn't be long, he thought, before the missives were reaching the group's chairman or managing directors.

Instant investigations were set in motion. Much deranged (this kind of thing agitated him greatly), Hill discussed the best course of action with Bader. The service of fuel on the airfields abroad, the provision and maintenance of the equipment, were Douglas's baby. An important and valuable contract might be at stake. How to mollify the chairman of BSAA?

Douglas was in no doubt. An unfortunate mistake had been made in the dark. His honest and uncomplicated mind, allied to an innate common sense, told him that it was no good mucking about with convoluted and detailed explanations, still less excuses. 'There's only one thing for it,' he said, 'laugh it off! It was bloody lucky that so much water got through quickly rather than a few gallons of the stuff flowing into the feed halfway across the Atlantic. Laugh it off, it's the only way in the circumstances.'

He could see it wasn't going to satisfy Hill. It did nothing to lessen his unease. Douglas chanced his arm again. 'Don't worry,' he said, 'let me talk to Don Bennett.' Bennett was a 'chum' and a practical aviator.

All was quickly mended and a somewhat bizarre happening put behind; but not before Bader and his colleagues had seen to it that, in future, no more aircraft could be fuelled with Shell's 'special mixture'.

Douglas enjoyed his overseas visits with Snodgrass. They weren't as frequent as those with other colleagues like Miller; but when they arose they were always good value. Snoddy's humour and the precision of his mind were used to make the most of their experiences. There was one droll episode with the French in Algiers which took them nearly 1000 miles to the south, deep into the heart of the Sahara.

Their destination was a newly established Shell exploration camp at Getafe, far down beyond El Golea, in P. C. Wren country. Snodgrass was to cover the last part of the journey by truck. The way south into the desert was strictly controlled by the French. It was open for only six months of the year, from October until March. This applied to light aircraft using the 'corridor' over the surface track just as it did to desert trucks and jeeps following the *piste* itself. The authorities had wearied of sending out rescue parties for travellers who had lost their way over the vast land tracts and in the air above them. Apart from the nuisance of it, they found they had been noticeably unsuccessful in recovering the considerable costs either from insurance or other sources. So the first hurdle for Bader and Snodgrass was to get over the problem of permission.

As usual Douglas went to the top. Having reached Algiers, via Bordeaux and Barcelona, he made contact with the French general who commanded the local air forces. Yes, *le général* would be glad to accept *le colonel*'s invitation to dine that evening and bring his *chef d'état-major* with him.

It turned out to be a hilarious party which got off to exactly the right start when Snodgrass discovered that the chief of staff, one Colonel Challe, had beaten the record for a timed flight from Paris to Saigon in 1928. Snoddy, who had then only just joined the company, had been responsible for the paperwork that supported the refuelling arrangements which Shell, or the Asiatic Petroleum Company, as it then was, had made along the way.

Bader, sustained, as was his custom, by nothing stronger than a few glasses of mineral water, dispensed all his winning charm. 'Have you ever heard him talk French?' Snodgrass's question to the author, as he recalled the incident, was rhetorical. 'He spent the evening telling these two senior French officers typically risqué English stories in his own special brand of French with an accent which rivalled Churchill's. Each one was richer than the last. He was quite superb, totally unselfconscious and uninhibited.'

After three or four hours of it, the general and his chief of staff, limp with endless laughter, made their farewells. The general took Snodgrass to one side as they parted. 'Do you think that Shell realize', he asked, 'what a great man this is?' Another door had been unlocked. Permission to fly was now only a formality.

El Golea was within 4 hours' flying time from Algiers in the

Gemini, cruising at around 125 m.p.h. Getafe was another $2^1/_4$ hours on beyond that. The *piste*, which in the fine and clear visibility could be seen sharply from the air, stood out like a furrow in the brown sand and as a narrow strip of white ribbon laid across the black rock of the desert.

At El Golea they were met by the Shell superintendent who was in charge of the movement of desert trucks and other vehicles in the area. He was steeped in local knowledge. A former NCO in the French Foreign Legion, he knew the Sahara as well as anyone from his service days. Over dinner in the local hostelry, he gave Douglas detailed instructions about how to reach the camp at Getafe and its precise position. He sketched out on the back of the menu the route which the trucks took with the exact distances in kilometres between the various points. Bader converted it all into miles and flying times, working out with minute care the ETA (estimated time of arrival) at each landmark. It was a rough-and-ready way of doing it, but there was no alternative. There were no large-scale flying maps of the neighbourhood. The sketch on the menu was all that he could rely on. With this, he made his meticulous plan.

The verbal directions which backed the diagram were quite clear. 'Suivez la piste' was the first commandment of the desert. Anyone disobeying this doctrine in a light aeroplane did so at his peril. So the *piste* had to be followed down to Fort Miribel which was no more than a pull-in for the truck drivers.

'Don't take the left fork there,' said the ex-Legionnaire, 'but head straight on for Belbel. After 270 kilometres turn right where the tracks cross. Go on for another 120 kilometres and you should see a great cairn of stones. Turn right again there and in 7 kilometres you should see the camp ahead of you.' He might have been directing a truck driver, not an aeroplane pilot.

Douglas and Snoddy spent the following day in El Golea, and the two of them agreed that the number 2 in the team should go down to Getafe in a desert truck, an uncomfortable eight-hour journey through the dark. The temperature, which at the height of the day rose to 70° C in the bright and clear sunlight, fell sharply to zero at night.

Douglas was anxious that Snoddy should go on ahead, find the camp and choose a 'safe' 300-yard landing strip close to it. 'We don't want to get down there and find we're stuck fast. And you can then set off the smoke at the up-wind end of the landing path and I'll come in and put the Gemini down.'

236

The following morning Bader set course for Fort Miribel at a comfortable 3000 feet and 125 m.p.h. The menu was beside him. After checking each pinpoint and still following the *piste*, he started to look for the 'great cairn of stones'. It was due to show up after 1 hour and 33 minutes' flying. Circling what should have been the mark, he could find no sign of the cairn. He thought it unlikely, but he could have made a miscalculation. What to do?

Dropping down to well below 1000 feet for a final search, he suddenly caught sight of a jeep approaching from the west with a wake of dust behind it. It turned north just as Douglas was himself momentarily turning north over the top of it, going in the same direction. It must also be going to the camp, he thought; there was really nowhere else for it to go. He guessed the cairn of stones probably wasn't visible from the air, anyway. It was a truck driver's mark, not a pilot's.

He headed north for a couple of minutes and there straight ahead, just as the Shell superintendent had said it would be, was the camp, with its little huts, tents and caravans. It had been partially hidden behind a bluff. In a moment the smoke was rising from the strip. One good look round and Douglas was putting the Gemini down softly on three points on the spot Snoddy had selected for him. The look on his colleague's face left no doubt about his pleasure at the aircraft's arrival. One eight-hour drive through the night and down the *piste* had plainly been quite enough for him.

They made their way together over to the lunch tent; 40 minutes later, just as they were finishing their cold chicken and salad, the jeep pulled into the camp. Its crew came rushing over to the tent. 'Où est le pilot?' the driver cried. 'Où est le pilot . . . le pilot?'

An emotional greeting revealed their secret. They had been lost, hopelessly and utterly lost, when they saw the Gemini turning north over the top of them at 500 feet. They had felt sure the pilot was leading them to the camp. The blind and the legless were at one.

Flying for Shell in a light aeroplane in Africa was usually eventful. One or two flights which Bader had made with Bill Swerdloff, the company's aviation manager in West Africa, had clearly deserved the credits they were given in his log-book.

Swerdloff, who was based in Lagos, was a 'character'. A White Russian by derivation, he was a fluent speaker of languages. His colleagues tended to call him the 'Baron', sometimes with the prefix

237

'Bogus'. With a plain glass monocle worn in his left eye, he looked the part. The pseudonym fitted his personality perfectly.

One day, he and Douglas, sitting side by side in the Proctor, with the African sun pouring into the cockpit, were flying down the coast from Lagos to Port Harcourt, in southern Nigeria, a run of some 2¼ hours. Cutting inland on the second half of the flight, they were passing over thick scrub, bush and jungle when all of a sudden the motor stopped dead. They were just under 3000 feet. Bader thought instantly of his passenger.

'Bill, if we have to crash in the jungle, brace yourself with your hands against the front of the cockpit. The impact will throw you forward.'

Swerdloff, who was wearing a bush jacket and shorts, responded with an unconcerned and condescending grunt. Thereupon, quite deliberately, he removed the monocle from his eye, polished it with his silk handkerchief, wrapped it up and put it in his breast pocket. It was all done without flap and without hurry. It certainly impressed Douglas. 'He would have calmed anyone.'

As the eye glass was being placed safely away, the pilot spotted the simple cause of the trouble. The outboard fuel supply had emptied and he had forgotten to switch over before the motor cut. As he turned on to the main tanks, the engine caught reassuringly. Swerdloff registered no emotion at all at the sudden revival of their fortunes. He continued to stare straight ahead, unmoved. But he left the monocle wrapped up in his pocket.

Niamey, in the French Sahara, was between 700 and 800 kilometres from Lagos. Douglas and the Bogus Baron decided to fly up there together. A 2000-gallon Shell tanker had recently gone up in flames on the airfield and they wanted to try to find out why.

The facts were difficult to credit. Arab bedouins from the Sahara were employed around the airfield to perform the more menial tasks. One of them had acquired from a traveller, by one means or another, a cigarette lighter. In the heat of the sun it soon ran dry. What better way of replenishing it than from a Shell tanker during night duty? Dammit, he worked for the company.

Underneath these vehicles was a water cock. If it was removed any moisture content in the fuel, having sunk to the bottom, could easily be drained off. During the night the Arab had crawled under the tanker, loosened off the cock and saturated the lighter with fuel. After drying it off and waiting for the air to get to it, he gave it a couple of quick, exploratory flicks to see if it was working. The spark from the flint touched the vapour fumes. Immediately flames shot up inside the tanker and, within seconds, were out of control.

The last that was seen of the bedouin was his slim, dark body streaking away into the night, hot-footing it as fast as he could for the obscurity of the desert.

Living an international life with Shell could never be dull. Whatever the first ten years or so of Bader's post-war time with the group may have lacked in personal authority and command, they certainly made up in variety. There comes a time, however, when even endless travel and activity cannot satisfy an impatient, searching, demanding mind. Something more substantial and more mentally rewarding is needed.

The last dozen years of Douglas's time with Shell offered him, with his new-found authority and responsibilities, and the continuing free-dom that went with them, the chance to deploy his remarkable talents and attributes on an increasingly demanding world stage. With the renown which the spread of his story was bringing him, invitations to speak at this public dinner or that, or that summer fête or this, or so-and-so's speech day, or someone else's summer ball, flowed in with the postman's every knock.

Many he accepted – particularly for charity and the disabled, for he had developed an easy, breezy, boisterous and essentially conver-sational way of speaking in public. He did not find it difficult, as some do, to pick up the tenor of a function and catch the mood. He could ad-lib readily and improvise. It didn't take much out of him.

Occasionally, when he was specially anxious to do proper justice to an address, he would write out what he wanted to say in full in his own hand. He admitted to doing this three times in the 1960s and 1970s: when he spoke at the memorial service for Keith Park at St Clement Danes in the Strand; at the dinner the National Sporting Club and Charles Forte gave him at the Café Royal; and, again, when he addressed Cambridge's Hawks Club at the Savoy, in London. Each time the text was comprehensively prepared and mem-orized. And each time he achieved the result he sought. The prac-tised ear – and eye – can always tell when real trouble has been taken.

But, mostly, his speaking was done from a few cross-headings written on a single sheet of paper with no more than the general framework for the speech determined beforehand. Years of experience had taught him to 'think well on his feet'. He did not have difficulty when he found himself having to speak unprepared. It was often happening. ('I'm sure, group captain, they would all be delighted if you . . .')

All this, in a sense, became a part of his job. Shell was an international company, and Bader, now, was an international figure, flying the Shell flag at the masthead. He was just as much at home addressing an ex-servicemen's reunion in Toronto, Auckland, Salisbury or Sydney as he was speaking at the Union in Cambridge. The fact is that the hard school of experience has turned Bader into an effective public speaker. He is versatile and lets his audience feel his personality. He is often dogmatic and recurs to 'bulldog and empire' themes which are simple and provocative. He is for Britain, not party; but his stance is to the right of centre.

The biographer, standing back, with all the advantage of impartial and direct discussion with the subject's former – and sometimes critical – principals and colleagues, is left with a plain impression. Shell knew quite well what it was about with Bader. His masters recognized that, as the managing director of the aircraft subsidiary, he wouldn't be a conventional, pliable executive as others might be; he wouldn't be 'cosy' to deal with; more likely, he would be awkward to handle, often abrasive and not much given to yielding to compromise or to finding 'accommodations' and the 'middle way'.

They understood the retort of the minister who was asked by a member of parliament to consider Bader as a possible director of British Overseas Airways. 'Put Douglas on the board of BOAC? It's a marvellous idea – but there'd be a row with the chairman within a month!'

One time, when the group's seven managing directors were looking for large-scale economies within the organization, their committee asked the aircraft company's executive what contribution he thought he could make to cost savings. He gave his answers. They were pursued by one of the more persistent among his questioners. 'What about your own aircraft,' he asked, 'couldn't you, perhaps, give that up and draw on the pool that the executives use when they need an aeroplane?'

Douglas took an undeniable risk. 'How, then,' he countered, 'would I be able to get up to Prestwick to play golf?'

It's a safe bet there wasn't another in the company who would have chanced it. But he still kept his aeroplane.

They knew – or, at any rate, most of them did – that he was something of an 'odd ball', a law unto the laws of Bader, an outspoken and forthright man who would always be, in a business context, a 'card'. They also knew, however, and here came the breadth of Shell, that in Douglas they had a being who possessed qualities which were not the property of other men. His unrivalled experience and knowledge of the *practical* side of aviation were undoubted. But they saw much more in him than that. Here was now a national and international figure, who, by his status, achievements and personality – controversial though it was – could bring significant and material benefits. Here was a leader who could inspire and who, because he *was* a leader, could quickly recognize a 'happy ship' when he saw one, or, perhaps more importantly, an unhappy one.

No great multinational company gave more thought and importance to what may loosely be termed 'staff and personnel relations' than Shell. No worldwide group has a more telling record in human affairs. It is worth saying here that when, as the managing director of the aircraft company, Bader was reporting to Loudon, he was required to give his superior, after each overseas visit, his own impressions of the 'staff relations' he had encountered at the Shell posts *en route*: the abilities which had struck him, and the shortcomings he might have seen. This was a service which extended beyond his remit as, purely, the managing director of Shell Aircraft. Loudon laid store by the accounts he received.

Douglas always felt that he could 'manage people'. It was this confidence which persuaded him to propose to Fred Stephens, one day, that he might be considered for the vacancy which would shortly arise for a new personnel manager within the group. 'I would like to have a shot at it as my final job with the Shell Company. I'm sure I could do it.' Bader had then been managing director of the aircraft subsidiary for six or seven years. He felt he was ready for the responsibility.

'I'll talk to my colleagues', said Stephens, 'and let you know.'

A few days later, the chairman sent for him. Douglas has always had a cordial and easy rapport with him. He admired him greatly, and liked him. 'Steve was a lovely man,' he would say, 'charming and always friendly.'

Stephens came straight to the point. 'Douglas,' he said, 'I have spoken to my colleagues about the matter you mentioned to me the other day. The answer is no.'

241

Just that: no. Bader's reaction was unequivocal. 'I think you're quite wrong.'

Stephens, who knew the aircraft company's managing director as well, if not better, than all his senior colleagues, was ready for it. 'I thought you'd say that,' he said, and smiled at the accuracy of his forecast.

The collective view was, of course, that, having reached this stage in the journey, Bader's faculties – and message – were best employed in other ways. Best from the standpoint of the company; and best for those for whom, across the world, he had already become a light to lighten the darkness. Douglas was convinced they were mistaken; but history will give Shell the credit.

26
Nightmare

Kenneth More met Douglas only twice before Danny Angel, with Lewis Gilbert directing, started shooting *Reach for the Sky*. It was quite deliberate. He knew that Bader, apprehensive, anyway, at the prospect of the film being made, was worried about being caricatured – 'guyed' – and made to seem like an unreal, absurd figure. As an accomplished professional, he was afraid that if he got to know him too well beforehand, he would begin, unconsciously and unintentionally, to see in the character he was playing a caricature of the man.

More's friends had already started to warn him off the part. Alexander Korda and Laurence Olivier, both trying to be helpful, had told him they thought he was mistaken to take it on. 'It's ridiculous,' Korda said to him, 'a young and active man like you playing a hero with no legs. It's absurd.'

But More was confident he could do it. Looking back one winter's afternoon in his London home twenty-four years later, he was still quite definite in his feelings about taking on the part. He *wanted* to play Bader. He felt an identity with him, with his philosophy and his attitude to life. His character was quite clear to him. He could see the man and how he should be played.

I admired him. He was to me a Rudyard Kipling figure; you don't find them any more. I understood him. He was a harder man than I am. To me he represented everything that every Englishman wants to be – courageous, honest, determined – but knows he hasn't the nerve or the capacity to be.

He had got his faults – who hasn't? He suffered fools badly – not gladly. He was difficult, impulsive, strong-headed; he was all these things. But I just felt that someone had to give him to the world.

From the start I knew – I was certain – I could do it. It was the part of a lifetime. I felt – *felt* – I could play it. As an actor, you had to run the

243

whole gamut in the part. Wearing the steel plates that Roehampton had contrived for me to keep the joints in my legs, knees and ankles stiff was exhausting and made my legs sore where they rubbed. I was terrified of falling backwards. But, mentally, it was no strain.

Emotionally, it wasn't difficult. I swam through it, swam through it.'

Deep down, Kenny knew he was the right actor in the right part, whatever Korda and Olivier might say. That's where the confidence came from.

I like to think that Douglas felt he was in good hands. My worry was that I might let him down, missing some Service detail. I have always loved the Services and I was determined with Lewis Gilbert that we would try to get even the minutest detail right.

By the time they had reached the release from Colditz in the shooting, and the first post-war, Battle of Britain fly-past, More had dispensed with the clamps on his legs. He had the rolling, clattering gait fixed in his mind.

The two meetings they had were carefully chosen. They met, first, over lunch and talked for a couple of hours. Then they went up to Scotland, to Gleneagles, and played a couple of rounds of golf together on the Queen's Course. Two rounds of the green – thirty-six holes – in the same day; seven miles of walking on artificial legs. It was Bader's usual golfing ration – what he was in the habit of doing at the Berkshire most Saturdays and Sundays. No question of a buggy or an electric cart to ride round in. His two tin pins were intended for walking: 'That's what they're made for.'

The meetings were all that Kenny needed. He had memorized Douglas's image like he did his lines. He never had any trouble learning his lines. He could master them in front of the television. His wife, Angela, agreed that he could learn them with a programme going.

For Bader, the time they spent together served a different purpose. He found, from the start, that he and Kenny got on. He quickly and spontaneously felt he could trust him. Had he taken against him – and it was just the sort of thing that he might have done – God knows what would have happened. As it was, he was doubtful and demanding and insistent that every detail be got right.

These were still the 'difficult years', when the unsettled aftermath of prison still kept recurring, reluctant to be banished. The film did nothing to mollify him; if anything, it made him tetchier. But the fact that More was playing the lead certainly helped. 'Ken,' he said, generalizing, 'I don't trust these film people. I trust you. I know you'll do a good job and do your best to stop them making a complete balls of it.' He saw More as his ally.

Very sensibly, Danny Angel had agreed to Douglas's suggestion that Harry Day, 'Pricky' Day, his first flight commander in 23 Squadron at Kenley in 1931, who had also been shot down early in the war and taken prisoner, should advise on Service detail. It was one way of stopping the clangers.

Day became the go-between, shuttling back and forth from Douglas to Angel, Gilbert and More. Even so, there were myriad problems. For one thing, Bader wanted all the real-life characters who mattered in the story to be individually represented in the film. He was, for instance, horrified over one detail in the casting. There was the fine strapping Australian, Jack Cruttenden, a pupil pilot at Woodley at the time of the crash, who had lifted him out of the wreckage and travelled with him in the ambulance to the hospital pressing his thumbs down on the femoral artery of his right knee to stop the flow of blood. In the film, Cruttenden had been turned into Douglas's great friend in 23, Geoffrey Stephenson. Stephenson had been nowhere near the ambulance. 'What the hell are they going to say when they see it?' The thing was a nightmare to him.

He accepted, only under protest, the director's diktat that there must be a doubling-up, a telescoping of the parts. Otherwise there would be a proliferation of actors, and audiences would become totally confused by the multiplicity of characters.

There were times in the making of the film when Danny Angel, at his wits' end with exasperation, used to appeal to the family and Douglas's close friends to intervene and allow reason to prevail.

But in all the ups and downs there was always Kenny More, the perceptive, goodnatured, brilliantly able professional, to convey to Douglas, via Pricky Day, the impression that in the film industry there were still a few left with compassion, humanity and reason.

Bader never once visited the studios while the film was being shot. He had decided he would have – and be seen to have – nothing whatever to do with it. The cast took it amiss. They were hurt that he hadn't been to see them at Pinewood. They thought he might have gone once.

Then came the première, attended by Prince Philip. It was the usual illumined evening of colour and sparkle, of celebrities in glamorous dresses with jewels twinkling, of flashing cameras and surging crowds. Bader wasn't there. He had categorically refused to go. No one, not even Thelma, could have moved him. He was utterly resolute about it. It simply wasn't for him and that was that.

Thelma and her sister, Jill, slipped into the trade show, unseen, at 10 o'clock in the morning. They could barely bring themselves to believe that Kenny wasn't Douglas. They sat there alone, enveloped in their own emotions, mesmerized by his performance. They didn't have to hide the tears; no one noticed them sitting there on their own.

Then it was over. The apprehension which had been mounting in the family for weeks suddenly fell away. The storm which had been rumbling to a crescendo had passed. All was now quiet. Only the occasional rumble from Douglas (it had become a habit) punctured the relief.

Nothing would induce Bader to go and see the film, even after the tumult and the shouting had begun to die. Years passed and still he hadn't seen it. Then, one evening, he was caught in front of a television set. The next item on the programme was Angel, Gilbert and More's masterpiece. Surprisingly, he was prepared to sit through it.

When it was over, someone asked him, timorously, what he thought of it. He took two matches to light his stubby pipe before replying. 'Rather good, old boy,' he said; and at once changed the subject.

The success of the film gave a new fillip to Kenneth More's and Douglas Bader's careers. 'It turned the corner for me,' was how Kenny put it. Under a deal with Rank and 20th Century Fox, he signed to make two films a year. As for Douglas, everywhere he went now he was recognized, a target for every autograph hunter within sight. The film had injected a fresh stimulus into the legend. Speaking engagements multiplied.

At the Lloyd's Golf Club dinner, five or six years later, in London, Pat Milligan, the chairman, in an inspired reference, introduced the guest of honour to the assembled underwriters and brokers: 'Douglas Bader. . . . Some of you may remember he played Kenneth More in *Reach for the Sky*.' Such was the likeness of actor with character.

In the high noon of his popularity, they put a picture of More on the front cover of the paperback of *Reach for the Sky*. When Douglas saw it, he was quite surprised. 'Why the hell, Ken,' he asked, with a quizzical naïvety, 'did they stick *your* face on the front of that book?' It had become a sort of double act.

Attention was now being focused increasingly on Bader's newspaper articles. The then proprietor of the *News of the World*, Sir William Carr, who, with his wife Jean, often entertained Douglas and Thelma at their home at Halland, in Sussex, had persuaded him to contribute articles on aviation, military and civil, to the Sunday newspaper with Britain's largest circulation.

The pieces he wrote were, like his speeches, well informed, dogmatic, opinionated and often provocative. He took great pains over his writing and set real store by it – more than he did with his addresses. He wrote slowly, correcting, scratching out, rewriting and revising until he felt he had got the copy right. It was the antithesis of the procedure he adopted with his run-of-the-mill speeches, which were only superficially thought out beforehand.

Some felt it surprising that Shell, who weren't given to letting their employees engage in outside, paid activities, should allow him to write for the national press on air matters. To criticize the nationalized airlines (which he was not averse from doing) could well conflict with the interests of the supplier of petrol.

When O. P. Jones, then the doyen of the great airline captains, retired from BOAC, Douglas, in a forceful and objective story, suggested that he should be put on the corporation's board. It would give encouragement to the other aircrew to see his extensive record and experience recognized and used. It was a fertile theme which Vere Harvey (Lord Harvey of Prestbury), the member for Macclesfield and the chairman of the Tory Party's aviation committee, pursued with his customary vigour and persistence on the floor of the House of Commons.

Much incensed, Miles Thomas, BOAC's chairman, who was allergic to criticism in parliament and the press, wrote a strong letter to Bader's boss, making veiled references to the importance of maintaining good relations between customer and supplier. Little came of it. Shell wasn't the sort of company to be much moved by that kind of stuff.

There was another by-product of the public notice he was now attracting both at home and overseas. The weight of the mail which was delivered to his office in St Helen's Court and, later, in the Shell Centre, on the south bank of the Thames, mounted. With the faithful

Joan Hargreaves, the secretary who managed him (and managed is the word) for most of his post-war years with Shell, he devoted thought, care and humanity to handling it.

The letters came from all over the world. Mostly they sought advice on disablement; often they came from distraught parents, worried about offspring who, through some misfortune, had lost the use of limbs. He replied meticulously to each one. He invested his answers with feeling, with personal experience, but also with directness. Douglas is very firm and objective with his fellow disabled. 'You've got to make up your mind you will live with it. It's there and there's nothing you can do about it. So you've got to make the best of it. You must never, never give in.' It was a forthright and realistic stance; but that was the way he had himself played it – and conquered. He had no time for softness and self-pity. He knew that would get them nowhere.

Almost best of all he liked the letters he received from children. Little boys want to write to their heroes and get their autographs. Lots of them wrote to Bader after seeing the film on television.

'Dear Douglas,' one of them wrote, 'Next to Tom and Jerry you are my favourite person. Will you please send me your autograph? Signed Andrew (aged 9).'

'The boy', said Douglas, 'had obviously got his priorities right.' He wrote back by return. 'Dear Andrew, You are quite right, Tom and Jerry are my favourite people, so here's my autograph. Signed Douglas Bader.'

27

Playing with Hogan

Between Ben Hogan, the great American golf player, and Douglas Bader there has existed an appealing affinity. Each came back from the dead after suffering lacerating hurt, one in a 'written-off' motor car, the other in a disintegrated aeroplane; and each, thereafter, lifted himself up on to the summit of the world in an extraordinary act of human resource. In their own way, their two stories are without parallel. One recovered to strike a golf ball with a precision which, some say, has never since been matched – 'like a machine stamping out bottle caps'. The other took a 100 per cent disability into the air and made flight its servant.

After they had met, briefly, at Wentworth in Surrey in 1956 during golf's Canada (now the World) Cup, Hogan and Bader resolved to meet again. Each held a fascination for the other, as men of rare accomplishment often do. There was a mutual urge to talk and play when the crowds weren't about, and they could exercise and reflect alone. Golf and the conquest of adversity made a bond between them.

The chance to get together again had to wait eight years. Then, Douglas and his opposite number in Shell in the United States, George Hughes, were in Fort Worth, Texas, Hogan's home base, seeing about a new Grumman Gulfstream, 'a lovely aeroplane', which the company had just purchased for its fleet. Thelma was with them.

It was at Shady Oaks, on a warm and cloudless Texan day, that the two legends picked up the game where they had left it. The detail is still sharp in Bader's mind. There were six present: Douglas and Ben Hogan, their two caddies, and Thelma and George Hughes. Thelma and Hughes rode round the course in a buggy. Bader and Hogan, whose legs were never the same after his accident in 1949, walked. Ben, who was fifty-two then – two years older than Douglas, and largely 'retired' – was still subjecting himself to his rigorous regimen of other days, hitting a few score balls of a morning before playing his daily eighteen holes.

Euclid stood proxy for Hogan that day, draughting his shots for him with a ruler and pin-sharp pencil, according to his lasting definition of a straight line. Each drive, standing out white against blue, finished in the dead centre of the fairway, and each iron shot appeared destined to knock the stick out of the hole. The flags on the greens flopped down limp from the pins like drunks slumped against the wall, so there was no wind to influence this marvellous geometrical progression. Shady Oaks seemed to be intent on having everything right for these two somewhat unusual men.

Douglas had played with many of the game's greats in his time, from James Braid onwards, but he had never seen a golf ball hit quite so accurately as this. 'It was extraordinary, really; quite extraordinary.' But even in the tranquillity of this sunlit scene Hogan's putter became a fiend in his hands. The stroke which once had rolled in the putts that mattered had taken its early leave. Once or twice there seemed to be a hint that the gremlins might be starting to jump up at him from the greens like children's firecrackers in the street.

Douglas, who has always putted well ('I have to, old boy') with an old, rusty, hickory-shafted favourite, noticed on the eighth or ninth green that Hogan's hands were snapped on to the putter grip like the jaws of a rat trap. 'Ben,' he asked, 'why do you hang on to the club as tight as that?'

The Hawk straightened up deliberately from his practice putt. Tapping, first, the side of his head and then pointing down at the putter head on the grass, he made the supplicant's penitent confession. 'Doug,' he said, 'I can't get it from there to there.'

After the round, during which Hogan offered Douglas no golfing advice, instruction or wisdom – they just played round happily together – the party spent the evening at the club. Ben's wife, Valerie, joined them for dinner.

Thelma, having heard from Douglas of the severe golfing routine to which Ben still subjected himself, asked Valerie where they liked to go for their holidays. The reply was positive. 'Thelma, we like to take our vacation in the winter and go to Palm Beach in Florida. Ben just loves the Seminole.'

Not too sure what the Seminole was (it's the dream of a golf course on the Florida coast), Thelma fished again. 'And what do you do there, just swim and laze about in the sun?'

250

'Why no, Thelma,' said Valerie, deadpan, 'Ben just likes to work on his game.'

It was an entrancing evening, with the two illustrious fighters comparing notes and experiences of life's vicissitudes and traumas. The time came to say goodbye.

'Ben,' said Thelma, giving her thanks for a treasured day, 'do try to come over to England next year and play just once more in the Open. Everyone would so love to see you again.'

The answer was considered with characteristic circumspection. 'Thelma,' he retorted, 'I will if I can putt.'

Few individuals, by their example, have filled the handicapped, the halt and the lame with greater impulse and spirit than Bader and Hogan. As in other things, there was an identity in their respective performances.

Within six years of taking up golf on his artificial legs, Douglas had holed Hoylake in 77 shots ('the most exciting thing that ever happened to me in my life'). Within four years of the surgeons' mending his crushed, torn body, Ben had become Open champion of the United States three more times and British champion once. Of those last victories Hogan was later to say: 'I think the Lord has let me win these . . . championships for a purpose . . . to give courage to those who are sick or injured or broken in body as I once was.'[1]

Alongside this there is the Bader doctrine: 'If you have been luckier than others and been able to get over your problems, you've got to put something back. That's the point.'

Douglas's golf, which, in terms of recreation, had sustained his morale and given him hope again in those first, dreadful years after the accident, brought him, in the three post-war decades, new friendships and a fresh challenge. It added enjoyment and lustre to his life. The game absorbed him rather as flying did. There was a feature which was common to both.

He could fly just as well with artificial legs as he had done with his own. While none who understood would ever suggest that he played golf as well on artificial legs as he would have done on his own, there was no denying that he managed the game incredibly well – better,

1. Gene Gregston, *The Man Who Played For Glory* (Prentice-Hall).

in the best years, than 60 per cent of the ordinary club golfers who regularly play it. He could take his place in any company and keep his end up. He earned a handicap of 4 at the Berkshire in the immediate post-war years and, with it, he could participate and compete. This was important to his demanding mind.

There is a social club in the West End of London called the Nineteenth Club. It has a golfing flavour. Three years after the war, Douglas won the club's annual meeting at Camberley Heath, an undulating, tree- and heather-lined course in Surrey, which none could say had been built for a legless golfer. He played with his friend and solicitor, Alan Garrow, who had himself been a fine games player at Oxford. His scratch, or gross, scores that day were 79 in the morning and, in the afternoon, 82. His net return for thirty-six holes of 153 (75 + 78) won the event. No one else – on his own legs – could match it. It is a feat of physical endurance to walk round a golf course like Camberley twice in a day on a pair of artificial legs. To have done it, to have scored like that at the same time, is hard for ordinary men to credit.

Douglas became a member of the Royal and Ancient Golf Club of St Andrews after the war and was soon a regular competitor in the club's spring and autumn medals. Mostly, he stuck to the same partners, playing often with Henry Longhurst, the journalist, whose golfing commentaries on television brought delight to millions in Britain, the United States and elsewhere; Sir Iain Stewart, the industrialist and a captain of the club, was another frequent playing companion. His best net score in a medal round the Old Course was 73; by then, with the gathering years (it was the 1960s), his handicap had been raised to 9. He took three putts on each of the last two greens and finished two shots behind the winner or, as the Americans prefer it, 'two shots off the pace'.

How did Bader get round Britain's long championship courses – St Andrews, Muirfield, Troon, Prestwick, Hoylake, Birkdale, Sandwich, and others, with all their humps and dunes and hollows, often twice in a day? The short answer is: he walked it. The only concession he would make to outside assistance was in a special situation, such as going up a steep bank or a sandy, seaside path. In fine, loose sand, he gets what he calls 'wheel spin' – like the wheels of a car spinning round and failing to grip. Then he would need a hand from partner or caddy. This had to be properly administered to suit his exacting taste. The aide had to continue moving straight ahead while stretching out a firm arm behind. The fingers of the upturned hand (this was an important refinement) had to be curled up so that Douglas, with arm extended forward, palm down and fingers also curled, could make a solid and secure link with the tug. The pull had to be evenly and consistently maintained; there could be no slackening off. The process worked on the same principle as a motor car being towed on a shaft rather than a rope.

Bader's regular partners and caddies had the drill buttoned up. All were alerted and ready to step into the breech. It became the normal routine; he didn't have to ask. Mounds and inclines were gobbled up without trouble.

There was another accessory which Douglas put to good use. He couldn't sit comfortably on a shooting stick as others do; at the same time it was convenient to be able to rest on the teeing ground while opponents and partners drove off. His golfing friend Sir Raymond Quilter, the parachute manufacturer – an improvisor if ever there was one – solved the problem. Quilter found among his father's possessions a low, three-legged, folding seat covered with a piece of fine but tough hide. His father had used it for shooting towards the end of his life when he could no longer stand and turn with a gun to his shoulder. Instead, he would sit on this low seat and swivel round to one side or the other, taking the birds as they passed to the left or right.

It assisted Douglas's rounds of golf. To be able to rest comfortably while others were driving or putting was a boon. The seat had been fashioned to the Quilter design and appeared then to be the only one in existence, being purpose-built for one man. Years later, and quite by chance, Bader happened to see a replica in a shop in Calgary, Alberta. He bought it, but within no time a third had been added to his collection. The proprietor of the Don Hotel in Darwin, Australia, presented him with one. The news, it seemed, had travelled far and fast.

By any test, eighteen holes of golf – let alone thirty-six – have been, for Bader, a trial of athletic endeavour. To see him stumble momentarily on a piece of uneven ground on a seaside links course, recover, regain his balance and drop readily again into the forward stride, is to recognize at once the speed, nimbleness and poise of the Rugby half-back.

If he falls – and it is very, very seldom that he does – the gymnastics he learnt at Temple Grove have remained so ingrained that he invariably pitches forward, never back. Then, the immensely powerful hands, wrists, forearms and shoulders take the load and, in a moment, he is up again and back into the rhythm of his rolling gait. He recovers his balance like a trapeze artist.

And, when the round is over, the swiftness with which he is able to shower himself, change his legs and his clothes – always remembering the liberal application of Johnson's baby powder to the stumps – cannot fail to surprise. When he gets up in the morning, he allows himself no more than half an hour to bathe, shave, secure his tin pins, and dress. It has all become a precisely disciplined, practised art.

Bader's caddies have, in part, personalized his golf. His relationship with them, as with others who have served him in Service and civilian life, is close, extrovert and totally without 'class'. 'Judge a man by his friends,' they say, 'and a master by his servants'; on that basis he shouldn't have any trouble with St Peter when the time comes to knock on the door.

In his best playing days, there were four caddies whom he regularly employed. There was Leslie at the Berkshire followed by the big, strong Tucker. When he played with the family at Brancaster, it was the one-armed Everett who would take his bag. At Troon and Prestwick, it was always Andy Anderson who would be ready to serve. The goodnatured ribbing and ribaldry that used to go on between them, ceaselessly, all the way round, became an element in the match.

The first time Everett took his clubs at Brancaster was in a Saturday morning foursome. It was the mid-1960s, and a motley crew had gathered on the first tee: Bader; Gus Walker, one of Bomber Command's wartime alumni, with an arm missing; Everett, in a similar fix; the Fifth Earl of Leicester; and the author. It was just the sort of unlikely situation that Bader is quick to exploit.

'Good God, Everett,' he said, 'whatever are things coming to? I've got no legs, you've only got one arm, so has the Air Marshal. . . . What are we all going to do? We'll never get round. . . . His Lordship and Mr Lucas are the only able-bodied men among us. . . .'

In forty-odd years of caddying, Everett had never encountered another like him. He was always inquiring afterwards when next we were expecting 'the group captain to be up'. It was as if some extraordinary apparition had entered his life. He found it difficult to believe that what he had seen was real.

There were stories about each of these splendid characters. There was the time when the faithful Leslie got knocked off his bicycle riding home in the dark one winter's evening from the Berkshire. He had been round the course twice with Douglas that day. When he woke up in hospital, he was asked his name. 'Leslie,' he replied.

The same evening, the hospital telephoned Bader at home. 'We've got your brother, Leslie, here,' they said. 'He's been knocked off his bicycle.'

Douglas was nonplussed. 'I only had one brother and he died in South Africa years ago.'

'Well,' they persisted, 'he says his name is Leslie and all his clothes are marked "Bader".' Thelma never could remember to take off the name tapes.

Of all Bader's caddies, Andy Anderson, one of the characters of Scotland's golfing west coast, was probably the most effective when it came to matching his endless banter. He even silenced Douglas at Troon one morning during a game which his employer was having with Ian Collins, the publisher. As they walked up the eighteenth fairway, Collins suggested that they might all go over the next day to Machrihanish, a delectable golf course 40 or 50 miles to the west across the water, overlooking the Mull of Kintyre. Bader's aircraft was at nearby Prestwick, and it wouldn't take half an hour to fly across.

'Andy,' he said, 'we'll pick you up at home at nine tomorrow morning. There'll be room in the aeroplane for all of us and the clubs.'

Andy stopped dead in his path. Dumping the bag of clubs down defiantly on to the turf, he stood his ground. 'I wouldna fly with ye, ye mad bugger.'

So Douglas never did get to play Machrihanish. . . .

Douglas's forty-year friendship with Henry Longhurst, like so many others among his closer relationships, sprang from golf. Longhurst was one of the select few who, in the daunting and testing post-accident days when Bader was a nobody, encouraged him to persevere with the game. The times they had together on the golf course, particularly at St Andrews, were happy affairs with Henry's ever-ready wit to adorn them.

Longhurst, in his time, had played golf well. After captaining Cambridge, he had later gone on to win the German championship in Hitler's time. Latterly, his game rather fell away. 'Sunk without trace' was the exaggerated epithet he applied to it. Like Hogan, it

255

was the putting that killed him. His handicap, once scratch or better, moved up – 2, 3, 4, 5. . . .

One brisk and sharp autumnal morning, he started out with Douglas on the Old Course in the medal 5, 5, 5, 5, 5; with a stiff following wind, it was too many for a player of his class. Another missed putt gave him his sixth consecutive 5. The familiar nasal voice put it nicely into perspective. 'There it is,' he said, 'another 5 . . . everything's 5 . . . my handicap's 5 . . .'

Douglas, loyal and constant to a point in adversity, was one of the last of Henry's old friends to see him before he died. He went down specially to see him in his Sussex home. The long illness had taken its toll. There were only a few days to go. The next day, a Sunday, Longhurst sent him a card of thanks and affection. The handwriting, by now, had become uncharacteristically weak and thin.

Marvellous to see you, old boy, and your journey much appreciated. Wish we could have had more time to cover what is now more than forty years! Many of them I would like again – but not all. It won't be long now before I shall know the answer we have been waiting for. Will try & let you know. All the very best.

The sequel followed almost exactly two years later – in the summer of 1980. Douglas and his wife were visiting one of the Cheshire Homes near Banbury, in Oxfordshire, to officiate at the annual garden party and fête.

Having made his 'few remarks', Bader started on the rounds. He stopped for a talk with the clairvoyant. She was attracting an inquisitive clientele. After following a few fertile leads, the lady found a receptive point. 'I am in touch', she said, 'with someone called Henry . . .'

'Good heavens!' exclaimed Douglas, warming to it. 'Go on let's have it.'

'He says he went to sleep for a little while and then woke up. . . . And now he's speaking. . . . His words are quite plain: "The grass is a lot greener this side, old boy." '

The golfing visits to St Andrews had other associations. After Douglas's mother-in-law had died in the early 1950s, the response and feeling which illness, loss and loneliness stir in him were soon evident in his concern for Thelma's bereaved stepfather. To provide change as an antidote to sorrow, he would insist that they took Mervyn

256

Addison with them whenever they could on their journeys away from London. Now and then he would take him to St Andrews for one of the meetings. For an old professional soldier there was a friendliness about the place. It touched us greatly in the family to see such thoughtfulness being shown.

For Mervyn Addison, travelling about with Bader, with all the attentions and honours which were paid, reminded him of his resplendent Service days in India in the 1920s. One of the family asked him once what he was doing the following week. 'I'm travelling with "King" Bader,' he said.

It was a fortunate convenience for Douglas that the Royal Air Force station at Leuchars was so close to the 'auld grey toon' on the Fifeshire coast. With the facilities and welcome which the Service offered both him and his aeroplane, he could be checking into his hotel overlooking the Old Course the same morning or afternoon that he had left his house in South Kensington. Moreover, because the autumn medal coincided with the annual Battle of Britain anniversary, he often used to make a point of calling in at Leuchars on its public days.

It was through one of these visits that he came to make contact with Arthur Smith, a patriotic and well-tried Scot, from the nearby town of Kennoway. Enlisting in the Army in 1935, while still under seventeen, Smith had joined the Lanarkshire Yeomanry as a trumpeter. 'Converted to Field Artillery in 1940 and privileged to serve with the Eleventh Indian Division for ten gloriously battered weeks from the Siam border to Singapore', he had been taken a prisoner by the Japanese. Much of his subsequent captivity was passed doing hard labour in a 'damp-ridden copper mine that ran under the South China Sea . . . at Kinkasski, in North Formosa'. There, Arthur Smith began to write his moving poetry.

After spending a Battle of Britain day at Leuchars, wandering among the aircraft, old and new, he 'sketched out' these sensitive and appealing 'lines of consolation' to the ageing Spitfire – and to the 'indomitable war-horse of a pilot' who had once added glitter to its name. Writing under the pseudonym of Clyde Sinclair, he gave his verses the title 'Address tae an Auld Spitfire'. When he had finished the poem he sent Douglas a copy care of the Royal and Ancient Golf Club of St Andrews. The old Duxford wing leader numbers it among the most treasured of his personal papers.

257

Whit' maks' ye look sae sad and lost, Auld Spitfire: Whit's the maitter?
These Jets beside ye canna' boast o' Deeds like yours, or better.
You've had yur' Day, and proved yur' Worth, in Fearless, Firm Formation,
And smashed Armadas o' The North, tae save an Island Nation.

Don't pout yur' 'Prop', nor wilt yur' Wings because the people pass ye
Tae look at Supersonic Things wha's vanities harass ye.
When Tyranny, at Freedom's Door, in Armoured Might, wis knockin',
Ye made a Nation's 'Finest 'Oor' – The Tyrant's Blade wis Broken.

Though streakin' Jets reflect the sun – The people don't forget ye. –
You're staunin' noo on Hallowed Grun', – A Monument we've set ye.
You've Banked and Spun, at Battle's height when greater numbers matched
    ye,
And cleared the skies o' Fascist Blight, while Freedom lovers watched ye.

Noo au' yur' Supersonic Brood kin' frolic, frisk and play
In skies where once in Balance stood, The Scales o' Destiny.
– Yur' youthful Dash, and Fortitude, and sense o' Service – True.
– Has won the lastin' Gratitude 'o' mony for The Few'.

Ye seem tae ken' yon man that walks, on artificial Limb. –
– He strokes yur' side, and gently talks – YE SEEM TAE TALK TAE HIM
– Ye seem tae me, withoot a doot', attached tae yin' anither: –
– Ye maun' hae much tae talk aboot. – Ah'll leave ye baith the gither.

Which professional helped Douglas most with his golf? After the war,
when his handicap was coming quickly down, there was Arthur
Lacey at the Berkshire and Archie Compston at Wentworth. He
played regularly with each.

In later years, he has benefited from the simple doctrine of John
Jacobs, one of the world's most sought-after teachers. John, like
Bader, is quite tough about disablement. The advice, as ever, is
distinct and decisive. 'Now come along, group captain, ball further
back at the address and shoulders square. . . . Clear that right
shoulder out of the way in the backswing and let your arms swing up
to the top. . . . That's the position I want. . . . Now, go on, hit it as
hard as you like from there – hit the ball with the clubhead, that's
what it's there for.' Douglas has always had a regard for the blunt,
Yorkshire approach.

Compston was dedicated to improving Bader's golf after the war.
He knew what the game meant to him in his life. But he didn't say
much about the mechanics. His pupil had a good eye and he was a
games player. He tended to let him get on with it. Douglas recognized
Archie's strength.

Where he helped me was in showing me how to get the ball round the course in a reasonable score; how to play sensibly, not doing damned silly things, not trying for too much. He warned me off taking a wooden club out of the rough instead of a 5 iron, or taking too straight a club out of a bunker. He taught me to *think* round a golf course. . . .

This tousle-headed, rugged, swashbuckling buccaneer became 'a great chum'. His forthrightness – particularly when he got exasperated with a pupil – appealed greatly to Bader. There was some similarity in their two temperaments.

They were playing together one afternoon, long after Archie had left Wentworth, at the Mid-Ocean Club in Bermuda. An American insurance broker and his young and attractive Dutch wife had joined them. The girl, a pupil of Compston, was making heavy weather of it. She teed up another ball as the mentor's patience ran out.

'Go on, lady,' said Archie, 'for Christ's sake hit the fucking thing.'

Bader smiled to himself when later he heard the lady had become the Bermudian champion.

28

Colleague and subordinate

Those who were at the top of Shell in the 1960s, as Bader played out his time, have a definitive recollection of him as both a colleague and a subordinate. The similarity of views, as well as the conviction which supports them, is striking. It greatly assists an assessment of the estimation in which he was held by his masters.

Douglas had completed thirty-six years with the company, war service included, when he retired from it in 1969, a few months short of his sixtieth birthday. His final years as managing director of the aircraft subsidiary, carrying the name and image of Shell abroad, presented an arresting paradox.

His standing as a public figure was at, or near, its height. His international work for the group took him to virtually every major country outside Russia, the Eastern Bloc countries and China. Yet he remained extrovertly and staunchly British, in thought, word and deed. He rested his principles on his allegiance to queen and country just as he did on his loyalty to Shell and the Royal Air Force. He would willingly have gone to the stake in defence of any one of them.

When he wrote or spoke in public, at home or overseas, he did so – or he *felt* he did so – as a private individual and as a Very British Person. His views, often widely represented, and now and then misrepresented, were his own. He spoke for himself, but his unequivocal, uncompromising and individualistic attitudes to the more controversial of the world's issues were sometimes inimical to Shell's interests. His vigorous and outspoken championing of Britain, its institutions and traditions – flavoured, frequently, by a pugnacious, imperialist approach – was not necessarily always consonant with the company's declared theme.

Consistent towards those whom he was intent to uphold, he delivered, on one of his last visits for Shell to southern Africa, a spirited defence of his friend, Ian Smith, the Rhodesian Prime Minister. It was in the controversial aftermath of Smith's announcement of Rhodesia's UDI. Included in the address was a pointed assault on the British government's determination to impose sanctions. The press in London picked up the speech: 'Shell Chief Blasts Sanctions – Bader's Outspoken Attack . . .' The headlines were predictable.

David Barran, the managing director to whom he was then reporting, asked to see him on his return. 'Since when', he inquired, 'have you been a Shell chief?' The need to reconcile public utterance with corporate interest was stressed. It was a playback of an incident which had occurred ten years or so earlier in New Zealand.

Douglas had been in Christchurch in 1956 (the year his public service had been recognized with the award of the CBE) talking to the Tin Hats, an association of ex-servicemen, vociferous supporters of the British cause. The Suez crisis was in spate, with all that it meant to the interests of Britain's oil producers in the Middle East.

He had given the assembled company a sharp piece of his mind (strongly applauded) about Nehru's offensive strictures upon Britain's action. He had been told that the press would not be there; but his remarks were seized on and headlined. The embarrassment was compounded by a current meeting of the Colombo powers and by Bader's appointment to see the Prime Minister, Sidney Holland, in Wellington, the next day.

Douglas came straight to the point as he began his meeting with the New Zealand leader. 'I must apologize, sir,' he said, 'if my remarks about the Indian Prime Minister in Christchurch yesterday have caused you and your government embarrassment. I had been told I would not be reported.'

'That's all right, boy,' replied Holland. 'Someone had to say it.'

But it hadn't gone with quite the same swing in Shell's offices in London. A managing director's cable was dispatched to Bader leaving no doubt about the company's reaction to the publicity which had come at a delicate moment in its relations with the Arab world. Everything had subsequently been amicably explained and resolved, but it was a further manifestation of the problem he had in reconciling his vehement personal views with corporate interests.

The nub of the problem was plain. Douglas's standing and renown as a national and international figure, whose words and actions were 'news' wherever he went, was out of balance with the level at which he was operating within the corporation. Add to this his well-known characteristics – his dogmatism, his dislike of compromise and consensus, his disposition to see things as black or white – never grey; his acute sensitivity and aversion to criticism; his need to be told when he had done a good job; the impulsiveness of his mind – and there was a mix which did not easily fill a multinational mould.

The extent to which he rubbed shoulders with the world's leaders was not publicly revealed. He did not talk about it, nor did he discuss his perambulations along the corridors of power, except in private, and then only among close friends and family. Yet the catalogue was far-ranging.

There was Sir Harold Wilson, confiding in him at 10 Downing Street during the critical run-up to Rhodesia's UDI: 'Tell him [Ian Smith] from me when you see him in Salisbury to do nothing and to go on doing nothing for as long as he can. . . .'

There was an early post-war meeting with the impressive Jan Smuts, and the South African leader's moving valediction as they parted: 'I'm always pleased to see a good man.'

There were his exchanges with Churchill and his stays with other Commonwealth leaders – with Roy Welensky, Prime Minister of the Central African Federation, and his wife at their home in Salisbury, and their thought in inviting to breakfast one morning the two be-reaved sons of his friend, Johnny Plagis, the most brilliant of Rho-desia's wartime fighter pilots, who had then, sadly, just died; with Robert Menzies in Canberra, and so on. It was seldom that a Shell visit to a Commonwealth country took place without Douglas re-establishing contact with the governor-general or high commissioner, particularly if he happened to be 'an old chum'.

Then, again, there were the little gestures in high places. There was the fulfilment of a promise to Giles Wilson, the Prime Minister's schoolboy son, made one evening when Douglas and Thelma were upstairs in the Wilsons' flat at No. 10. There, the teenager, sur-rounded by his model aeroplanes, was offered a flight from White Waltham in the 'real thing' – Shell's Beech Travelair, with its two 180 h.p. Lycoming engines and its cruising speed of 195 m.p.h. at 9000 feet. The boy was given his treat (with his parents' slightly concerned consent) one memorable Saturday morning when academic studies did not interfere. The pilot officer in Douglas also admitted to some rather special motoring. 'We got the Alvis[1] up to 108 m.p.h., coming back along the M4 to Downing Street from the airfield.'

1. Bader's Type TE 21, 3-litre Alvis. Tended and nursed, it completed 253,000 miles on the same engine.

262

It was all, in a sense, part of the broad sweep of his outside public relations work which he combined with his routine, but varied, activities within the company. Put together with his continuing support of the disabled, which Shell encouraged, and his preoccupation with the visits to the group's outposts in jungle and desert, it made, as John Loudon had it, 'quite a package – in fact, a fascinating package'.

Loudon saw the job from the standpoint of an overseeing managing director.

Douglas had a very special position in Shell. He had his own aeroplane. He was largely his own boss. We all recognized that his usefulness and value extended well beyond the function of the aircraft company into public and personnel relations. As a booster of morale at the isolated points of operation – oil exploration and production – he did a wonderful job. He wasn't always right; quite often, as a matter of fact, he was wrong; but he gave people confidence and spirit when they were far away from home. There are very few men who could have done that.

Nor was the service restricted to Shell. The Iraq Petroleum Company turned to Bader when the Iraqi authorities stopped it from using its own aircraft in support of its operations. They had insisted that Iraq Airways' aeroplanes be employed instead. He went to Baghdad to see his 'old chum', Brigadier Jenabi, the head of the state-owned airline. They had been contemporaries together at Cranwell.

'Ah, Dooglass,' cried Jenabi, in friendly embrace, 'what can I do for you?'

In ten minutes the oil company had won back its right to use its own aircraft.

Few outside the company were aware of the contribution that Bader had made to the introduction of the helicopter into Shell's exploration and production work.

No pilot, particularly a purist, brought up as he and the wartime flyers had been on conventional, powered flight, took readily to the concept of the rotor blade or autogyro. In his early dislike – even mistrust – of the principle, he was to be numbered alongside many of his contemporaries. For him, and for them, it could be no more than an acquired, a necessarily acquired, taste.

But times change. As the latent potential of this 'unnatural' form of air transport stretched out from the 1950s into the 1960s and beyond, Douglas became a strong proponent of its application for Shell.

In the first post-war years of development, the cost of constructing a mile of road through a dense African jungle to a virgin exploration point worked out at around £21,000 (at the money values of those days). The provision of access, without which there could be no progress, was thus a heavy part of the outgoings in opening up a site. The helicopter became a prime 'cost saver'. Rectangular landing pads, cut out of tall forests, were forerunners of the erection of the rigs. The supply of more portable drilling equipment, capable of being lifted by this means, followed on from any plan. Thus did the helicopter take its place as an essential element of Shell's aircraft fleet.

In the military metaphor, the corporation's senior executives saw Douglas as a field commander, a man who dealt in the currency of human and public affairs and the more practical issues of life. They never saw him as a 'chief of staff' or an administrator. That wasn't his line. Unremitting attention to detail (except flying detail) has not been one of his strengths.

Who else, for instance, could have gone into the local businessmen's club in Hong Kong with Dick Frost, Shell's general manager, and in less than ten minutes raised not the £100 which was needed but something closer to £1000, to help a nineteen-year-old Chinese girl get two new artificial legs made for her at Roehampton? She had lost her own, both below the knee, as a small child in the bombing of Canton in the 1930s. Hitherto she had been managing with a make-shift pair which a local Chinese mechanic had run up for her in his workshop. Douglas asked him where he had found the design. A pleased smile exposed a mouthful of teeth: 'I find velly good advertisement in paper.'

A year or so later, Douglas went to see the girl with her new legs. She was still living with the Australian couple who had originally contacted him. They were Salvation Army workers. 'There she was, old boy, terribly pleased, striding round the room as mobile as anything. . . . No trouble at all.'

Bader had a knack of striking up friendships with the locals on his travels. There was Joseph, the Hauser, who used to drive him out to the airfield at Ikeja, whenever he was staying in Lagos. Douglas took him flying one morning in his aeroplane.

As they climbed through a thin layer of cloud which the sun's heat had not yet had time to disperse, Joseph was bewildered as they lost sight of the ground. 'Master,' he inquired quizzically, 'how you find your way? There are no signposts up here.'

Bader tuned in the radio compass to the unseen airfield. 'In a moment, Joseph, we will be going down through the cloud and you will see Ikeja straight ahead of us.'

The young man's eyes stayed glued to the compass. As they broke cloud, there was the airfield ahead. A grin transformed the wondering face. He pointed to the amazing instrument. 'That's white man's juju, master,' he said.

As they drove back into Lagos, Joseph became silent. He was pondering this new and wonderful experience he had just had. After a while he spoke. 'Master,' he observed, 'there's not much foot-palaver in an aeroplane.'

Nigeria had usually proved to be an eventful hunting ground for Douglas. It was from there that he and Bill Swerdloff used to fly up into the French Sahara. The desert held a fascination for him. It reminded him of Beau Geste and all the other Wren novels he had read with delight in his younger days.

One time, the two of them flew up, via Niamey, to Timbuktu. He had never really believed the place existed. He wanted actually to see it for himself. Like Joseph and his 'white man's juju', for Bader this was a mystery to be unravelled. Once they were there, there was little to be seen. To travel hopefully is often better than to arrive.

Amid all the travels and other work, a worry now beset Douglas – and the family. Thelma's health began to worsen. The first traces of the emphysema which seized her lungs and was so soon to cut short her life had been diagnosed. Her heavy smoking gravely exacerbated it. Breathlessness and, with it, a growing inability to take even light exercise, became the outward and visible sign of the advancing malady. Visits to specialists and to King Edward VII Hospital at Midhurst, in Sussex, increased. Douglas's concern mounted. The outlook was bleak. But Thelma had the courage and bearing of a Stoic. These attributes marched side by side with her for such time as remained.

Meanwhile, Douglas continued his multifarious activities with expected zeal and zest. His speaking engagements took him all over the country. Important among them was his speech at the dinner given earlier in his honour by Sir Charles Forte and the National Sporting

Club, at the Café Royal in London. It was a distinguished evening. The guests, specially chosen from among his friends, old comrades and colleagues, were drawn from a wide cross-section of British life. Shell's alumni were there in strength.

Dermot Boyle, now a past chief of the air staff, proposed Bader's health from the wealth of material which their long years of friendship had provided. Douglas, much moved, spoke – as he always does – shortly and with the effect which his personality conveys. The care he had devoted to the preparation of his remarks quickly showed through as he developed his theme.[1]

He was, for a change, anxious as he got up; not nervous, but concerned that his words should fit the mood and the occasion. It wasn't an easy speech to make, but when he sat down he felt that the room had been with him. If such is a speaker's feeling, he has a right to rest content.

Nearly four years after the National Sporting Club dinner, on the day of Sir Winston Churchill's funeral, an incident occurred which bridged the years. Bader was driving with the Shell Company's chairman, Fred Stephens, and Frank Hopwood, one of the other managing directors, to St Paul's for the service.

As the catafalque passed through Trafalgar Square and into the Strand on this searchingly cold February day, the escorting units which were to join the slow-moving procession prepared to take up station. Precedence of position was given to a small but illustrious contingent – no more than a dozen strong – of Battle of Britain pilots, worthy representatives of Churchill's 'Few'. Led by Al Deere, who, with his countryman the 11 Group AOC, Keith Park, had brought undying glory to New Zealand in the battle, the distinguished posse had spent several hours on the previous day on the square at Uxbridge, under the critical eye of a drill sergeant, trying to recapture some of their pristine smartness and shine. Now, dressed in their ceremonial regalia, they stood there in the searing east wind, shrivelled with cold, anxiously awaiting the moment to move off.

The Shell Rolls Royce came to a silent and unnoticed halt exactly opposite them. Douglas, dressed in a morning coat and striped pants and comfortably protected from the elements, wound down the window. A lowered, but unmistakably familiar voice penetrated into a dozen pairs of receptive ears. 'For Christ's sake,' he said, 'stand up and look as if you bore the brunt in 1940.'

*

1. The text of the speech is in Appendix A.

Bader had 5360 flying hours in his log-book when he made his last flight for Shell. It was now forty-one years, almost to the month, since he had first flown with Pearson in the Avro. In the twenty-three years which had passed since his return to the company after the war, he had completed 100 hours short of 4000. The last 850 had been amassed in the Beech Travelair, a beautifully stable and advanced aeroplane, with all the modern aids. Things had moved on since 1946 when he and Jimmy Doolittle, sitting jovially side by side together in the tiny Proctor, had made their goodwill tour of Europe and North Africa.

There wasn't another pilot, anywhere in the world, who had had greater all-round experience of flying light aeroplanes – and navigating them. The truth is that, taking everything into account, Bader was, by now, out on his own. His flying with the company in the 1940s, 1950s and 1960s had mirrored his lifestyle. It was tailored for him and for the era. It will never be repeated in Shell, that is quite sure. There are, however, questions to ask.

Had this massive, multinational corporation wanted to do so, could it have used Douglas in a more conventional, stereotyped, line-management way? And, had it tried, would he have been prepared, *twenty years before*, to stick the routine? Would he have stomached the admin. and the management processes and chores?

Most of his colleagues say no, it would have been totally out of character. David Barran, the last managing director to whom he reported before leaving the company, stiffer and stricter by inclination than the others, is by no means so sure. If, instead of having the latitude to play things his way after the war and flying about all over the world, Douglas had been required *then* to conform with the customary staff and management sequences, Barran believes it might well have worked. Moreover, he thinks it quite possible that, taking the long view, it might have provided him with greater fulfilment in terms of personal satisfaction and gain.

It is a nice point, coming, as it does, from a group chairman and the occupant of the chair of one of the four great joint-stock banks. Bader, when taxed with the hypothesis, will not commit himself to a view; indeed, one is left with the faintest hint that perhaps, on the whole, he is thankful that the choice did not have to be made at the time.

It is probably true that Barran played Bader on a tighter rein than his predecessors. It would have been in his manner to do so. 'I made up my mind when the aircraft company came under me that I would treat Douglas just as I would treat any other Shell employee at that level.'

The resolve was soon put to the test. Some matter had come up for decision while Bader was on a visit abroad. The managing director had asked for him – only to find he was in West Africa and wasn't expected back until the following week.

Barran put the question to him on his return. 'To whom do you normally report when you go away?'

Douglas gave his reply. He wouldn't expect to have to bother a managing director with that sort of point.

'Well,' retorted Barran, 'in future you'll bother this one with it.'

It was an isolated example, but it might be thought that such a relationship would have been destined to founder. Not so. Barran, apart from other things, had recognized acutely what flying represented to Douglas in his life, and what it had come to mean to him in terms of mobility.

The Beech Travelair was a sizeable asset in any company's books, but he determined that, when he left, Douglas should be given the aeroplane to take with him into retirement. There would then be no break in the continuity of transport to which he had been accustomed for nearly a quarter of a century. It would, furthermore, be a fitting way for the company to mark its respect for one of the most extraordinary men it had ever employed. In this single, magnanimous gift was invested the humanity of a great corporation.

There was a poignant postscript to this farewell act. A young cousin of Sir David's wife, an art student, had stepped off the pavement in Trafalgar Square and been hit by a bus. The girl had lost a foot and now lay recovering in a ward in Westminster Hospital. At nineteen, she was learning for the first time how forbidding can be the darkness of despair.

One afternoon, a thick-set, stocky and sturdy figure, with a rolling, clattering gait, came swinging down the aisle towards her. His face was familiar from his pictures; his infectious bravado and spirit seemed unconsciously to fill the ward. He sat down on the bed and talked positively and easily for half an hour. In those minutes he changed a young girl's attitude to adversity.

'I realized', she said afterwards, 'that I was now looking at life differently.'

David Barran gave expression to a family's feeling. 'It was an act of true Christian charity.'

The day after Douglas retired from Shell, he was interviewed on BBC radio. The reporter rounded off the exchanges with a final question. 'Has the loss of your legs', he asked, 'been a great handicap to you in your life? Has it prevented you from achieving some ambitions?'

The spontaneous answer is often the most revealing. 'Well, if it had,' he replied briskly, 'you wouldn't be here talking to me now.'

29

There was youth and gaiety and laughter

Bader attacked his 'retirement' with uninhibited spirit and purpose. Having left Shell after handing over the managing directorship of the aircraft company – as he had always hoped he might do – to Roy Snodgrass, his lifelong colleague and friend, he now started to assemble a portfolio of new interests.

As he entered his sixties, he had a wealth of aviation experience to offer; his mechanical flair, which had first been applied to stripping down and tuning the engines of his various motor cycles at Cranwell, and which had been freshened during the years with Shell, was an additional asset. It was natural, therefore, that he should establish a consultancy base on which to rest his services.

His newspaper articles continued. With the Murdoch and News International takeover of the *News of the World* in 1969 Douglas slipped across to the other side of Fleet Street and started writing intermittent features for Express Newspapers. And when, in due course, the ownership of the *Express* passed from the Beaverbrook interests into the hands of Nigel Broackes's and Victor Matthews's Trafalgar House group, Bader's association with the papers continued.

It was in contrast to his position with the Cunard Steamship Company. There, Sir Basil Smallpiece, the chairman, after a long run with BOAC, had retained him as a consultant in the field of aviation and, in particular, in the use of the helicopter. But Cunard, in its turn, fell a victim of Trafalgar House. In the inevitable clear-out which follows every takeover, Douglas had his anticipated meeting with Victor Matthews, the shipping company's new executive chairman.

He made the parting easy for the chief executive by telling him first, in his usual jocular way, what he knew quite well he was now going to be told – that there was no place for him in the reorganized and slimmed-down company. In the brief and good-humoured exchanges that followed he added a salutary rider. 'Now that you have got hold of Cunard, my advice to you is to get out of civil aviation altogether.' His realism appealed to Matthews.

It was the start of a friendship which has blossomed with the passing of control of the *Express* to Trafalgar House and Lord Matthews's accession to the chair of the newspaper group.

There had been other consultancies, among them with Trusthouse Forte and Hunting Percival; but most of them had to be surrendered with his appointment to the statutory Civil Aviation Authority where, under Lord Boyd-Carpenter's dominant chairmanship, he was to make a significant impact with his conduct of the committee which had been set up to examine the critical issue of pilot fatigue.

John Boyd-Carpenter soon recognized that in Douglas Bader he had a man whose experience and knowledge commanded the aircrews' healthy regard. They wouldn't easily get the better of someone with that sort of background and personality. He had too many of the answers for the airline pilots to try to put anything over him. There wasn't anything they could tell him about flying – *real* flying.

From the air to the road: his Royal Air Force and Battle of Britain association with Patrick Barthropp opened the way for a seat on the board of the personalized and successful London car hire firm which bears its founder's name. A wartime fighter pilot, Paddy Barthropp had had his full share of the air shooting when, one day in 1942 over Saint-Omer, a Focke-Wulf 190 returned the compliment and he spent the rest of the war at the Germans' expense. But, having once placed his trust in the Rolls Royce Merlin engine, it was on the products of the famous Derby-based company (he started with a Bentley and then added a Rolls Royce) that he established his private business enterprise in the second half of the 1950s.

Sitting quietly up in the sun, south of Hyde Park, with plenty of tactical height and surprise, the wing commander started picking off the business of the older and more staid competitors around him. With a series of nicely timed sallies against the enemy, he made his mark and later found advantage in adding Douglas's name to his opportunist and spirited board. It had the ring of a fighter squadron about it.

Finally, when Bader's time on the Civil Aviation Authority came to an end, it was with Norman Angel's air component firm, Aircraft

Equipment International, at Ascot, that he established a connection and made his working base.

Such was the new crop of interests which the post-Shell years had yielded. With the activity thus provided, and with the mobility which the Beech Travelair continued to afford, Douglas maintained a style and a tempo which was little changed from the life he had been leading in the quarter of a century that had passed since the war.

It was, of course, strange to be working for himself after being caught up, for so long, in the currents of a vast, multinational corporation. But if the commercial backdrop had changed, there was at once no adjustment in the sweep and thrust of Douglas and Thelma's social life. Since they were first married they had always been practised weekenders, staying away with their friends in the country. A reciprocal consequence of their own entertaining in London, these visits had become a feature of their life together.

Bader was, by any test, an unconventional and often unpredictable guest. His restlessness had probably got something to do with it. For the uninitiated and anxious hostess, his eccentricities could be unnerving. The old hands, however, had long since come to know what to expect – and what not to expect. His idiosyncrasies were understood and accepted as a normal hazard of a Bader weekend.

How, it may well be asked, does Douglas get away with his wayward and highly 'personal' behaviour? It's a good question. He has been walking, untouched, away from it for years. True, age and wear and tear have mellowed him and brought stability where, in middle and earlier times, there might be turmoil. Some scars may remain; but, mostly, it has been his charm which has spirited away devils and melted outrage. He has unreasonable reserves of the commodity.

Edward Bromley-Davenport, one of Douglas's old golfing partners, got it exactly right one Sunday morning years ago when the group captain had just made a muddle of a golf date. Exasperated, Edward turned to the others in the game: 'Why *are* we so fond of Douglas when he *is* so *terribly* tiresome!'

All was now being overtaken by the cumulative weight of Thelma's gathering sickness. But such was the measure of her fortitude that even close friends like Annie Griggs, Ben Cadbury, Dixie Mackintosh and Pip and Nick Harrison could not penetrate the disguise. None save her relatives and advisers knew how truly ill she was. Nor would she defer to the insistence of her physicians, Lord Hunt and Sir Geoffrey Marshall, that she should give up her heavy smoking. Two packets of twenty a day remained, by and large, her quota.

It was during her last visit to Midhurst in the latter part of 1969 that the medical head of King Edward VII's Hospital conveyed the incontrovertible message. Dr Geoffrey Todd, who had so many times bestowed his care upon her, went into Thelma's room with Douglas. With an admirable Australian bluntness and courage, he set the niceties aside. 'Thelma,' he said, 'it's as simple as this. If you go on smoking you'll die. If you give it up we shall keep you going for a bit.'

With all the demands upon him, Douglas's frequent visits to Midhurst from London became a time-absorbing burden. Their friends, the Duke and Duchess of Richmond, understanding allies in a crisis, offered him open sanctuary at nearby Goodwood, leaving him free to come and go as he pleased. In his motor-racing days, Freddy Richmond had displayed several of the attributes which had taken Douglas into the skies. And in the General Strike of 1926 his daily transport of the continental mail from London to the Channel ports was in character with his natural verve, wiriness and energy. The drives through the night in the old 3-litre Bentley, leaving Buck's Club at 1 a.m. with the other cars, and reaching Dover well inside two hours, was stamped with the mark of Le Mans and the enduring resolve 'The Mail must get through.' In these sombre days, Douglas knew that with Betty and Freddy Richmond he was in gentle and sympathetic hands.

The end, when it came, came swiftly. As 1970 turned into 1971, a bad head and chest cold was sufficient to complicate the emphysema from which Thelma suffered. She was moved hurriedly to the London Clinic where Douglas also took a room to be near her. From there, with the family, he kept his vigil.

During the night her heart, taxed beyond endurance in the months-long struggle for breath, stopped beating. Only the attachment to the artificial heart and lung machine kept her alive and stayed the fall of the final curtain. But soon the play was over; the soul of one of the two leading characters in this astonishing drama had departed. The union of courage and unthinking faith, which she and the young, unknown flying officer, without means, legless and

273

devoid of prospects, had fashioned thirty-seven years before, had been severed.

Its total finality (Thelma died on Sunday, 24 January 1971) was tempered by an interlude of intense poignancy. It was as if the great days, the sunny days, the glorious days of Duxford and 1940 had returned to offer her their last salute.

Tim Vigors, unheralded, unannounced – and unknowing – who had fought side by side with Douglas in Treble-Two over the Dunkirk beaches, was in the London Clinic seeing his wife who had been seriously injured in a riding fall. Tim Vigors – the same young Royal Air Force officer who had turned up at the Pantiles, near Sunning-dale, with Douglas that June morning after the withdrawal and, with him, had fallen asleep in the chair within ten minutes of setting foot in the house – spent and utterly drained. The same Tim Vigors: good-looking, gallant, engagingly Irish and attractive, courting Thelma's nineteen-year-old sister, Jill; a sure-fire knockout for any young girl. The same decorated officer who, with the war over, and before each had left the Service, had become one of Bader's station commanders in the North Weald sector of 11 Group. Now, as in other days, he took up station at Douglas's side.

But the battle was different – and so, too, were the odds. Then, there had been struggle and fighting and loss, of course; it was inevitable. But so, also, had there been youth and gaiety, love and triumph, laughter and romance. Now, there was nothing. Life echoed its emptiness. All at once it seemed to strike cold, like coming in from the warm sunlight and entering a long, damp cave.

30

Second marriage

Douglas faced up to his loss with evident resolution and grit. He was, by now, experienced in meeting adversity. His philosophy owed something to disablement. No one can change what has happened; one has to live with it and accept it. Once more his realism took command.

One of his first concerns was for Thelma's memorial service which his friends had urged him to allow them to arrange. It was held on 6 March 1971, at St Clement Danes. Crowley-Milling, still then a serving officer, with the spirit of 242 in his heart, played the leading role in its organization.

There was a capacity congregation. The music and the singing, which bore the stamp of the selective taste of Thelma's brother, Jock (John Addison, the composer), stirred the mind. Flowers adorned the setting, and in an address of simple, moving dignity, Sir Dermot Boyle made words live.[1]

The London *Evening News* carried a headline on its story: 'The Few Salute Thelma Bader'. The spirit of 1940 burned brightly in the capital that day.

Golf continued to be Bader's ally in these days, just as it had become in the rough times before the war. It had brought him many friends over the years. They were friendships he greatly prized. With them he had played so often at the Berkshire, Sandwich, Troon and St Andrews. The regular partners came from a close circle: John Beck and his wife, Baba; Jack Mellor, Gubby Allen, Edward Bromley-Davenport and Peter Clapham; Sir Iain Stewart, Ian Collins and

1. The text of this address is in Appendix B.

Guy Jamieson; between them, they embraced singular accomplishments in diverse fields of endeavour. Some were soon to depart, but all offered him the companionship which his life has always needed.

It is golf, also, that he has to thank for bringing him, in due time, his second wife. Douglas had partnered Joan Murray (they were both members of the Berkshire and had met there, first, in 1960) in the mixed foursomes competition in one of the annual meetings at Roehampton organized in support of the British Legless Ex-Servicemen's Association. She had taken the place of Douglas's original partner, Diana Critchley, who had had to drop out.

Each, at best, had played to a relatively low handicap – Joan, a championship competitor, off a Ladies' Golf Union handicap of 2, and Douglas off 4. Between them, they made a formidable combination, sufficiently strong that day to win the scratch prize for the best gross return.

Joan Murray (née Hipkiss) was born in Worcestershire, the daughter of the owner of a successful steel business in the midlands. From childhood, spent in her native county and at Borth, near Aberdovey in Wales, horses had absorbed her days. With an innate aptitude, and all the opportunities which were open to her, she soon developed into a proficient horsewoman, riding well to hounds, competing regularly in point-to-point meetings and eventually making her mark as a competitor in showjumping events.

It was her love of horses, and riding, and her work for the disabled, which equipped her to be one of the original volunteer supporters of Riding for the Disabled, a charity of which Princess Anne is the patron and Douglas Bader an honorary life vice-president. It is a movement which, within two decades and under different banners, has become established worldwide.

With this background, and with golf, which came very much second after riding, Joan Murray had common interests with Douglas. When they married quietly on 3 January 1973, at Earlsdon, near Coventry, the vicar who officiated was an unusual entrant into the Church of England. A wartime pilot in the Royal Air Force and a friend of Bader, the Reverend Tom Knight had finished up as a group captain in charge of a Bomber Command station at Gaydon in Warwickshire. Having, in due time, retired from the Service, he had then taken holy orders.

After their marriage, Joan and Douglas Bader made their home near the small village of Marlston, in the Berkshire countryside. There, in a farming environment, Joan could pursue the interests which have been so much a part of her life – riding, animals, the country. For Douglas, Withers Farm is 30 miles from his office in Ascot, and the same from his golf at the nearby Berkshire. Driving at the speeds he does, he can normally reach his house in South Kensington in little more than an hour.

Thus, for the family (Joan has three children by her first marriage, all now grown up, with two married, each with a child), the living arrangements suit varying needs and tastes. And tastes is the word, for there is no better table kept in all England than the one Joan Bader offers her guests at Withers Farm.

Their respective – and combined – work for the disabled has given the Baders a joint and abiding concern. There is, demonstrably, a similarity in their approach to the problems of the handicapped. It rests upon a base of firmness, allied to understanding.

Joan's work as an instructor for the Riding for the Disabled Association is, for the most part, centred now on the Royal Mews at Buckingham Palace or, as Douglas will have it, 'opposite the Girl Guides' shop in Buckingham Palace Road'. Although all ages are catered for, her concern is primarily with the young.

The children, who range from five to six upwards, and who are brought to the Mews by minibus once a week for their riding lessons, are drawn from special schools in the East End of London. Mostly they are cerebral palsy cases and come from seriously deprived, mixed-up and often broken homes. The doctor and physiotherapist at the schools pick out the children whom they consider are most likely to benefit from the therapy which the weekly riding sessions offer.

Generally, the children are confined to their wheelchairs. They are accustomed to being looked down upon by their elders and others. Put them on a pony and their vantage point is dramatically elevated. It is they, and not others, who now have the advantage of superior height. It offers them their only practical chance of being able to place a hand on top of an adult's head. It is this, and the independence that riding gives them (they can then cast off their wheelchairs and crutches), which offers a new outlook on life. And when there is added the contact with the ponies, and all that this means in their young lives, the effects of the therapy upon them can be profound.

The degree of the mental and physical indignity to which the children have often been subjected is barely credible. The instances

277

are poignant in their consistency. There was the red-headed boy of ten who, when he first started coming to the Mews, wouldn't let Joan Bader – or anyone – touch him; nor would he speak. The story was that, when he was three or four, his mother had had twins, one of whom had died. After the death, the child was told by the parent that it was he who should have died because there was something wrong with him. He was an abnormal child whereas the baby was quite healthy. After that, he never spoke again either at home or at school.

After two or three weeks of riding in the indoor school, there was still no improvement. Then one day, after his ride, Joan said firmly but persuasively to him: 'Come on, touch the pony and say "thank you".'

The boy went up to the animal, gave him a pat and in a clear and distinct voice said 'thank you'. The physiotherapist could hardly credit it.

As the weeks went by his condition steadily improved. Whenever he got out of the school bus, he would run up to Joan and hug and kiss her. ('He really quite hurt.') All the while he was speaking in long and coherent sentences. The patting of the pony and the uninhibited words of gratitude had liberated his constricted mind and tongue.

Then came the depressing reverse. One afternoon when he arrived for his ride he was back where he had started. Not a word came from his mouth. The weeks of effort seemed to have come to nought. Joan asked the physiotherapist what she thought could have happened. 'Oh,' she said, 'his mother had a boyfriend staying in the house last weekend and because there was a man around the boy was ill treated as usual to make him keep quiet. It's always the same. When that happens he reverts to his old condition.'

It took three or four more weekly rides, with patting and thanking the pony at the end, before the hurt had been exorcized and the sentences began to flow again.

Bader received his knighthood in June 1976. James Callaghan was by then at No. 10 and Douglas appeared in his list. Forty-five years had passed since the crash at Woodley in 1931. During the interim, he had, by his actions, often exceeded what, in the cliché, is termed 'the normal call of duty'.

Recognition of his achievements – in war and in peace – had

already brought him several accolades: two Distinguished Service Orders, two Distinguished Flying Crosses, three mentions in despatches, and, from the French, the Croix de Guerre and then the Légion d'Honneur. It was now twenty years since his appointment as a Commander of the British Empire. He was thus no novice at investitures. The conferment of the knighthood, however, which required him to kneel before the monarch, posed an altogether new set of physical problems not satisfactorily covered by the Queensberry Rules.

General Gillett, secretary of the Central Chancery of the Orders of Knighthood, who was responsible for the arrangements, telephoned Bader beforehand. He had been alerted to the possible difficulty by Douglas's 'chum', Frank King, then the General Officer Commanding the British Army of the Rhine, who was himself to receive the GCB at the same investiture. With a fine, selfless prescience, he had thought about his friend's predicament.

'How are you for kneeling?' Gillett asked Douglas.

'Flat on me face, old boy,' was the immediate – and predictable – rejoinder.

'All right, then,' said Gillett, 'come early and we'll have a run through before the others arrive. . . . You'll see the lift to bring you up . . .'

Douglas and Joan, with two of her children, Michael and Wendy, arrived at Buckingham Palace in plenty of time. While Joan and the children were led away, the 'recipient' was taken to the room which was to be the scene of the ceremony. A stool, with an inconveniently placed handrail, offered little confidence.

'Damned silly. The only knee I've got was the one wanted for kneeling. I made a nonsense of everything and finished up on the floor with the stool on top of me.'

By now, John Mills and Neil Cameron (Marshal of the Royal Air Force Sir Neil Cameron), two more 'chums', had arrived. It all appealed instantly to Mills's humour. 'I say,' he said, full of his usual spirit and twinkle, 'let's have a go.'

There then followed the actor's brilliant impersonation of the new knight trying to resolve his physical difficulty – legs splayed awkwardly all over the place, half kneeling, half standing, the long right leg stuck out ridiculously from the stool, until everything collapsed, hopelessly, in a heap. It was a sight seldom witnessed in such a setting. 'Worth five guineas a minute.'

Douglas gave Gillett his irrevocable verdict: 'Look here, old boy, I'm not going to risk bringing Her Majesty down with me. . . .'

The view was at once accepted. 'Very well,' he replied, 'I will explain to the Queen. You'll have to receive it standing up.'

As the decade of the 1970s passed into history, there was little let-up in Sir Douglas and Lady Bader's visits overseas. Invitations to attend this or that public function (and a lot of private ones as well) flowed in. The long journeys were now made by airline, not by private aircraft.

Australia, central and southern Africa, the United States, Canada: the spread was wide, and repetitive. Almost everywhere they went, the main purpose was to assist the cause of the disabled. There were other public, and private, engagements to fulfil, but this was always the first priority.

When they were in Adelaide in 1978, they spent the day at the Regency Park Centre for Physically Handicapped Children on the outskirts of the South Australian city. It was a fine, modern, state-aided creation in which its principal, Sir Dennis Paterson, had embodied the best design features of comparable institutions in Scandinavia, West Germany, Britain, the United States and Canada. Here, parents could bring their handicapped children at 8 o'clock in the morning and leave them, content and happy, to be collected again at 6 o'clock in the evening. All was provided within the complex – schooling, medical needs, sport and recreation. Douglas does not remember having seen an establishment to compare with it anywhere in the world. It is a model of its kind.

During their visit, the Baders had a question-and-answer session with the children. Nothing was barred. The exchanges reflected the open and uninhibited way in which the principals ran the centre. Before long, Joan became aware that one of the girls, an exceptionally pretty fifteen-year-old, was following her in her wheelchair wherever she went. Both her legs had been amputated just above the knee. As the time approached to leave, she asked the girl whether there was something she wanted to say, some question she would like to put.

'Yes,' said the girl. 'Had he' (pointing at Douglas who was some distance away) 'got any legs when you married him?'

She got her answer: no, he hadn't any legs when they were married, but this was something that was well known.

'Didn't you mind?'

Joan Bader responded with a counter-question. 'Are you worried that because you haven't got any legs no one will marry you?'

The admission was given straightly. 'Yes,' she said.

The comment was equally direct. 'I don't think you should worry about that at all. You are a very pretty girl. You have a lot to offer a man. That won't be affected by having no legs. And, what's more, any boy who gets you will be very lucky.'

As they were leaving, one of the teachers said the girl had been trying all day to pluck up her courage and ask these questions. It was only when Joan put her on the spot and asked her straight out whether there was something on her mind that the barrier came tumbling down and the questions poured out one after the other.

The following year, 1979, four months after his 69th birthday, Douglas piloted his own aeroplane for the last time. The entry in the log book is, as ever, explicit and terse:

4 June,   Beach 95   Travelair   GAPUB   White Waltham, local flying
50 minutes

He had by then amassed a total of 5744 hours and 25 minutes flying – and what flying! He was in good company. Around the same time his old mate and adversary, Adolf Galland, after a lifetime in aviation, had decided to hang up his gloves – or should it be his helmet?

In terms of aerial experience, military and civil, in peace and in war, there will never again be such a pair.

31

'He impressed me very much'

Sir Douglas Bader was completely taken in by the secrecy of the party his wife gave him on his seventieth birthday. Joan had intended that he should know nothing about it, and so things remained.

It wasn't until he walked into the President's Suite of the Bristol Hotel, at the corner of Berkeley Street and Piccadilly, around 6.30 p.m. on Thursday, 21 February 1980, and found eighty of his oldest and closest friends, comrades and colleagues waiting for him that he realized what was afoot. The CIA and MI6, between them, couldn't have improved on the cover plan. It was a gathering of unusual distinction and talent, classless and representative of Douglas's life and interests; its collective achievements were outstanding.

Sir Denis Crowley-Milling, in a few telling phrases, proposed the health of the guest of honour. He touched on a delicate point: 'Douglas has reached threescore years and ten. . . . But we do still allow him his one piece of vanity – that he still believes he can see to read without the use of spectacles. . . .'

Bader has never used a stick in his life, nor, so help us, will he ever wear spectacles. He would much prefer to go on misreading the dates he has made with his friends in his diary to having to resort to so mundane an aid.

The extent to which Bader's name has reached out to the extremities of the community was demonstrated in a chance comment overheard at an English League football game by one of the younger friends of Douglas and his family. Christopher Smyth, son of Michael, whose surgeon's skills won him in his lifetime the respect of Harley Street, was standing in the crowd at one of Millwall's home games in the 1960s. Two dockers stood right in front of him.

A clever, weaving run by Cripps, the Millwall striker, left him with an easy shot at goal. With the crowd roaring, he put the ball over the bar. 'Cor,' exclaimed one of the dockers, 'Douglas Bader would have done better than that!'

An incredulous spectator, standing in front, who had half heard the remark, turned round. 'Didn't know he was playing. Could I have a look at your programme?'

In fact, Bader has long held a strong appeal for ordinary working people. A week or so after his seventieth birthday party, a letter, date-marked 25 February 1980, was delivered to his London home. There was no proper address on the envelope. Instead it carried a request. 'Post Office – please forward this to Sir Douglas Bader, our war hero. I do not know address.' It had been posted at Harlow, in Essex.

The Post Office obliged. Inside was a note from a woman, asking him if he would send her mother, 'a true Cockney lady, living in the East End of London', who had just had both legs amputated, a signed photograph. She was eighty-two and had lived 'in the same little house for over sixty years and stayed there throughout two world wars'. The details were given:

> Mrs Nellie Wallpole
> 127 Corporation Street
> Plaistow
> West Ham
> London, E15

Douglas drove down to see the old lady the same morning that he received the letter. The daughter answered his knock. 'My name's Douglas Bader. Could I see Mrs Wallpole?'

Quite unmoved, the daughter called back over her shoulder. 'Mum, here's Douglas Bader.'

The old lady, legless but undaunted, was full of spirit. She hadn't yet got her artificial legs. She was moving about on her bottom, propelled by still strong hands and arms. After a cup of tea and a good talk, Douglas offered her a choice. 'Which would you like, my dear? A photograph of me as I am now, or one when I was young?'

The eyes smiled out of a face of true English character. 'I'd like the young one.'

So there it is: the life and times of a remarkable Englishman. Perhaps history will say that his greatest achievement was to show that, in human affairs, almost any goal is within reach if the will is there. It would be a fair assessment.

Towards the end of 1980, his friend and near-neighbour in the country, Anthony Montague Browne, Sir Winston Churchill's private secretary for thirteen years, sent Douglas a copy of a sale catalogue of Sawyer, the booksellers of Grafton Street. He covered it with a note in his own hand. 'You may be interested to see page 10. I remember that meeting in the House of Commons.'

The item for sale, price £150, was a letter, dated 2 April 1954, written by Churchill on 10 Downing Street notepaper to Sir Gerald Kelly, then at the end of his time as President of the Royal Academy. It recommended, in the words of the catalogue,

... Peter Portal as spokesman for the Air Force at a forthcoming banquet, and alternatively suggesting Group Captain Douglas Bader, whom he had just met [in his room in the House of Commons] and who 'impressed me very much'.

Within twelve months of writing the letter, Churchill, who was then eighty, had made his last great speech as Prime Minister. Those of us who sat behind him in the House of Commons that afternoon will never forget the mastery and majesty of his rhetoric in defending the West's possession of the nuclear weapon as the best deterrent to a third world war. He ended his deeply moving peroration with a final call:

Meanwhile, never flinch, never weary, never despair.[1]

It is the message of Douglas Bader's life.

1. Hansard, 1 March 1955.

Appendix A

Speech by Group Captain Douglas Bader at a dinner held in his honour by the National Sporting Club, at the Café Royal, London, on 24 April 1961

Responding to the toast of the guest of honour, proposed by Marshal of the Royal Air Force Sir Dermot Boyle, Douglas Bader said:

Mr Chairman, Your Grace, Mr Minister, my lords and gentlemen:

Thank you for your reception of that toast. I know you will be understanding and not expect too much of me tonight. It is manifestly impossible to expect me to answer a speech by the Marshal of the Royal Air Force who has just told you that I am a decent chap. If I were to try, it is possible that I might become emotional; and, judging by the amount of alcohol most of you have consumed, it is reasonable to suppose that you, too, might also become emotional – and the result would be a disaster.

When the National Sporting Club first invited me to this dinner, they asked me, with great kindness and courtesy, if I had any friends – and, if so, would I like them invited. As a result, some of you may find yourselves sitting alongside various disreputable characters whom you do not know. Indeed, you may already have made a mental reservation that you do not wish to know them. Gentlemen, these are my friends.

I have worked with them, played with them; I have been in prison with them – correction, in a prisoner of war camp with them; I have nearly been court-marshalled with them, or because of them. In the bad times and the good over the years, they have always been around. I thank God for them and, particularly, for their presence here tonight.

I like people and I love the warmth that friendship brings. As we grow older and the years roll on we find the pattern of our lives changing. The violence, the vigour, the impatience of youth, gives

285

place to the more settled and tranquil state of mind and body. Our memories multiply with the years and we have more time to enjoy them.

Among our memories we treasure many 'firsts'. The first time, for instance, as a boy at school, we saw our name on the notice board to play for the 1st XV or the 1st XI. The first time we made a hundred runs at cricket or broke 80 strokes in a medal round of golf. The first time we climbed into a boxing ring and won an important fight. The first time a Messerschmitt 109 shot us up the arse. Memories like these linger as the years gather; they stimulate our minds and give us a lot of laughs.

Mr Chairman and gentlemen, may I raise my glass to you all and wish you happy days? Thank you for coming here tonight and supporting this dinner; for bringing into this room in this short space of time the warmth of your friendship.

By your presence here tonight you have made this a tremendous occasion for me. You have given me a magnificent 'first' to add to my store of memories. It is one which I shall recall many times in the future and it will bring much warmth and happiness as the years unwind.

Appendix B

Address by Marshal of the Royal Air Force
Sir Dermot Boyle at a service of thanksgiving for the
life of Thelma Bader held at St Clement Danes, in
the Strand, on 5 March 1971

We are assembled, appropriately in this beautiful Royal Air Force church, to pay tribute to a gallant and much-loved lady whose father was an airman, whose husband was an airman and who herself became involved in the human drama inseparable from the lives of those who fought in the great air battles of the last war.

Thelma's life cannot be described by a catalogue of achievements; indeed, any such approach would be to belittle her whole attitude to life. Instead, we must realize that at an early age she acquired the qualities which enabled her to lead the life of a true Christian – generosity, courage, unselfishness, loyalty; intelligent interest in the things that mattered and a happy chuckle for those that didn't. It was the way she applied these gifts to the turmoil of living that endeared her to everyone.

There are several examples of her strength and wisdom. When she met Douglas, she was quite clear that he was the man for her; she was equally clear that there were difficulties, indeed, very great difficulties. From these she did not shrink but, instead, solved them by a mutual bond of unselfishness, wisdom and devotion with the result, as we all know, that these two strong-minded people had the happiest of married lives.

Again, during the war when Thelma was inevitably, because of Douglas's activities, living amongst those engaged in the critical air battles of the time, she became a continuous source of comfort and encouragement to everyone. Many of the young pilots were a long way from their homeland, some of them were tired and saddened and even disillusioned by the futility of war. She gave so generously of her help and affection at this time, the fact that her anxieties were much greater than theirs tended to be overlooked and when Douglas went missing for five long anxious days she devoted herself so

287

wholeheartedly to comforting the pilots who had lost their wing leader that it was hard to realize that it was she who had lost a husband to whom she was utterly devoted. Thelma's life was a shining example that to give is better than to receive.

And then, in the final stages of her life, when she knew better than anyone how ill she was, Thelma continued to live to the limit of her physical endurance; continued to give those charming dinner parties in her happy home and remained gay and interested in the affairs of others – always giving out help and encouragement to the exclusion of any idea that it was she who needed help. In fact, triumphantly Thelma did not need much help because she did not fear death.

To those who were nearest and dearest to her we extend our deepest sympathy at their great loss but I would hope that this lovely service – in this friendly historic church – with its majestic music, and in the presence of so many warmhearted friends, will prove to be, as well as a memorial to Thelma, a source of strength to those who mourn her.

It would be wrong for us to go forth from here in the belief that this is in any way a final tribute. The last tribute to Thelma Bader will not have been paid until time has removed from this earth all those privileged to have known her.

Appendix C

Address by Group Captain Douglas Bader at a service of thanksgiving held at St Clement Danes, in the Strand, on 12 September 1975, for the life and work of Air Chief Marshal Sir Keith Park, commander of No. 11 Group, Fighter Command, during the Battle of Britain

We are here today in our own Royal Air Force church of St Clement Danes to pay our final tribute to a great fighting airman, an outstanding leader, and a distinguished senior officer of the Royal Air Force – the late Air Chief Marshal Sir Keith Park. I first saw him in the mess at Northolt when I was a pilot officer in 1931. He stood there, tall lean, upright, immaculate: every junior officer's idea of a fighting airman, this decorated wing commander. He died earlier this year in his native New Zealand at the age of eighty-two. Keith Rodney Park was born in 1892. He joined the New Zealand Territorial Army in 1911. In 1914 he went overseas with the New Zealand Expeditionary Force. He first saw action in Gallipoli and then in France. In 1917 he transferred to the Royal Flying Corps. He flew with 8 Squadron, 38 Squadron, then was given command of 48 Squadron in April 1918 after the formation of the Royal Air Force. During those last two years of the Kaiser war he was awarded the Military Cross twice, the Croix de Guerre, and the Distinguished Flying Cross – in that order.

This active fighting background was to be of inestimable value twenty-two years later when, as air officer commanding 11 Group of Fighter Command in 1940, Keith Park was to assume operational control of all the Hurricane and Spitfire squadrons defending this country against the massive German air attacks from occupied France over our south-east coast. I suppose every squadron in Fighter Command was involved in the Battle of Britain. Some came down from the north to replace badly mauled squadrons in the south; others operated from airfields like Warmwell in neighbouring 10 Group and Duxford in 12 Group. Every single one of these squadrons was under the operational control of 11 Group headquarters at Uxbridge and its outlying-sector Operations rooms.

289

Flying Colours

The late Air Chief Marshal Lord Dowding, Commander-in-Chief, Fighter Command, from 1936 until the end of 1940, has often been acclaimed as the saviour of this country. Rightly so, because in the pre-war years he laid down an air defence system which in the event proved to be impregnable. Nevertheless, the Battle of Britain had to be fought in that high summer exactly thirty-five years ago. It is right and proper for me to say on this occasion and in this place something which I do not recall has been said before. It is this. That great and vital air battle was controlled, directed and brought to a successful conclusion by the man whose memory we honour today. The awesome responsibility for this country's survival rested squarely on Keith Park's shoulders. Had he failed, Stuffy Dowding's foresight, determination and achievement would have counted for nought.

During the battle this splendid officer flew himself around in his Hurricane to see what was going on. He had done the same during the Dunkirk episode earlier in 1940. This was leadership indeed of the sort that was to become traditional in the Royal Air Force.

I saw Keith Park in December 1940. He was lean, upright, immaculate as usual, but haggard with fatigue from the colossal strain of the events of the preceding months.

This tired officer was rested in Training Command during 1941. His subsequent career continued with distinction and resolution, but always overshadowed by his tremendous Battle of Britain achievement.

January 1942, AOC Egypt; July 1942, AOC Malta – an operational command once more at which he was in his element. When the North African campaign ended and Malta became a stepping stone for the invasion of Sicily and Italy, Keith Park was appointed AOC-in-C, Middle East. As the European war receded he was posted to South-East Asia as Allied Air Commander in 1945. He retired from the Royal Air Force in December 1946 to his beloved New Zealand.

I last saw him there in 1969 in his house. He had just come in from sailing. He was wearing rope-soled canvas shoes, shorts, a short-sleeved shirt: lean, bronzed, upright, immaculate. He carried his seventy-six years with disdain.

This is no sad occasion. Rather is it a time during which we can let our memories drift back to those halcyon days of 1940 when we fought together in English skies under the determined leadership of that great New Zealander we are remembering now. They were busy times, exhilarating times, argumentative times; with never a thought that we might lose the battle. Keith Park was one of us. We all shared the great experience. That is what we remember today.

British military history of this century has been enriched with the names of great fighting men from New Zealand, of all ranks and in every one of our services. Keith Park's name is carved into that history alongside those of his peers.

Index

* Denotes dual usage – Service and civil

292

Index

West, Warrant Officer Bernard, 107, 108
West, Flight Lieutenant Jeff, 179, 185
West Kensington Court, 81
West Fulham parliamentary constituency, 212
Westminster Hospital, 268
Wilson, Rt Hon. Sir Harold, MP, 262
Wilson, Giles, 262
Withers Farm, 125, 277
Wolcough (Wolkoff), Alexander, 75

Wood, Derek, 123
Wood, Rt Hon. Sir Kingsley, MP, 165
Woodhall, Group Captain A. B., 119, 130, 133, 136, 140, 154, 157, 188
Woods, Stanley, 43
Woollett, Squadron Leader H. W., 46, 108
Wootton, Frank, 191
Wright, Robert, 123, 161, 168, 171

Zemke, Colonel H., 46

303